SNEAKONOMIC GROWTH

SNEAKONOMIC GROWTH

SCARCITY, STORYTELLING, AND THE ARRIVAL OF SNEAKERS AS AN ASSET CLASS

DYLAN DITTRICH

NEW DEGREE PRESS

COPYRIGHT © 2018 DYLAN DITTRICH

SNEAKONOMIC GROWTH

Scarcity, Storytelling, and the Arrival of Sneakers as an Asset Class

ISBN   978-1-64137-184-1   *Paperback*

         978-1-64137-185-8   *Ebook*

CONTENTS

THE TOUR
DEPARTS NOW

Deploying capital is tricky.

On the one hand, you want your balance sheet to grow over time, but on the other, you'd like to preserve your hard-earned wealth.

How do you walk that fine line between risk and return? Between safety of principal and mouthwatering returns?

Do you pile all of your chips into the latest hot offering or do you steer for the reliable industry stalwart? The new kid on the block with underrated potential or the blue chip that's reliably held its value for years?

In either case, your decision boils down to one simple question, the answer to which must be carefully constructed from painstaking market diligence on a vast array of critical factors.

When I'm ready to sell, will somebody be willing to pay an even greater price for my asset than the price that I paid for it?

Look, you could just allocate $5,000 to the Nike Air Yeezy 2 "Red October." Yes, you heard me correctly.

Five. Thousand. Dollars. One pair of sneakers.

And yes, I said *allocate to*, not *spend on*.

It sounds crazy. It *is* kind of crazy. And yet, the value has endured at those elevated levels since the sneaker released in 2014. Moreover, there's reason to believe it will *remain* propped up. More shares...er, I mean pairs...are not coming to market; Yeezy is an Adidas brand now, and surely existing supply is drying up. Then again, it's tough to know for sure whether Kanye West's politics might unduly influence prices in years to come.

Sure, it could be the sneaker industry's Mickey Mantle rookie card, but diversification is probably for the best.

You could turn your attention to the flavor of the moment, the Off-White Air Jordan 1. That might have been a sound use of capital back in November 2017 when prices troughed at around $1,200. You would've doubled your money in a year if you had the foresight to buy low.

A triple digit return. In twelve months. On a pair of sneakers.

No connections or inside information necessary. No tricks. No scams. All that was needed was the conviction that demand would overwhelm supply in the months to follow.

Well, conviction, a spare $1,200, and the willpower to abstain from...you know...actually wearing them.

It all sounds so silly. Surely, this is Tulipmania. This is Beanie Babies all over again. This is...nonsense, it simply has to be.

Is it though?

***

I live in two worlds that I'd never thought to combine:
- High finance, investment analysis and management
- The sneakerhead community

I was so sure that everything I've learned in the former should convince me that the economy of the latter is sheer folly. I certainly wouldn't be alone in thinking so – that is the *safe* line of thinking after all.

Over the course of writing this book, though, I've become *more* convinced of the sophistication of sneakers, the asset. Moreover, I've become wholeheartedly convinced of the sophistication of the economy that has risen around them.

Look, that doesn't mean every individual (or frankly, any individual) should be carving out a 5% allocation to sneakers alongside their equities and bonds. That *is* patently ridiculous. For a plethora of reasons.

The "market capitalization" is big and getting bigger, but it's not *that* big. The sneaker asset class is in its nascence; we're not at a stage where historical data on risk and return is robust enough or reliable enough to inform allocation and investment decisions of scale. We may never reach that stage.

We are at a stage, however, where this asset's value can be measured, understood, and shaped in real time by free market forces with the benefit of timely, accurate information. *That* is a level of sophistication never attained by failed collecting fads of the past.

Part of my aim in writing this book is indeed to destigmatize the view of sneakers as both fashion article *and* valuable asset. In the process, we'll offer collectors a framework to better understand their fashion statement's behavior as the latter.

There's a reason that investors of major repute *are* flocking to the businesses powering this sneaker economy in droves: it's real, it's growing, and it's not going away.

***

Let's start with the simple facts. Per *The Financial Times*, the secondary sneaker market was in excess of \$1 billion in sales volume annually...in 2015.[1] Today, *individual* market-

---

1   Thompson, Ryan. 2015. "The Footsy Index: How Sneakers Became Very Big Business | Financial Times". Ft.Com. https://www.ft.com/

places are closing in on that run rate. We're into the *billions*, rather than billion. And that's *just* the transacted volume.

Just look at eBay. Though no longer the darling of the sneaker resale world, the secondary market stalwart still has 1.2 *million* sneaker listings daily, processing a sneaker purchase every 1.5 *seconds* as Jeff Chan, the head of the company's sneaker category, told *GQ*.[2]

While eBay may still lead in scale, the emergence of fierce new competitors over several years has changed the sneaker economy forever and for better. StockX, the stock market of things, facilitates more than 10,000 transactions daily according to *The New York Times*, amounting to greater than $2 million in daily sales volume.[3] CEO Josh Luber notes that the company's volume run rate has indeed reached $1 billion, with sneakers making up approximately 70% of the marketplace's merchandise. According to *TechCrunch*, secondary sneaker marketplace, GOAT, boasts 8 million members, 100,000 sellers, and 400,000 listings.[4] Those numbers are likely exploding as I write this.

---

content/b3ea93b2-d48d-11e4-9bfe-00144feab7de#axzz3WBgYkYUg.

2   Wolf, Cam. 2018. "Ebay Wants To Be The Place You Sell Your Sneakers—Again". GQ. https://www.gq.com/story/ebay-sneaker-resale-competition.

3   Shapiro, Bee. 2018. "How Much Is That Sneaker In The Window?". New York Times.

4   Panzarino, Matthew. 2018. "Sneaker Market GOAT Hires COO Lizzie Francis And Makes A Play For Women Sneaker Shoppers". *Techcrunch*. https://techcrunch.com/2018/06/19/sneaker-market-goat-hires-coo-lizzie-francis-and-makes-a-play-for-women-sneaker-shoppers/.

***

While the sneaker world of the present day has grown more orderly, more civilized, and more mature over the years, don't mistake that for waning fervor and affection. Line-up skirmishes (and all-out riots) at brick and mortar stores have largely been replaced by furious screen mashing on the Nike SNKRS app. The underlying intensity of lust for the right pair of sneakers – the ones that combine trendy, timely design with the forces of hype – remains as strong if not stronger than ever.

Look no further than releases of the past 1-2 years. Countless Off-White x Nike collaboration pairs garner well in excess of $1,000 on the secondary market. The Tom Sachs-designed NikeCraft Mars Yard 2.0 sneaker fetches close to $3,000 consistently. Yeezys remain coveted statement pieces in the right models and colorways. The appetite for sneakers persists, and it's not always limited to the ultra-limited releases.

Glance at the iTunes App Store's ranking of free shopping apps. Of the top 100 at the close of 2018, eight are directly tied to and centrally focused on the sneaker economy. Countless others bear a looser connection to the space. Nike SNKRS, which centers solely on new sneaker launches, has climbed as high as 10th in the shopping application rankings. Nike has a stand-alone application, but new sneaker launches necessitate an application of their own, with the SNKRS team consistently developing new, exciting, and innovative ways to connect product with consumer. There are three applications in the top 30 providing access to the secondary sneaker market, and sneakers are the focal point of two of those applications, GOAT and StockX.

Such a reality is not a surprise; the secondary market is undoubtedly the rocket ship of sneaker economy growth.

How do you make sense of a market that large, that diverse, and that emergent? Because while there has been significant maturation, inefficiencies remain plentiful. Fear not, though, as those inefficiencies are slowly but surely being mitigated by the increased proliferation of reliable and valuable information. The sneaker economy is not short of voices, and those voices are certainly not short of people ready and willing to listen.

Take for example the Instagram followings of various sneaker blogs and publications. Sneaker News boasts 7.9 *million* followers. Nice Kicks has 3.2 million. KicksOnFire isn't far behind at 2.9 million. Again, those numbers are a mere snapshot in time, likely climbing rapidly as you read. We're talking about *millions* of people anxious to digest the most recent sneaker news as swiftly as possible, to be ready for the latest release, to know what's going to sell quickly and what won't.

The Instagram followings of sneaker leakers, those that divulge inside details on upcoming releases, number in the hundreds of thousands. Those follower bases *should* grow into the millions swiftly as savvy consumers learn to exploit informational disparities. KicksDeals, a service centering on providing interested consumers with timely updates on recent discounts and sales, has a Twitter following of over 350,000 people.

The content isn't solely handy information, however. Sneaker YouTube is a vast network of highly impactful, highly entertaining digital content with devoted fanbases. Sneaker Shopping, the crowd-pleasing show from pop culture brand *Complex,* features several episodes that have eclipsed 10 million views and countless others that aren't far behind. YouTubers like Jacques Slade and Foamer Simpson boast subscriber bases of approximately 1 million and 375 thousand respectively, with daily videos providing highly authentic opinions and reviews of new releases, profiles of underappreciated sneakers, and other fun detours creatively concocted.

There is a voracious appetite for sneaker content, whether for information, for entertainment, or otherwise.

While sneaker media and sneaker journalism have grown into full-fledged professional arenas, mainstream publications are taking notice. More and more frequently, sneaker stories, primarily centering on the resale space, grace the pages, physical or digital, of *The Wall Street Journal, The Washington Post,* and *The New York Times,* among many others. The eye-popping checks written by investors of repute seeking access to the space render the industry glow-up difficult to ignore.

***

But let's pause there for a second – should we *really* look at sneakers as an asset, or are they just shoes? Why *aren't* they destined to become Beanie Babies? Through what lens should we examine them – fine art, baseball cards, comic books? Is value driven by novelty, with that value destined to wane if the accompanying novelty fades?

I wasn't entirely certain either – and my interest in sneakers, like most, certainly was *not* spawned as a means for financial gain.

I've been on the lookout for fresh sneakers since high school, but I got into – and I mean *into* – sneakers when Jordan Brand re-released the "True Blue" Jordan 3s, which harken back to MJ's time with the Washington Wizards.

From that moment, I was thrown headfirst into the sneaker economy and all that comes with it – the apps, the blogs, the Instagram accounts – *everything*.

But for sneakerheads like me — the ones that love it not just for the fashion statement but *also* for the market dynamics that influence value — looking at them as *just* shoes isn't enough. I wanted to understand and analyze the sneaker market just as if I was analyzing the investment implications of the demand for the services of a tech company about to go public, oil sanctions, or the increasingly competitive cloud storage landscape.

It's one thing to understand and another to explain. In providing a framework to better understand sneakers as asset, as well as the business ecosystem that has grown to serve that concept, we'll dive into topics including:

- The importance of right-sizing supply in the primary market
- The influence of rapidly growing secondary market supply
- The impact of deadstock profiteering on the market at large
- The growing importance of speed and agility throughout a product lifecycle
- What it means for retail to be truly differentiated in an online world
- Why demographic barriers no longer loom as large
- The evolving role and origin of "influence"
- The power of authentic storytelling

Throughout the book I'll attempt to offer a fun, insightful tour of the sneaker economy — with some sophisticated financial and investment analysis mixed in along the way. A dry investment memorandum or economics text this is not; the goal is to enlighten and enthuse.

My aim is not necessarily to persuade or dissuade you from thinking of sneakers themselves as a vehicle for capital appreciation or even preservation, though for *most*, it's probably best not to think of them in either regard for reasons we'll touch on later. Still, principles of investing, of competitive and economic forces, and of market dynamics can be utilized to great advantage in better understanding how the sneaker economy functions. That understanding grows stronger still when accompanied by the inside knowledge of those who are making the sneaker economy such a beacon of growth and innovation. I have sought out those individuals in the development of this guided tour.

I may be your guide, but my hope is to stay largely out of the way, drawing your attention to the insights of the brains behind the marketplaces, the consignment shops, the boutique retailers, the content creators, the brands, and other ancillary service providers – the economic constituents of import. These folks are the real story of the sneaker economy: really bright people doing really impressive things that are changing and will continue to change not only the sneaker arena, but commerce as we know it.

There are unbelievably powerful lessons to be learned from the decisions being made daily across the sneaker economy: lessons of economics, yes absolutely, but also marketing, influence, consumer engagement, and authenticity. Passionate, smart, ingenious people are working tirelessly to change the way that brands and consumers interact, the way that consumers buy products, where they buy products, how consumers make informed decisions, even how prices are determined. It's sneakers now, but there are few boundaries to the reach of these innovations, which will assuredly disrupt broader retail for the better in years to come.

Who belongs on this tour? First and foremost, this book is for the sneaker fanatic that wants to progress into a more savvy, discerning market participant. If you're running out of storage space for your next pair and wondering how it came to this point, you're in the right place. Unfortunately, I can't help with the storage problem – my own is keeping me busy enough – but I can present thought-provoking questions that may help you reconsider what you're acquiring and how you're offloading those pairs deemed surplus to requirements.

The tour is not for the sneakerheads of the world alone, though. Rather, importantly, it's also for the outsider who has had his or her curiosity piqued by the occasional mainstream news coverage and wants to look under the hood to better understand how the sneaker economy became too large to ignore. Don't worry, we won't sneer if you're not yet fluent in sneaker-speak. You too are in the right place.

One of the beautiful things about travel is the tourist's tendency to bring elements of the foreign land's culture home with them. My hope is that the same holds true here. Marketers, strategists, finance professionals, designers, buyers, retailers – all can gain.

No matter your place in the sneaker economy, whether consumer, reseller, retailer, industry insider, or total outsider, there are powerful lessons to be learned from an intimate understanding of how all these constituents coexist, interact, and relate, particularly with regard to the ways in which economic and competitive forces shape decision-making. The sneaker-collecting hobby is replete with valuable intel.

So lace up, and let's go.

PART 1

HOW THE WILD WEST GOT LESS WILD AND MORE EFFICIENT

CHAPTER 1

PIVOTAL MOMENTS – HOW SNEAKERS BECAME MORE THAN SHOES

"On September 15th, Nike created a new, revolutionary basketball shoe. On October 18th, the NBA threw them out of the game. Fortunately, the NBA can›t stop you from wearing them. Air Jordans, from Nike."

The year was 1984, and the revolutionary basketball shoe highlighted in Nike's marketing campaign was the Air Jordan 1.

While many trace the roots of sneaker culture to the 1970s, this was the pivotal moment that set the sneaker collector's economy in motion in earnest. The National Basketball Association banned Michael Jordan's use of red and black sneakers, which violated an NBA uniform standard necessitating the inclusion of only primary team colors on sneakers. While Jordan had actually worn a red and black colorway of a model known as the Air Ship in catching the league office's attention, Nike seized upon the ban and made it a focal point of the Air Jordan 1 campaign nonetheless.

With His Airness sporting the "banned" sneaker in the 1985 Dunk Contest, the Air Jordan 1 quickly became a bedrock of sneaker folklore. A May 1985 article in *The Chicago Tribune* by George Lazarus details the sneaker's commercial success, with an expectation of three to four million pairs sold over the course of that year. The AJ1 debuted just a month earlier, in April, and yet Nike had already shipped 1.5 million pairs, amassing $55 million in retail sales and orders in the process.[5]

Nike's initial sales expectation was a mere 100,000 pairs.

How did it happen? How did the Air Jordan 1 become an overnight icon and defy expectations in the process? Explanations are offered within the *Tribune's* article, with many quotes foreshadowing things to come for the sneaker economy:

---

5   Lazarus, George. 1985. "Michael Jordan Shoe Also Having Big Rookie Season". *The Chicago Tribune*, 1985.

"Air Jordan has become our Cabbage Patch doll," said the Nike spokesman. "It's one of the best things that's ever happened to us."

"A lot of people obviously are wearing Air Jordan for basketball footwear, but we're also finding that the shoe is not being worn exclusively playing the sport but rather as a 'hip' shoe as something fashionable," said an advertising agency Nike account supervisor.[6]

Just like that, through terrific product design, an exemplary marketing strategy led by storytelling, a transcendent athlete, and a little bit of luck, the Air Jordan 1 became a collector's item, an *asset* with value beyond its on-court utility.

The growing sneaker buzz was not exclusively Swoosh related, however.

One year later, Run-D.M.C. released their hit song, "My Adidas," generating a wave of hype around Three Stripes products, particularly the Adidas Superstar sneaker. The group inked an endorsement deal with Adidas shortly thereafter, setting the stage for a long (and complicated) future of business relationships between pop culture figures and sneaker companies.

Fast-forward two years to 1988. Michael Jordan was entertaining the idea of leaving Nike, disgruntled and uninspired by the brand's follow-up efforts to the Air Jordan 1. That's when legendary Nike designer, Tinker Hatfield, introduced

---

6   Ibid.

him to the Air Jordan 3, the first Jordan to feature visible Nike Air and the iconic Jumpman logo.

Obviously, Jordan elected to stay put.

He went on to win the Dunk Contest in the White Cement colorway and the All-Star Game MVP award in the Black Cement colorway in front of his adoring Chicago fanbase. The rest of the relationship between Jordan and Nike is, of course, history, and extremely lucrative history at that.

The same Nike Air inhabiting the midsole of the Jordan III aroused a frenzy of its own in running shoes, with Nike Air Maxes playing a dominant role in the sneaker world during the late 1980s and especially the mid-1990s. So intense was the fervor that Japanese store owners were embarking on "scavenging trips" to the United States in a quest to locate and purchase Nikes at a reasonable price and resell them for a dramatic profit back in Japan – nascent cross-border resale.

"Police throughout the country report a rash of thefts and holdups the Japanese have dubbed 'Air Max hunting,' according to press reports," detailed Michael Lev of the *Chicago Tribune* in a 1996 article. "No one has been killed for their fashion choice, as has happened in the United States, but in several reported incidents, youths have been beaten or threatened while their Nikes were taken."[7]

---

7   Lev, Michael. 1996. "'Air Max Hunting' Shocks Japan – Holdups, Beatings Blamed On Mania For Used Sneakers". *The Chicago Tribune*, 1996. http://community.seattletimes.nwsource.com/archive/?-date=19961117&slug=2360191.

Why the rash of theft and crime? Because those Air Maxes were selling for in excess of $1,000.

Already, in the mid-1990s, we had widespread, global reports of sneaker-induced crime and violence, incited not just by the cool look of the sneakers, but more importantly by the reality of their increasing value. Word was spreading, and the race to acquire and acquire quickly was heating up.

Around the same time, in the fall of 1995, Pierre Omidyar founded a company named AuctionWeb. The premise was simple: internet-based auctions for goods that people were looking to offload. In 1997, the company's name was changed from AuctionWeb to eBay. Concurrently, Beanie Babies exploded in popularity, contributing to eBay's growing user base and amounting to 10% of the site's listings according to *Fortune*.[8] In time, eBay would become a hotbed of sneaker transaction activity, with the internet dramatically widening the scope of available buyers and sellers participating in the secondary market.

In 1999, Nelson Cabral established NikeTalk, an internet forum created as an online destination for the discussion of sneakers and sneaker collecting. With the increasing popularity of the site, information no longer lived exclusively in magazines, at malls, and on street corners. Without incentive, forum posters provided other posters (and commonly,

---

8   Vandermey, Anne. 2015. "Lessons From The Great Beanie Babies Crash". *Fortune*. http://fortune.com/2015/03/11/beanie-babies-failure-lessons/.

lurkers) with valuable intel – what was being released, and when and where it was happening – in hopes that somebody else would feel comfortable doing the same. A sharing economy of information was created, and word of mouth broke free from the confines of locality. Like an airborne virus, hype spread, and the sneaker frenzy intensified.

In the late 1990s and early 2000s, many of our beloved streetwear and sneaker boutiques were opening their doors for the first time, offering a less sterile, more culturally fluent alternative to the mall-based Foot Lockers of the world. For example, Concepts opened for business in Cambridge, Massachusetts in 1996. Alife was founded in New York City in 1999. Across the country in Los Angeles, Undefeated launched in 2001. The story was similar overseas in Europe and Asia, where well-known retailers like Fragment Design, Sneakersnstuff, Titolo, Size?, and countless others were preparing to surf the wave.

With the mid-2000s came the arrival of sneaker media, born from the popularity and success of forums like Nike-Talk, which served as proof of concept for the robust demand for sneaker-focused content. Sole Collector, Hypebeast, Nice Kicks, Sneaker News, and others entered the fray, and a cottage industry that would later shed the cottage label was formed. Impressive page view totals followed, editorial staff were hired, and sneaker media became an actual phrase that could be uttered without leaving laughter in its wake.

However, traditional media began taking notice of sneaker buzz as well, with eye-popping resale prices finding their way onto the headlines of reputable newspapers, often by nature of the violence and crime that ensued. Nonetheless, the resale profits were captivating. Surely, adding sophistication and structure to the pursuit of these profits was an area of promising business opportunity.

In that vein, vintagekicks.com was established in 2005. The site would later evolve into two brick-and-mortar locations for the sneaker consignment business we now know as Flight Club, which facilitates the buying and selling of rare, highly-coveted sneakers. Flight Club's current NYC and Los Angeles locations opened in 2010 and 2008 respectively. With those locations came the elevation of resale to an experience more closely resembling traditional retail, eschewing the mainstream perception of resale as a shady business.

It wasn't just the who, the where, and the how of resale that imposed a cap on its growth prospects, though. It was the information, or lack thereof, associated with the transactions that served as a source of friction. In 2012, an IBM consultant named Josh Luber set out extracurricularly to provide transparency, data, and structure to a resale market that was indeed somewhat murky, disjointed, and difficult to navigate. He founded Campless, which sought to aggregate and track resale price data so that users could have some idea of the price for which they should buy or sell their shoes. The company generated revenue through eBay affiliate marketing, offering direct links to product pages, and by packaging and selling its data to market researchers.

For the first time, the addition of robust data to the sneaker economy was contributing to a more efficiently functioning secondary market, as market efficiency is always improved by the wide availability of timely and accurate information.

In 2015, Daishin Sugano and Eddy Lu founded sneaker marketplace application, GOAT, after a series of less successful entrepreneurial ventures. This idea, however, would stick, as the marketplace, based on the idea of an intermediary offering authentication services, proved immensely popular. That same year, Stadium Goods, founded by John McPheeters and Jed Stiller, opened its doors in SoHo, and another consignment juggernaut specializing in sophisticated retail experience was born. In 2016, following investment from Cleveland Cavaliers owner, Dan Gilbert, Luber's Campless became StockX, the stock market of things. The data angle would remain in place, but StockX would also function as a marketplace for buyers and sellers of sneakers and other limited goods, buoyed by that robust pricing data. The maturation of the secondary sneaker market had begun.

Perfectly coinciding with the expansion and maturation of the secondary market was the launch of the Yeezy collaboration between Kanye West and Adidas. 2015 saw the release of both the Yeezy Boost 750 and the Yeezy Boost 350, and suddenly, Jordans and Nikes were not the only sneakers lusted after for their resale value. Unquestionably, the surging popularity of Yeezy would provide a tailwind to resale markets in the years that followed.

But the retail market, which we'll also refer to as the primary market, was ripe for change in the digital age. Nike debuted the SNKRS application in February 2015. Acquiring limited releases was suddenly possible from the palm of our hands, and sneaker acquisition was forever changed – no matter where they were, what time it was, and what they were doing, sneaker seekers were able to tap to buy with ease.

Over the years to follow, with the erosion of friction proceeding relentlessly through the pursuit of capitalistic enterprise, the immense popularity of the sneaker-collecting hobby continued to grow, particularly as newbies aimed to discover whether they too could reap the profits of successful sneaker acquisition.

Spoiler alert: most could not.

Still, the resale businesses proved valuable, with demonstrably impressive growth trajectories capturing the attention of major investors and eliciting, in aggregate, hundreds of millions of dollars in investment. GOAT and StockX alone raised more than $100 million in 2018.

That's where the crash course in the history of sneakonomic growth to date ends. It's a punctuated timeline of pivotal moments, but all of these pivotal moments have led to the development of a vast sneaker economy. In this economy, success is not the exclusive windfall of large sneaker brands and sneaker retailers, but also of entrepreneurs, individual resellers, bloggers, YouTubers, and numerous other parties. Sneakers are a 24/7 global business, unbounded by geographic borders and the demographic stereotypes of old. Though sneakers help to shape the future of retail, they remain somewhat reliant on the history that brought us here.

They say you should never forget your roots, and sneakers certainly haven't. After all, the Air Jordan 1 "Banned" colorway just re-released on the Nike SNKRS app in 2016. It sells on StockX today for in excess of $400. Respect the past. Embrace the future.

CHAPTER 2

SNEAKER COLLECTORS – FROM ANARCHY TO ENTREPRENEURSHIP

———

"Before the riot, sneaker culture was underground and kind of nerdy. After that, we had investment bankers coming into the store telling us, 'We used to buy cigars and wine. Now we're just going to buy sneakers.' It changed overnight."

—Jeff Staple, Founder of Staple Design and Reed Space, to Jeff Block[9]

———

9   Block, Justin. 2018. "Jeff Staple's Oral History Of The 2005 Nike SB "Pigeon" Riot In NYC". *Medium.* https://medium.com/@ jblock49_6777/jeff-staples-oral-history-of-the-2005-nike-sb-pi-geons-riot-in-nyc-446f518a7fe3

Riots played an invaluable role in the increased sophistication of today's sneaker economy. It sounds counter-intuitive, such an uncivilized and chaotic event leading to sophistication and order. Nevertheless, violence and crime brought the jaw-dropping numbers of sneaker resale into the mainstream limelight.

The sneaker economy wasn't always this civilized, this sophisticated, this professional. In fact, it was quite the opposite. Sneaker releases were mayhem. Reliable information was difficult to come by. The secondary market existed, certainly, but it didn't inspire confidence. Really, in the early 2000s, the forces of capitalism and of entrepreneurship had not yet sufficiently strengthened to gently guide the sneaker economy to a more orderly, structured existence.

It really was an underground economy, not to the same degree as the drug trade, but unregulated by efficient market dynamics. Sneaker culture was raw and untamed, existing mainly where it had its roots: the street. Without blogs to guide tastes, Instagram to reinforce and amplify notions of cool, and a robust e-commerce world to provide access to boundless variety of offerings, the sneaker enthusiast took to their local malls, boutiques, and catalogs to discover the new and unique, that which would capture the envy and respect of local peers.

None of that is a bad thing, by any means; it was just... different. In fact, in those early stages of the sneaker economy, participants were, if anything, more empowered to express their individuality absent the echo chambers of social media, and more justly enabled to acquire that which they desired at a reasonable price, undeterred by the bot arms race and seemingly unwinnable raffles.

Had you built connections or not? Were you in line early, or weren't you? These were the simple questions that determined whether or not you acquired successfully. Those questions still matter today, but as we know, the equation is no longer so simple.

So how did we get here? How did we make this transition from relative anarchy to a bustling economy? Just as entrepreneurs and investors are now flocking to the cannabis industry as it gains mainstream acceptance, so too did capitalism rush to embrace the mainstream acceptance of sneakers; the difference of course was the lack of legality hurdles requiring clearance.

In many ways, sneakonomic growth is the product of a perfect confluence of events: the rise of e-commerce, the arrival and popularity of social media, and a new generation of technologically-savvy entrepreneurs. While these events were inevitable, their application to the sneaker world was amplified and expedited by the mayhem that preceded them.

CURBSIDE CALAMITY AND MALL MALICE

Perhaps the most renowned sneaker release in history, the one that is considered to have catapulted sneaker culture into the mainstream and the sneaker economy into an accelerated stage of growth, took place in 2005 when Jeff Staple's New York City based Reed Space retailer launched a collaboration with Nike: the Nike SB Dunk "Pigeon". The "Pigeon" release has become sneaker canon, its story recounted often as the pinnacle of kicks-induced hysteria.

Staple's New York City roots inspired the Pigeon; he wanted the New York City inspiration not to be an obvious nod to the Statue of Liberty or to the subway, but instead to something that true New Yorkers would understand, something that might make outsiders scratch their heads and raise an eyebrow.

In an interview with Justin Block, Staple explained how the gritty sneaker inspired such a frenzy: "It's those kids on the forums and the boards. They are so CSI knowledgeable about sh*t. They know stuff we don't. We actually didn't know when we were going to get the shipment of Pigeons into our warehouse. The day it arrived, I remember I sliced open the box and I was like, 'Here it is!' And then we got phone calls like immediately."[10]

The forum hype machine is perfectly emblematic of the era. Sneaker blogs and sneaker media were still a newborn endeavor. Sneaker subculture remained somewhat underground, but those involved boasted an unparalleled amount of dedication. Through an admirable amount of sleuthing, an economy of information sharing, and a commitment to

---

10   Ibid.

the forums, acquiring the Pigeon Dunks quickly became a proposition for only the brave and the in-the-know

Once the sneaker faithful discovered the release date, they wasted no time. A queue was quickly formed outside of Reed Space days in advance of the launch. And, oh by the way, the launch was in February, and a blizzard ravaged New York City that week. Therefore, these individuals, mainly youths, pitched tents and waited *in a blizzard* outside of the store *for days*. Staple recounts that he bought pizzas for the kids each night, marveling at their willingness to brave the elements.[11]

Eventually, the crowd grew so large and unsettling on the day of the launch that the police arrived to disband the gathering. Naturally, those that had endured a blizzard for four days did not take kindly to this suggestion and refused to exit the queue. Escalating levels of police involvement followed, including SWAT participation.

Line inhabitants clinging desperately to the gates of the store were pulled away and, in some cases, arrested.

It wasn't just the police that caused Reed Street concern for their patrons, though. Due to the well-understood hype around the sneakers, any successful buyer walking away with the Pigeons would essentially be holding hundreds of dollars of value in their hands. So, Staple enlisted taxis to wait outside of the back of the store, where the lucky recipients

---

11 Ibid.

would be funneled out and whisked away from the potential harm and theft awaiting them out front.

Indeed, when interviewed, Staple often recounts finding baseball bats and even a freaking machete on the ground outside of the store once the dust had cleared.

The next day, the front page of the *New York Post* read "Sneaker Frenzy," with a picture of the Dunks beside the headline. Inquiring minds, previously blissfully unaware of sneaker culture and its economic power, wanted to know:

- Why were people risking harm for sneakers?
- What was it about *these* sneakers that elicited such a reaction?
- How much were they re-selling for?
- *How can I get a pair worth that much?*

The event, and particularly the questions above, catalyzed sneaker culture's transition into the mainstream. Today, the Pigeon Dunk is listed on StockX with an asking price in excess of $10,000, and that *New York Post* cover is immortalized on the outsole of a "Panda Pigeon" Dunk, released at the start of 2019.

While the Pigeon riot of 2005 is certainly the most notable example of release mayhem, it's far from the only one. In 2012, lines for the Nike Foamposite One "Galaxy" caused melees across the country: riot-gear police involvement in Orlando, a stabbing in Jersey City, a shot fired in Richmond, California, police discharging pepper spray in the Seattle area, and reports of other incidents.[12] In 2014, the release of the Supreme Nike Foamposites resulted in a near-riot outside of Supreme's SoHo location, with police resorting to the use of mace to calm crowds that had grown unruly.[13]

News of these events served only to amplify the hype; they brought word to the mainstream that limited sneakers commanded resale prices far in excess of their retail price tags. Four-figure resale values dropped jaws nationwide, recruited new followers, and perhaps most importantly, captured the imaginations of executives and entrepreneurs who knew that there simply had to be a better way.

News of sneaker riots, mall melees, and pepper spraying no longer grace the headlines as frequently today. These things do still happen, though. Just in the fall of 2018, the planned release of the Canary Yellow Nike Diamond Dunk at ComplexCon was postponed due to rowdy crowds, with the 250 pairs escorted out of the building by police (rightfully so – that's approximately $500,000 in value).

These incidents, unfortunately, still take place, but in lower quantity, and for good reason – the sneaker economy has evolved. The bright lights of capitalism have pulled the economy above ground.

---

12 "Nike Shoe Launch Sparks Melee At Florida Mall". 2012. *Twin Cities.* https://www.twincities.com/2012/02/23/nike-shoe-launch-sparks-melee-at-florida-mall/.

13 Rosario, Frank, and Aaron Feis. 2014. "Sneaker Release Nearly Causes Riot At Soho Store". *The New York Post.*

OFF THE CURBS AND ONLINE

First come, first serve lineups for highly limited releases have largely become relics of an era gone by. They still occur, but not nearly as frequently. Given the events just detailed, I don't think I need to explain why. Undoubtedly, line-ups persist, but mostly for releases that won't command resale premiums of several hundred dollars, the kind of premiums that don't warrant physical altercations and police involvement. The sneaker industry has built better release vehicles for the most valuable of sneakers. While those vehicles may often feel more complex, less just, and bereft of hope, they are at least safer.

Nikes which were once the subject of hotly contested curbside lines now find their way to owners based on who has the most nimble thumbs, as sneaker seekers furiously mash their iPhone screens to acquire pairs via the SNKRS application at the strike of 10:00a.m. on a Saturday morning. Of course, in the ceaseless sneaker-seeking arms race, nimble thumbs are one-upped by superior bots, devised by coding wizards to tip the scales in their favor. If one could riot against a bot, I'm confident that we would see more headlines than ever. Alas, we're left to sigh with exasperation as sneakers sell out in mere seconds, but that exhalation certainly bests the inhalation of pepper spray.

Moreover, those retailers, the ones that played arena to sneaker melees of the mid-2000s and early 2010s, have devised new ways to bring eager patrons within their confines without necessitating the use of police force or weapons. Today, consumers hoping to purchase at their local shops can visit in advance of a release to enter a raffle, which, I hate to say it, they will almost certainly lose. Absent that in-store victory, they may tempt the fates by turning their attention to that retailer's online raffle, which cleverly suggests that the consumer subscribe to the retailer's e-mail list, follow its Instagram account, and like its Facebook page to gain multiple entries. With the maximum number of entries gained, they will still almost certainly lose. The retailer certainly wins: they've gained access to many new potential customers with whom they can directly engage via e-mail and social media to sell other, less limited products.

The warm consolation accompanying this multitude of Ls taken by sneaker seekers is the reality that the sneaker that got away never truly escapes our reach, thanks to the maturation and sophistication of today's secondary market. Sure, eBay and the forums existed when sneaker riots were at their most intense, but those secondary mediums of exchange lacked trust, uniformity, and confidence of transacting. The only way to be sure you were acquiring authentic product – brand new, fresh, real sneakers – was to acquire them at launch. That's not the case today.

Today, the ship has never sailed, thanks to the growth of GOAT and StockX, secondary marketplaces offering authenticity-verifying intermediaries and a purchasing experience that very closely resembles online retail. Why despair over missing out on a coveted release when you might emerge victorious on the next one? Even if you don't like the next one, you can sell it and allocate proceeds towards purchasing the one that eluded you, all with a few taps of your finger.

Technology has brought sneaker-seekers off the curb, retailer closer to willing consumer, and consumer closer to their grails or to profits. The ease with which we can transact, buying and selling with mere taps, has rendered sneakers less an article of clothing and more an asset, that value determined only by how many consumers want it more. The growth of listings on the secondary marketplaces underscores this reality: by nature of the fact that the pairs are listed, the likelihood is that they were purchased not to wear at all.

Wants, desires, and consequently, values, are shaped constantly today by the inundation of information and impressions on offer from the countless sneaker blogs, YouTube channels, and the sneaker Instagram accounts. We know exactly what is releasing and when it's happening. We know exactly what we want and where to get it. We take not to the mall to scour the shelves, but instead to our various online emporiums of choice, not to discover new product – we already know what we're looking for – but to uncover the most favorable price. We see which sneakers, when captured in that perfect Instagram post, command the most likes.

We're beginning to form patterns from the quantity of likes, of blog posts, and of favorable YouTube reviews that better inform our projections of a sneaker's secondary market value. We subconsciously construct an equation that includes all of these variables and others to answer a vast array of questions. Should I buy these from Nike now? Will they be discounted? Can I flip these for more if I decide I don't like them? Are these not going to rise in price – should I, gulp, actually take them out of the box and wear them? How much should I list this pair for if I need to sell them now? What if I can afford to wait?

Knowingly or unknowingly, these are the questions that sneaker enthusiasts are constantly asking themselves and answering to the best of their ability, equipped with an aggregation of data cataloged from the daily onslaught of content. Simply put, things are a lot more complex now. With complexity comes frustration, yes, but also opportunity. Many of those that have embraced the complexity, that have tried to wrap their heads around it, have become successful entrepreneurs, whether as a purveyor of a service or as a large scale or smaller scale reseller.

Capitalistic pursuits do create a somewhat unfortunate reality: the sneaker purist, who views sneakers as footwear or expressions of self and not an engine of profit, gets squeezed. This is not a new reality, just one felt more intensely. People who want to wear the sneakers have been losing out to people who want the profits for many years. The economic evolution of the hobby need not be viewed as a net negative for the purist though, and the story of the sneaker economy need not begin and end with the fact that there are sneakers out there selling for four (and even five) figures.

Sure, those headline-grabbing figures are really freaking interesting, but that's the surface level view of the story. That's where the story starts. The real story is that there's this economy sprouting from that phenomenon, and in that economy, really bright people are innovating in ways that will advance not only sneaker commerce, but broader consumer retail. They're bringing brand and retailer ever closer to the consumer and products more frequently into the hands of those who covet them most, often at prices that more efficiently balance supply and demand.

The lessons on offer from the sneaker economy originate not just from the decisions being made by the sneaker titans, but by the entrepreneurs, the content creators, and the consumers themselves. The future of commerce is developing constantly right before our eyes, and I believe that the sneaker economy is a microcosm of that future.

StockX wasn't developed as "the stock market of sneakers", it was developed as "the stock market of *things*". The SNKRS app won't be the last to creatively connect consumers and fans directly with products that they value. Foot Locker won't be the only iconic retailer to take cues from boutiques in pursuing leaner physical footprints and deeper community engagement. The frameworks provided by Sneaker YouTube and sneaker Instagram for forging authentic connections with audiences and consumers are in many ways rewriting the definition of "influencer".

All of these innovations and these developments are *micro* – changing the sneaker landscape in the present moment – but they have the potential to induce change on a more *macro* level.

Thinking on even more micro terms, the individual sneaker consumer is developing an entrepreneurial spirit. Even that purist, like the enterprising market participant, is striving to make sense of the complexity simply for the purpose of acquiring their targets with increased savvy. To be a savvy consumer in today's sneaker economy requires critical thought, diligence, and a pinch of strategic instinct.

A savvy consumer is one that has a relatively firm handle on the supply and demand dynamics for a given release, has a hunch of where the price will ultimately end up, and avoids becoming the sucker that pays too much for a sneaker that will inevitably be a bargain bin dweller. To take it a step further, a savvy consumer that participates in the secondary market, as buyer or seller, understands how the bid-ask spread, the depth of each side of the market, and liquidity needs should impact his or her decision making.

These are considerations that, when addressed, may have the power to not only make us better sneaker collectors, but more informed consumers, negotiators, investors, and critical-thinkers outside of the confines of the sneaker economy.

Look, it sounds exhausting, and I recognize that. It sounds exhausting because it is exhausting.

At present, efficiently and effectively sneaker seeking is, quite frankly, pretty tiresome. But does it beat waiting four days in a blizzard? I'd say yes, but of course, everyone's entitled to their opinion....and then again, Jeff Staple did provide pizzas.

**

The growth of the sneaker economy coincides with the persistent escalation of the sneaker seeking arms race. With increased media coverage, we came out from the underground and into the mainstream. With the proliferation of more sophisticated technology, we've come in out of the cold and onto the internet. As it turns out, it's complicated in here.

Those with a passion for sneakers and an entrepreneurial spirit have provided us with all the information and the tools we need to transact with confidence; it's up to the consumer to digest the information and to put the information and the tools to good use. The brands and retailers are bringing us ever closer to the products that each of us personally covet via technology, but our odds of acquiring are shaped by dumb luck, timeliness, or a combination of both. No longer, though, is our safety a persistent variable in questing for those most limited of sneakers.

So far have we evolved that sneaker acquisition is less a quest of physical endurance and toughness and more a resemblance of research and due diligence seemingly fit for Wall Street. It's more sophisticated but ever so calculated, somehow colder than those city curbs despite the hollow illusion of warmth provided by all of those Instagram likes. We're off the streets, but the sneaker economy is more cut-throat than ever.

It's for this reason that those that still embrace the culture – the retailers ingrained in their communities, the YouTuber that cultivates authentic relationships with their followings, and the designer that takes inspiration from the street rather than vice versa – attain higher levels of success. They understand something that the rest don't: the only thing propping up those dollar signs, at the end of the day, is the culture that allowed the sneaker economy to grow in the first place.

It's a lesson not to be ignored by any business dealing with rapidly changing consumer tastes.

TAKEAWAYS FROM THE SNEAKONOMIST:

- Chaos, crime, violence, and rioting played a significant role in the acceleration of sneakonomic growth.
- These events drew mainstream headlines, and those mainstream headlines inspired more widespread interest.

- Newer market participants lured mainly by the promise of profits have had a diluting effect on sneaker culture as it once existed, further crowding out the sneaker purists.
- Despite the additional frustration for purists, entrepreneurial ventures have meaningfully lessened friction within the sneaker economy.
- Capitalistic pursuits led to the development of businesses that rendered sneaker acquisition safer, more orderly, and more sophisticated BUT also more complex.
- Effectively navigating this more structured sneaker economy requires the digestion of an abundance of data.
- Sneaker economy constituents can carve out successful niches by rising above the data and acting as purveyors of culture, ingraining themselves in their respective communities.

CHAPTER 3

THE OTHER ASSET CLASSES – HOW OTHER COLLECTIBLES FARE AGAINST THE TEST OF TIME

———

"If you really think of it, when a stock doesn't pay dividends, there really isn't a whole lot of difference between a share of stock and a baseball card.

If you put your Mickey Mantle rookie card on your desk, and a share of your favorite non-dividend paying stock next to it, and let it sit there for 20 years. After 20 years you would still just have two pieces of paper sitting on your desk.

The difference in value would come from how well they were marketed. If there were millions of stockbrokers selling baseball cards, if there were financial television channels dedicated to covering the value of baseball cards with a ticker of baseball card prices streaming at the bottom, if the fund industry spent billions to tell you to buy and hold baseball cards, I am willing to bet we would talk about the fundamentals of baseball cards instead of stocks."

—Mark Cuban[14]

Buy low, sell high. Simple enough in theory, extremely difficult in practice.

Nonetheless, we have a long societal history of individuals turning their attention away from the financial markets and towards the markets for other, nontraditional assets, performing their very poor and very misguided Warren Buffett impersonations in hopes of attaining attractive returns.

As sneakers continue to shift ever so slightly towards pure asset on the spectrum from article of clothing to asset class, it's important to keep in mind that they are far from the

---

14 Cuban, Mark. 2008. "Talking Stocks | Blog Maverick". *Blogmaverick.Com*. http://blogmaverick.com/2008/09/08/talking-stocks-and-money/.

first asset or collectible unusually characterized as a store of value or a vehicle for speculation, and they certainly won't be the last. Wherever there is both scarcity and demand, a market for collectibles is born. While the degrees of staying power vary, even momentary hype can catapult an asset from ordinary object to investment opportunity, no matter how ill contrived and under-researched that opportunity may be.

Those with the best information stand to profit, while others without it, blinded by the promise of profits, are the prey of the better informed. Many of the same principles apply to asset purchases both small in dollar value and enormous – from baseball cards to Da Vinci paintings.

There is much to be derived from the travails of trading in these other collectible commodities in terms of their relevance to the sneaker market. By examining the liquidity of each market (how easily and often one can sell their asset), the forces influencing value, and the informational asymmetries dictating market dynamics, we can better understand what the future may look like for a sneaker collection. Can an Air Jordan pass the test of time like a 1952 Mickey Mantle baseball card? Or will we be desperate to offload them for pennies on the dollar like Beanie Babies, just to free up space in our attics?

TRADING CARDS: FROM INFATUATION
TO SATURATION AND BACK

The most fabled baseball card in existence, the Honus Wagner T206 card, was printed and included in cigarette packs by the American Tobacco Company from 1909 to 1911. Topps, which started in principal as a chewing gum company, began producing baseball cards in 1952, the same year that the similarly precious Mickey Mantle card was produced. It was during that decade that the baseball card collecting frenzy started in earnest. That frenzied pursuit of new packs of cards from the various companies – Topps, Fleer, Upper Deck, and Dunross among others – lasted decades, with new fans taking up the practice, drawn by the suddenly eye-opening values of the rare cards from the industry's early days.

In the 1980s, collectors clung desperately to the rookie cards of players like Darryl Strawberry, Dwight Gooden, and Jose Canseco, believing that they had unearthed the next Mantle or even the next Wagner. They would protect them dearly, ensuring that they remained in mint condition for the alluring riches certain to greet them in the future.

Of course, collectors knew not that those careers would be far less illustrious than the Mick's. Far more importantly though, they didn't realize just how many copies of their precious treasures had flooded the market.

Importantly, by virtue of exclusive agreements facilitated by the Major League Baseball Players Association, Topps maintained a stranglehold on licensed baseball cards from the mid-1950s until 1980, when Fleer won an antitrust court case that ultimately broke the exclusivity. With that break in exclusivity and the significant increase in demand came the vast proliferation of supply in a market suddenly awash with new competitors.

The 1994 Major League Baseball strike, coupled with the production glut in the preceding decade, catalyzed the end of the collecting frenzy, at least in terms of buying newly produced packs at retail. Today, most of those cards from the 1980s and 1990s hold little value. They are but stacks of nostalgia-laden cardboard, littering the attics and basements of aging baseball fans across the country. There are select cases of cards from that era boasting impressive prices on the secondary market. Mostly though, those that were late to the hobby did not reap profits from those promising seeds that they nurtured for so many years.

Still, today, a robust marketplace remains for the baseball cards of the earlier era, and businesses adding structure, data, and services to the market are rising to benefit from the opportunity at hand. In 1998, PWCC, considered the leading marketplace for trading cards, was established to provide buyers and sellers with transparency, increased liquidity, and lower transaction costs. Additionally bolstering the legitimacy of trading in these assets was the emergence of an industry standard grading system, developed by the largest independent appraiser of sports cards, Professional Sports Authenticator. The company grades cards on a scale of one to ten, and these scores are widely accepted and widely utilized in assigning value.

As we'll discuss, the sneaker economy cries out for the presence of an independent, industry-standard grading system, particularly with regards to much older or used sneakers. Certainly, its arrival is not far in the offing.

PWCC touts the appeal of cards as an investment in a highly liquid alternative asset class, noting that according to the sales data that the company has tracked since 2008, trading cards have outperformed the S&P 500 by a large margin. The company maintains price indices for the top 100, 500, and 2500 cards, and all cards included in the indices must have been sold at least ten times in the last ten years, with at least two sales in the last two months. Such a parameter underscores the importance of liquidity; if these cards are to have appeal as an investment, buyers must be able to sell them swiftly and easily.

Exploring the performance of these indices on the PWCC website is highly fascinating. Yes, the top 100 have absolutely skyrocketed in value, registering a return on investment of 265% since 2008 through mid-September 2018, compared to the S&P 500 return of 98% over the same period. The top 500 registered a 164% return over the same period, and the top 2500 registered an 89% return, actually underperforming the S&P.[15]

---

15 "PWCC Market Indices". 2018. *Pwccmarketplace.Com*. https://www. pwccmarketplace.com/market-indices.

Where it gets really interesting is the exclusion of the top 100. The 100-500 ranked cards have returned 66% since 2008, while the 100-2500 ranked cards have returned just 27%, vastly underperforming the equity markets. Indeed, outside of the top 100, the growth in asset values leaves something to be desired, with values from 100-2500 actually declining from 2008 until 2015 before experiencing some modest resurgence.[16]

A glance at the top 25 cards in the index shows that just one card among them, a Magic Johnson and Larry Bird rookie card, was produced in 1980 or later. The rest hail from the 1930s, 1940s, and 1950s, when supply was far tamer and fewer people were going to such great length to preserve the cards, which of course means fewer cards with high graded scores.

For your curiosity, the previously mentioned Honus Wagner and Grade 10 Mickey Mantle cards are excluded from the indices, since they do not meet the liquidity parameter, though a grade 8 1952 Mantle tops the index. One Wagner card, previously owned by Wayne Gretzky, most recently sold for $2.8 million in 2007 and would fetch far more if sold now. A grade 10 1952 Topps Mickey Mantle card is said to be worth approximately $10 million today. [17]

---

16 Ibid.
17 Sullivan, Paul. 2018. "Trading Cards: A Hobby That Became A Multimillion-Dollar Investment". *New York Times*.

It's worth highlighting that when a marketplace grows as sophisticated and structured as the one PWCC is cultivating, ancillary services are bound to follow. To that end, PWCC is set to offer users new services at the end of 2018: PWCC Vault, a secure and insured repository for safe keeping, and lines of credit using collectors' card portfolios as the collateral, a practice that has long been used not only for investment portfolios of public securities, but also for unique alternative assets like art collections.[18] When you have sophisticated, timely, accurate data to accompany the trading of an asset, services offered alongside those assets can evolve far beyond what was thought possible.

So how can we apply what we learned from baseball cards to the world of sneakers?

Is the present moment akin to the 1980s in baseball cards? Certainly, the frenzy around collecting is similar, as buyers, sellers, and even investment funding flood the marketplace. It would not be unfair to suggest that due to both the great quantity of supply hitting markets today and also the great care with which collectors are preserving their sneakers, most pairs produced today are unlikely to appreciate meaningfully or even preserve their value over time. As has been the case with baseball cards, those rarest of gems will tower in value over the bountifully supplied and easily acquired. Suffice it to say, lessons from the world of trading cards suggest that

18 "New Alternative Asset Class". 2018. *Pwccmarketplace.Com*. https:// www.pwccmarketplace.com/alternative-investment.

sneakers bought and flipped today are likely best unloaded quickly for speculative profit than held for the long term as investment. However, those precious sneaker gems – the sneaker Mickey Mantles – few though they may be, *can* still be manufactured today should the story and design resonate strongly enough in conjunction with the provision of minimal supply.

Of course, there is a critical difference between 1980s baseball card collecting and the present sneaker moment that would prevent as severe a crash: *transparency.*

StockX CEO, Josh Luber, has long considered the parallels between the two markets, and sheds light on why sneakers aren't destined for the same fate as cards: "There was no transparency around supply. We didn't have the internet. Everybody thought that they were the only one with twelve '89 Upper Deck Ken Griffey, Jrs. But guess what? Everybody had twelve '89 Upper Deck Ken Griffey, Jrs. But nobody knew that, because we didn't have the internet. There was no way to really know that and have that amount of transparency in the market."

Transparency is a meaningful weapon at the disposal of today's sneaker collector. We have all the tools necessary to know if everybody else has the most recently released Air Maxes. Baseball card collectors didn't have that luxury. They just knew that Ken Griffey, Jr. was going to be good, that they had his rookie card, and that rookie cards had been valuable historically. They had no indication of the balance between supply and demand, beyond perhaps anecdotal evidence and word-of-mouth.

Transparency isn't the only difference though. It's really not even the biggest difference. The biggest difference is utility, a point underscored by Luber.

"Baseball cards are a pure asset. They're easy to have lots of from a storage standpoint. Condition doesn't deteriorate. With sneakers, the brands, the $90 billion part of the market, *that's* their focus. They want to sell as many products as they can. This [the sneaker collector segment] is just a small sliver of it that they leverage for marketing, for brand, and for PR."

The diehard sneaker collector or reseller often loses sight of the fact that they are but a mere piece of the overall revenue picture for the sneaker brands. An important piece, due to the implications for brand heat, but a small piece nonetheless. The vast majority of consumers buying sneakers are buying them not as an asset but for their utility as shoes. The vast majority of sneakers get used. This, of course, was not the case for baseball cards. While these differences are of great importance, we'll still discuss in detail later whether or not there is a bubble of sorts forming in the sneaker economy.

Still, differences though there may be, the rigor instilled around the baseball card marketplace provides an interesting blueprint for sneakers. In the short term, as the proliferation of robust sneaker market data continues to intensify, we may stay tuned for the arrival of new services – maybe even lending with sneakers as collateral – that once seemed farfetched but no longer feel quite so strange. Custodial services for sneaker "portfolios" are already in the works, and it's not difficult to envision the provision of a financing option for enterprise-level resellers, availing them of capital to acquire more supply, backed by existing inventory.

One may be cardboard and the other may be leather and rubber, but both trading cards and sneakers found their roots in sport and an unexpected future as an alternative asset class.

BEANIE BABIES: SCARCITY
WITHOUT LASTING DEMAND

Trading cards, at least those that were truly rare, stood the test of time, still commanding awe-inspiring amounts of money today. The American Tobacco Company didn't include Honus Wagner cards in their cigarette packs with designs of those cards being worth millions of dollars decades down the road, though. They just wanted to sell a few more packs of cigarettes.

But what about collectibles where rarity, scarcity, and mouth-watering future values were an intended purpose for buying in the first place?

Such was the case with the Beanie Baby craze of the 1990s. The stuffed toys exploded onto the market in 1994, and very quickly became a collectible phenomenon. People of all ages flocked to stores, ate ungodly amounts of McDonalds for the

Happy Meal Beanie Baby toys, and tucked their prizes away for safekeeping and the windfalls sure to follow.

The toys captured the profit-seeking hearts of many, with magazines and guides suggesting that many individual bears were worth hundreds of dollars and sets worth tens of thousands. As is often the case with nascent asset classes, entrepreneurial parties rushed to provide pricing data. Time and again, such a practice lends a perception of legitimacy to the marketplace and inspires the confident entry of new participants. Suddenly, people believed that they had not bins of bean-filled animals, but portfolios of valuable assets.

A *Wall Street Journal* article from 1998 tells the tale of two Beckys in Naperville, Illinois who had accumulated complete sets of the toys, valuing those sets at between $90,000 and $100,000 and planning to use them to finance their children's college educations.[19]

Ty, the maker of Beanie Babies, reaped the spoils of such stories for several years, amassing revenues estimated in the hundreds of millions of dollars as eager buyers shelled out $5.95 a Beanie Baby, not for their children to play with, but for the prospect of profits.

Of course, all this enthusiasm with regard to resale prices came without the benefit of timely and accurate information on actual asset sales taking place. That's where the "guides" were lacking. They provided value estimates without a

---

19   Gibson, Richard. 1998. "Ready For A Bear Market? Some Worry That The Beanie Baby Craze Is Going Soft". *Wall Street Journal*.

thorough, deep, and recent record of *actual* transactions. Sure, the listed values may have been realized in a sale or two, but what would happen when people really went to liquidate their portfolios en masse?

So people bought and bought, blissfully unaware of how, when, and to whom they would actually sell to realize their profits.

A quote from that same 1998 *WSJ* article really says it all: "And *Warman's Today's Collector Magazine* wondered recently: "Beanie Babies: trash or treasure?" *Warman's* went on to conclude that prices should stay high – unless collectors start to sell. A market in which people don't sell, of course, is no market at all."[20]

In that article, author Richard Gibson questions the value of the toys in a beautiful indication of the speculative nature of the era: "At those prices, Internet stocks seem cheap."[21]

Well, when collectors, seeing prices begin to top out and waver, finally went to sell, there wasn't really anybody left to sell to, at least not at attractive levels. People seemed to be coming around to the realization that these bean-filled toys were just that – toys. They had no real value, only value that had been assigned based on the idea of scarcity.

But when there's no demand left for a scarce item, whether because of a waning belief in rising values or otherwise, that scarcity means very little.

---

20 Ibid.
21 Ibid.

As we know today, people are no longer really engaging in the active trade of Beanie Babies, though not necessarily for lack of trying. Despite the occasional article cropping up that suggests that these toys are, in fact, actually worth incredible sums of money after all, Ryan Tedards, who runs a Beanie Babies price guide website, tells *The Wall Street Journal* that it's actually fake news: "There's just this cycle of fake news about Beanie Babies, some of them are the same article, copied and pasted, but they get a ton of traffic. It is always a bit of a battle. I have to explain to them that what they read or saw is not true."[22]

In fact, those who have recently unearthed collections in attics or basements struggle to offload them for any real value whatsoever, because there's simply no demand for it. Those surreal values of the 1990s are as surreal as the values were for many dot-com stocks during the same time. Those dot-coms aren't rising from the dead, and neither are Beanie Babies.

That 1998 *Journal* article does include a quote that draws a stark contrast to both today's sneaker market and to the trading card marketplace: "'They're all bubbles,' Robert Z. Aliber, professor of international economics at the University of Chicago, says of such instant collectibles markets. The informal nature of such markets helps propel prices up and can delay inevitable plunges, he notes. 'There is no New York Stock

---

22 Mahtani, Shibani. 2018. "Sorry, Collectors, Nobody Wants Your Beanie Babies Anymore". *Wall Street Journal*.

Exchange for this stuff' for immediate and widely shared price information. 'It's like real estate instead of stocks.'"[23]

What has been avoided in the sneaker market, thanks to the entrepreneurial efforts of those that have either catalogued eBay prices (the origins of Campless – predecessor to StockX) or developed marketplaces with robust data sets (StockX and GOAT), is that informality. Certainly, informality could characterize the sneaker economy of the past, but today, price information is, in fact, immediately and widely shared, and the depth of each side of the market, buyer and seller, is transparently conveyed.

Indeed, it's possible that some sneakers may go the way of Beanie Babies in the future, but it won't blindside those with sneaker boxes in their closets if they have their eyes open. Still, such a dramatic fall from grace seems unlikely, because unlike with Beanie Babies, sneaker collectors are selling and indeed selling all the time – and they are finding buyers.

Now those buyers could just be greater fools, but the significant volume of transactions suggests that the sneaker economy will not spontaneously drop off a cliff. Furthermore, consumers can use the significant information at their disposal to make an informed determination as to whether or not they should continue purchasing in the face of either increasing supply or waning demand.

---

23 Gibson, Richard. 1998. "Ready For A Bear Market? Some Worry That The Beanie Baby Craze Is Going Soft". *Wall Street Journal.*

Those Air Max 90s and Air Jordan models that graced feet on trips to the store for Beanie Babies in the 1990s may still fetch value in the present day, but don't expect to see those bean-filled toys, Tamagotchi pets, or Furbies on StockX anytime soon.

FINE ART: SNEAKERS FOR THE ULTRA WEALTHY?

Let's examine the properties of perhaps the most widely accepted, 'unusual' alternative asset class: fine art. Unlike the aforementioned assets, this one regularly commands an allocation in the portfolio of highly sophisticated institutional and ultra-high net worth investors. Whether for the diversification properties, the aesthetic joy, or both, investors are increasingly allocating portions of their net worth towards art.

Part of the impetus is the dearth of more attractive areas for incremental investment. With interest rates remaining low over the past decade, stock market prices reaching new highs, the possibility of inflation lurking on the horizon, investors turn with increasing frequency to the arena of tangible assets. A report from Deloitte and Art Tactic estimates that, in 2016, ultra-high net worth investors held $1.62T in art, with that figure projected to rise to $2.7T by 2026.[24]

---

24 "Art: An Asset Class To Be Reckoned With – The Sovereign Group". 2018. *The Sovereign Group.* https://www.sovereigngroup.com/press-room/art-asset-class-reckoned/.

Whether starting a collection to decorate the walls of a beautiful house or to generate returns, portfolios and demand are growing. However, the dynamics of this market are vastly different from the liquid trading of stocks and bonds. Liquidity for art is extremely thin. Buying is easy. Selling is an involved process, replete with meaningful costs and logistical hurdles.

Will a reputable gallery take on the task of selling the piece? What kind of cut would they like in order to do so? Will any new authenticity and condition issues crop up at the time of sale?

These are intricate questions that make selling complicated. Additionally, significant liquidity exists mainly for the most celebrated of artists. As noted by Doug Woodham for *Artsy*: "Works by 52,105 living and deceased artists appeared at auction in 2017, according to Art Basel and UBS's The Art Market | 2017 report. While this number gives a sense of the breadth of the market, what's much more interesting is that only one percent of these names accounted for the majority of sales value (64 percent). Like many talent markets, the art market is characterized by a winner-takes-all dynamic, in which the top names capture most of the rewards, with the rest selling for far less. As a result, there is very little liquidity in the art market, other than for the handful of stars whose works appear regularly at auction."[25]

---

25 Woodham, Doug. 2018. "What You Need To Know About Investing In Fine Art". *Artsy*. https://www.artsy.net/article/

Not only is liquidity itself a constraint, but the art market is also plagued by a dearth of recent and accurate information. This problem is somewhat mitigated by the increasing role of technology in the market, but persists anyways. The root of this problem is the arena in which most sales take place: gallery sales do not require public disclosure of price paid. It is therefore difficult to accurately assess exactly what your art is worth, particularly if it is not the work of an in-demand star or if it has not traded recently. Professionals with expertise in appraisal are available in surplus, but certainty of price is only realized upon sale.

Still, arming oneself with the best possible information is absolutely critical to sound investment decision making in the art market, a fact underscored by the travels of Da Vinci's *Salvator Mundi*. The original version of the famous painting lived in Louisiana for decades, after being mistakenly identified as a School of Da Vinci painting done by one of the artist's students. Relatives of those who brought it to the U.S. lived for years unaware of the painting's significance. Eventually, the painting was bought in an estate sale in 2005 for $10,000 by two dealers who then lobbied for its authentication as the original. They were armed with better information and a keener eye, and my-oh-my did they reap the spoils, selling it for $80 million in 2013.

---

artsy-editorial-investing-fine-art-investing-traditional-asset-classes.

And yet, others had even better information or a better sense of where the market was headed, and the painting immediately sold again for $127 million, and most recently for $450 million in 2017. In sum, one of the most famous paintings from one of history's most celebrated artists, a painting once owned by King Charles I, hung in the halls of a Louisiana home with its owners completely unaware of its significance, before selling for $10,000 and eventually nearly half of a billion dollars.

The lesson? Well first, if you have any unidentified art lying around, make sure it's not the work of a historical icon, but more relevantly, informational asymmetry is of grave consequence in the art market.

The parallels with the sneaker world are a bit more difficult to spot, but exist nonetheless. Value, of course, is based fairly subjectively on the appeal to and perception held by the masses, with those works boasting the richest stories with regard to their creation often commanding the richest values. There's clearly a magnificent disparity between a $450 million Da Vinci and a $40,000 Nike Air Mag, but they dominate their respective markets for similar reasons. Plus, you probably *could* make a case for Nike designer, Tinker Hatfield, as the industry's Da Vinci.

An additional parallel: it is those objects that have the widest followings and are most celebrated that trade with the most liquidity. Just as it's more difficult to move a piece of art by a relatively unknown artist for an attractive price, so too is it generally harder to quickly find a good bid for a pair of Diadoras or a Saucony pair relative to a pair of Nikes or Adidas.

Where sneakers do hold an advantage in market function, though, is in broader liquidity and in availability of information. Offloading a popular sneaker is the work of mere minutes via GOAT or StockX, and the pricing is quite transparent. Similarly, moving a less demanded sneaker or a higher volume of sneakers is accomplished with the assistance of the consignment gurus, Stadium Goods or Flight Club for example, who conduct all of the logistical legwork but at higher commissions – often 20%.

As these markets grow larger and more active, we are presented with immense data and transparency around current market dynamics, which better inform our ability to buy or sell with far less fear that we're selling a Da Vinci sneaker equivalent for $250 when it can really fetch $1,000. While I'm sure that there are rare exceptions, such a phenomenon doesn't really occur in today's sneaker world.

Are sneakers the every man's art collection? It's not a bad way to think about it. And even if they're not, all is not lost; at least collectors can offload their collection with confidence.

WATCH YOUR STEP AND TAKE YOUR TIME: STORING VALUE ON YOUR WRIST

What about fashion articles that, like sneakers, can be worn, used, and purchased for purposes beyond their capacities as a store of value?

Wristwatches may be just such an asset, somewhat bridging the gap between fine art and sneakers, but skewing in likeness more towards the former than the latter. In fact, for decades, the secondary watch market was characterized by the same opacity that can plague fine art. Watch trade took place mainly in two arenas: watch shops and auction houses. Watch shop transacting of course relies upon finding a dealer that can be trusted to purchase and sell at prevailing, fair prices, and acceptance by an auction house is reserved only for those most valuable of pieces.

At the very high end, watches can indeed fetch values comparable to the fine art market. Take for example the Rolex Daytona previously owned by Paul Newman, a watch collecting grail, which sold for nearly $18 million in 2017. That, of course, is an outlier of epic proportions, but the reality is that most watches will fail to hold their value, with certain exceptions.

Even with websites like WatchBox and Hodinkee aiming to provide increased transparency around vintage watch sales for the "masses," with values typically clustering in the $5,000-$20,000 range, two brands dominate the resale watch market: Rolex and Patek Philippe. These brands and their watches of eras gone by, for which supply is dwindling, boast robust transaction history and a proven ability to retain value.

However, one cannot simply walk into a watch shop, buy a new Rolex, and expect to flip it tomorrow for greater value. In fact, the second you walk out of the shop, your prize has likely decreased in value by almost half, given the significant mark-ups occurring throughout the distribution and sales process. Time has much work to do on the road to appreciation.

"After 20 or 30 years it starts to appreciate gradually in value—that's what's happened to almost all Rolex watches," Paul Altieri, CEO of Rolex Dealer Bob's Watches, told *Time* in 2015. "So we're starting to see the 16800 become collectible. That's the last Submariner made before the current one now."[26]

Resale value doesn't function in quite the same way that it does on the sneaker market. In many cases, if you successfully acquire a sought-after sneaker, you *can* immediately flip it for profit. This is the result of a market in which the challenge in acquiring is scarcity, rather than price. To be clear, Rolex doesn't produce their watches in large quantity by any means, but demand doesn't dramatically outstrip supply for the watches in the same way it does for the most limited sneakers. Rather, demand for the Rolex at a high price is

26 Wolff-Mann, Ethan. 2018. "Watches Are Bad Investments—With One Notable Exception". *Money*. http://time.com/money/4058109/ watches-value-rolex-investment/.

largely satisfied, so there's no immediate resale premium to be had as the equation is balanced.

Over time, however, as supply falls out of circulation and fewer watches in very good or new condition remain, appreciation begins. As with any other asset, the laws of supply and demand dictate value. These forces simply exert their influence at different times in the product lifecycle for watches and sneakers.

It is, consequently, not a tremendous asset for the impatient or for those with liquidity needs, though the online arenas like WatchBox are at least increasing the ease with which collectors can buy or sell.

Still, you cannot buy a brand-new Rolex today and assume that you are guaranteed returns or even protection of principal twenty to thirty years down the road. History would indicate that might be a safe assumption, but you would be wise to leverage the data and publications available today to better understand how often the manufacturer is coming to market with similar products and at what level of supply.

For most individuals, truly "investing" in watches is a losing proposition. Retailer and distributor markups simply erode return potential right at purchase, and the timeline for value recovery is both long and uncertain. A Rolex may be a better "investment" than an expensive television or a piece of furniture, in that it *should* hold some value over the years, but better than a traditional investment in stocks or bonds for most individuals? It's possible but not likely.

For those with expertise and capital though, the asset has proven to yield fruitful returns. Such has been the case for The Watch Fund. Essentially, the concept is this: an "investor" provides the fund with a minimum investment of $250,000. In return, that individual actually receives watches with a retail value of $500,000 to hold as collateral until they're sold. Predominantly because of its scale, access, and connections, the fund is able to identify and purchase sought-after watches at prices well below the levels at which collectors will ultimately be willing to purchase them.

According to a 2017 *Forbes* article, the fund boasts approximately $40 million in assets, and the fund's website suggests a return target of 20-30% net returns annually.[27] The fund, however, is really only for those with an interest in watches as a pure asset, not those longing for the sweet shine of a Rolex on their wrists.

In a world where transparency is rapidly increasing, it's perhaps difficult to gauge the sustainability of such a model, but the even more sobering reality is that success in such a strategy would not be attainable to anyone lacking the right connections and access to capital. It bears a striking similarity to the folly with which many ill-informed sneaker resellers enter the market. Without reliable "plugs" and the

---

27   Kaur, Tarandip. 2017. "Ones To Watch: How To Trade Timepieces For Impressive Returns". *Forbes.Com*. https://www.forbes.com/sites/tarandipkaur/2017/09/24/ones-to-watch-how-to-trade-timepieces-for-impressive-returns/#518e3d81b1a8.

ability to purchase significant inventory, the odds of mean-ingful financial success are low.

The lesson in both sneakers and watches is fairly similar for those without a deep Rolodex of connections and access to deep pockets – you're best served not viewing either item as a pure asset. That being the case, buy what you like inde-pendent of future value expectations.

Still, with sneakers, should you feel the need to speculate, your ability to liquidate your asset at a reasonable price is more assured, and twenty to thirty years of patience is not a prerequisite. With a strong feel for supply and demand dynamics and some luck, profits can be attained quickly, but perhaps not consistently. Even so, it's surprisingly difficult to argue that $10,000 could be put to better financial use in watches than in sneakers, at least in the short term, where a portion of those funds may also finance better connectivity to limited sneaker releases via bots or otherwise.

***

If sneakerheads are crazy for trading and collecting hoards of sneakers, it's at least nice to know that they indeed have company, though some company has proven smarter than others. We can see that the rise of sneaker collecting is not the manic fervor of accumulating Beanie Babies, and it's probably not going to become the acceptable long-term store of value into which the fine art asset class has evolved.

Perhaps, then, sneaker collecting is most likely heading in a similar direction to baseball cards: where collectors still treasure their nostalgia-laden pieces regardless of value, but the wheat has been separated from the chaff. That is to say, tremendous long-term values are reserved only for the scarcest of industry crown jewels, while values associated with issues of greater initial supply boast very little staying power.

In any case, the participants in the sneaker economy, the collectors in particular, have much that they can learn from the collecting of other tangible assets, those that derive their followings and value largely from subjective appeal and the laws of supply and demand. In many ways, we are not embarking on uncharted waters in the sneaker economy, but in others, namely through the creation of more liquid, efficient, informationally well-equipped marketplaces, the sneaker economy might just become an entirely different case study of its own.

We'll explore the various economy constituents and the strategic and competitive forces that guide them in order to better assess not only in which direction the asset class is headed, but also how the *economic* winners will distance themselves from the losers over time. I stress the use of the word *economic*, because remember: beauty is indeed in the eye of the beholder, and for those collectors not out for profits or economic gain, there is no losing in the accumulation of fresh kicks.

- Sneakers are not the first unusual collectible to be accepted as a store of value or a vehicle for speculation, and they certainly won't be the last.

- The difference between the present sneaker moment and the crashes of assets like baseball cards and Beanie Babies is two-fold: 1) we are the beneficiaries of significant market transparency today, and 2) sneakers are not yet regarded as a pure asset by the majority of consumers, with collectors representing only a small niche segment.

- The availability of standard grading or appraisal systems and recent, concrete transaction data contributes to the efficient function of a market.

- The liquidity for sneakers is actually vastly superior to that of many alternative, collectible assets. Many sneakers trade fairly frequently, and recent data is often readily available to support transactions.

- The way in which assets are released informs how their value will develop over time. If demand greatly outstrips supply at release, that asset will immediately increase in value. If not, it may take years or decades for that balance to shift in favor of capital appreciation. Sneaker values can appreciate in either manner, depending on the case.

PART 2

UNDERSTANDING SNEAKER MARKET (DYS)FUNCTION

CHAPTER 4

THE PRIMARY MARKET – HOW SNEAKER BRANDS NAVIGATE THE SUPPLY AND DEMAND BALANCE

———

"We are a derivative business. Our business relies on the ability of another business to create product that people want. Fundamentally, that's the thing that's most challenging in our business. It's about the ability of brands to continue to innovate and execute."

—Matt Cohen, VP of Business Development at GOAT

It's the bedrock idea upon which almost every other decision in the sneaker economy is made: the brands know what they're doing. The sneaker economy is big and it's growing, but that growth has been, at its heart, a derivative of the savvy of the sneaker brands.

The brands may not be able to hop in Doc Brown's DeLorean and travel back to the future, and they may not ace every decision, but at the end of the day, they know what they're doing. Their decision-making is well-informed, thoughtfully considered, and strategically rigorous.

This does not mean that they do not err. They do.

But it's very often due less to flagrantly poor decision making and more to the sheer difficulty of perfectly navigating the balance between supply and demand, a task which, when executed correctly, is both exquisite art and pinpoint-precise science.

As with any other market, the key to understanding the sneaker market at its core is developing a fundamental grasp of that delicate balance. Though it sounds simple enough, striking the perfect balance is an impossible task, even when solely considering the relationship between brand and consumer. Now, with the maturation of a robust secondary market, impossible may not even adequately express the difficulty of the task.

Certainly, we will discuss in great detail the implications of the secondary market on the primary, but for the moment, let's consider the pure dynamics of the primary market, the core relationship between brand and consumer.

Have you ever bought a sneaker that you were otherwise on the fence about, but the expectation of rarity swayed your decision? You know very well the role that scarcity (or the illusion of it) can play.

Have you ever lamented your decision not to buy a product that was incredibly available and accessible, only to find that it had vanished from shelves when your desire resurfaced? You know that absence makes the heart grow fonder.

Anticipating these consumer pangs, however, is a maneuver with an immeasurably high degree of difficulty.

Even the sneaker Goliaths, Nike and Adidas, typically best in class with regard to appropriately generating and projecting demand and addressing it effectively with commensurate supply, consistently grapple with this core challenge of balancing the two forces. They often fail.

Failure is commonplace. Perfection is rare.

Scarcity is often a key weapon deployed to confront this challenge. Scarcity, though, is a fairly abstract and variable concept, that elicits more questions than it answers:

- How scarce is too scarce?
- What quantity of sales is appropriate to leave on the table in the defense of scarcity?
- How does the definition of scarcity differ for a Jordan 1 and for a Stan Smith? Dramatically.

- How much *should* it differ? Maybe not as much as you think.
- Is scarcity alone enough to generate buzz?

These are all questions that must be critically considered to better understand the function of the sneaker economy, but at the core of our understanding must be a grasp of how the brands think about pulling the supply lever to influence momentum.

We'll explore some large-scale case studies to inform this understanding, but do keep in mind that the sneakerhead niche is just one relatively small subset of the mammoth customer bases targeted by the brands. It's undoubtedly an important subset, due to both the marketing buzz created by this segment and the demand provided by resellers, but we must be careful not to overinflate the impact of the sneakerhead on the broader market. When we discuss the financial results of a Nike or an Adidas, do be mindful of the fact that their quarterly revenue is multiples of the entire annual resale market.

CREATING AND MAINTAINING SCARCITY

Jordan Brand is the foundation upon which the sneaker economy was built – most would agree with this assertion. However, allow yourself for a moment to wonder what would happen if that foundation eroded, or if it was peeled away like a precariously placed Jenga piece. We all have that friend that gets just *a bit* too ambitious, knocking the Jenga tower over before the fun really begins – let's call him Steve. Dammit Steve!

Steve, in this case, was the plenitude of supply introduced to the market by Jordan Brand in 2016 and 2017. Steve, as always, ruined the fun early. The introduction of vast supply to the market, likely an attempt to harvest maximal revenue from a wave of success that rolled on in seemingly ceaseless fashion, eroded the perception of scarcity that had rendered Jordans so coveted in the first place.

But let's take a step back for a moment and consider the dynamics from a high level.

At the core of the sneaker market is the relationship between sneaker brand and sneaker consumer. Retailer success and resale fervor are, generally speaking, derivative products of those relationships. Those relationships are meaningfully shaped by the ways in which brands utilize the lever of supply to influence, react to, and generate consumer demand. When a brand pulls the supply lever, whether flooding the market or reigning in supply to create scarcity, the ripple effects are felt throughout the economy.

Scarcity has served as a central growth driver of the sneaker economy as we know it, and there is no better starting point for building an understanding of how brands use (or misuse) scarcity than with an examination of Jordan Brand's trials and tribulations from 2016 onward.

Whether you prefer His Airness or King James, its undeniable that Jordan's namesake sneaker brand has been a fundamental driver of the growing sneaker collector's economy. However, once unfathomable, the question now lingers: just how long can the stories of a transcendent athlete from twenty years ago continue to propel sneaker sales as we motor ahead toward 2020?

It's an entirely reasonable contention that Jordan Brand and its most iconic sneakers have long since transcended the athlete's popularity. In that vein, perhaps the brand can continue to grow independent of the GOAT's relevance in present-day basketball culture. After all, the athlete debuted the Air Jordan 1 in 1985, rarely wore it on court afterwards, and yet, Nike continues to produce new, fast-selling riffs on the model thirty-three years later. Still, the supply and demand balance and the freshness of stories remain delicate challenges for Nike to manage.

Those that have hurried to buy a Jordan release, their mouths still bitter with the taste of previous failures, know very well that scarcity begets demand. In the absence of scarcity, less celebrated silhouettes and colorways litter store shelves, retailer websites, and secondary marketplaces at discounted prices. Consequently, any brand can quickly learn the pain of a fall from iconic status should they err in their expectation of the supply and demand balance.

For Jordan Brand in particular, where the stories of the past fuel the sales of tomorrow, negotiating and preventing that fall is paramount.

The sneaker landscape shifts quicker today than ever before. One moment, collectors are huddling outside of stores for the chance at a limited sneaker. The next, they're returning it to that store because unexpectedly large supply, whether via restocks or otherwise, constrained resale prices. Before long, that sneaker is hitting clearance.

Critically, manufacturers must anticipate potential softness in demand and adjust supply accordingly, not necessarily for the success of any one release, but for the longer-term status of the brand. Such was the case for Nike and Jordan Brand as ominous supply and demand dynamics looming on the horizon of the company's 2018 fiscal year provided dark undercurrents to a largely successful fiscal 2017.

A journey through the transcripts of quarterly earnings conference calls, which typically focus on the positive while sufficiently and appropriately acknowledging shortcomings of investor interest, over those two years sheds light on a story of underlying tumult in Jordan Brand's standing in the sneaker economy.

Start in August of 2016 – the first quarter of the 2017 fiscal year (fiscal years are needlessly confusing – we'll stick mainly with months and years from here on out in this chapter). Former Nike President, Trevor Edwards, lauded the success of the brand, suggesting "It's clear, with continued double-digit revenue growth, the Jordan Brand is more popular than ever."[28]

One quarter later, Edwards again celebrated Jordan's continued presence in the sneaker world's spotlight:

"At the same time, Jordan footwear continues to electrify the marketplace with products that generate excitement through vibrant storytelling. In Q2, this was highlighted by the global launch of the much anticipated Space Jam 11 collection in both performance and lifestyle. And when combined with other releases this quarter like the Jordan 1s, the True Blue 3s and the XI in the original colorway, we surprised and delighted sneaker fans across the globe." [29]

Electrify! It's a strong word – one that feels a bit more awkward to associate with the brand today – but he was absolutely right in 2016.

Now, clearly there's a lot of "sneaker speak" in those quotes which may be somewhat foreign to an outsider, so for context, let's take a moment to provide some background on one of the sneakers that Edwards references above. It'll help to explain what made the quarter so electric.

---

28 "FY 2017 Q1 Earnings Release Conference Call Transcript". 2016. *Nike, Inc. – Investor Relations.* https://s1.q4cdn.com/806093406/files/doc_financials/2017/Q1/NIKE-Inc.Q117-OFFICIAL-Transcript-with-QA_FINAL.pdf.

29 "FY 2017 Q2 Earnings Release Conference Call Transcript". 2016. *Nike, Inc. – Investor Relations.* https://s1.q4cdn.com/806093406/files/doc_financials/2017/Q2/NIKE-Inc.Q217-OFFICIAL-Transcript-with-QA-FINAL.pdf.

The Jordan 11 is among the most celebrated and unique stories not only among Jordan Brand sneakers but also perhaps in the entire sneaker landscape. Following his brief retirement from basketball to pursue a baseball career, Michael Jordan returned to the Bulls in March of 1995 to aid the team in its pursuit of playoff success and an NBA title. As many basketball fans will recall, when Jordan returned, he opted to wear the number 45, which he had worn in his baseball pursuits, rather than his traditional 23, which had already been retired by the Bulls organization.

It was in the midst of a tightly contested Eastern Conference semi-final series against the young and talented Orlando Magic, led by the dynamic combination of Penny Hardaway (a Nike legend in his own right) and Shaquille O'Neal (a Reebok darling), that Jordan debuted one of the most storied silhouettes in Jordan canon, the 11. Sporting patent leather along the midsole of the sneaker, the 11 was both a futuristic and sophisticated model.

In games one and two of the tilt, Jordan donned the "Concord" colorway of the sneaker, with black patent leather, a white upper, and the number 45 stitched on the back. As the Bulls were obligated to wear black sneakers as part of their uniforms, Jordan was swiftly fined for wearing the "Concords" (ironic – given that the "banned" Air Jordan 1 was, in fact, black), and Jordan opted to return to the court for game 4 in a version with a black upper and a blue Jumpman logo.

The Magic eliminated the Bulls in six games, and over a year later, Nike released three colorways of the XI, including the "Concord," in advance of Jordan's big-screen debut in *Space Jam*. One colorway – the one debuted by Jordan in game 4 and sported against the Monstars in the film – was not included in the release and didn't make its way to consumers until the 2000 holiday season. Despite the fact that the sneaker retailed for $125 nearly twenty years ago and was re-released in 2009 and 2016, never worn pairs of the 2000 Space Jams still fetch in excess of $300 on StockX.

As Edwards alluded to, the Space Jams relaunched in time for the holiday season of 2016. Following the third quarter, it was declared by Edwards that "the Space Jam was the largest and most successful shoe launch in the history of Nike."[30]

In the history of Nike.

Let that sink in. The most successful sneaker launch in the *history* of the most successful sneaker brand. Not some hot, new technology. Not the signature sneaker of the most popular athlete of the moment. The most successful shoe launch in the history of Nike is a re-release of a sneaker from the mid-1990s, which was named after a Looney Tunes movie.

The sneaker economy is...different.

30 "FY 2017 Q3 Earnings Release Conference Call Transcript". 2017. *Nike, Inc. – Investor Relations*. https://s1.q4cdn.com/806093406/files/doc_financials/2017/Q3/NIKE-Inc.Q317-OFFICIAL-Transcript-with-QA-FINAL.pdf.

Notably though, that launch was indicative of a successful effort by Nike to connect predictably robust demand with an appropriate level of supply, as pairs commanded a healthy but not obscene surplus to the $220 retail price on the secondary market (most sales on StockX have hovered just below the $300 mark). This result was fairly optimal for Nike and Jordan Brand if we assume that the targeted outcomes were as follows:

- Generate significant revenue through high sales volume (a fairly obvious business practice)
- Accomplish goal #1 while still under-supplying demand (resale premium evidences success here)
- Protect the brand via preservation of the perception of scarcity

To many, the following is a fundamental rule of the sneaker economy: if everyone can get them, nobody will want them. Hyperbolic, absolutely, but not entirely inaccurate. Because the story was so iconic, and because Nike had released the specific sneaker (and other colorways) on several occasions before, the brand was likely armed with a relatively reliable projection of demand. Nonetheless, accomplishing those three goals in stride is daunting by any standard.

To illustrate why the Space Jam result was optimal, consider the parallels to an initial public offering of company equity. When a company comes to market, it generally does so to raise funds in exchange for selling an ownership stake in its company. Notably, after this offering, many of those who owned a stake in the company pre-IPO, including employees, executives, and private investors, will continue to own such a stake, and employees will be issued shares and stock options as part of their compensation going forward. Therefore, it's important to ensure, or make an effort to ensure, that the shares can trade at a relatively stable level or on an upward trajectory once public. Such an outcome allows existing shareholders the opportunity to liquidate at satisfactory levels once applicable restrictions on selling shares expire.

However, such a desire must be balanced against the desire to obtain a high level of funding from the offering. Often, companies want to avoid a significant "pop" in share prices on the first day of trading. A large increase in share price on the first day of trading indicates that the company has left funding on the table by setting too low an initial price.

It's a similar dynamic when a company launches a product and the principal goal is revenue generation, rather than hype building. If the sneakers begin trading on the secondary market for prices well in excess of the retail price, the company will have failed to sufficiently satiate demand, leaving revenue on the table by not offering commensurate supply. Offer too much supply and not only will secondary market prices drop, but future releases may also be met with less demand at retail. After all, part of the appeal to consumers is the very fact that they're owners of an object worth more than they paid for it.

It's a highly delicate balancing act, which is why the Space Jams were a monumental success. It's some of the strongest evidence on offer that the brands simply know exactly what they're doing.

As noted by Edwards on the 3Q call in March of 2017, the Space Jam launch "speaks not only to the obvious demand for our products but also our ability to connect greater numbers of consumers worldwide to the products they covet." [31]

In fiscal year 2017, Jordan Brand grew revenue by 13%, incredible numbers for a brand so mature and so large (the brand eclipsed $3 *billion* in wholesale equivalent revenue in that year). Yet, in the midst of all this success, Nike executives spoke more broadly about a dynamic and promotional landscape and the need to manage inventory levels.

A more challenging landscape was indeed evidenced in the results of another giant of the footwear industry, Foot Locker. On the company's earnings call in August of 2017 (just before the end of Nike's fiscal year), slower sell-through of Jordan sneakers was a frequent topic of discussion.

"Reflecting the increased pace of changing consumer influences, sales of some recent top styles fell short of our expectation," explained Foot Locker CEO Dick Johnson. "In North America, for example, the sell-throughs of certain

---

31   Ibid.

Jordan models slowed considerably compared to historical rates." [32]

Why the slow down? Well, recall how rich the story behind the Space Jam XI is. The reality is that it's difficult to create a story half as rich for most models released. When pressed by an analyst on the Jordan sell-through, Johnson offered the following explanation:

"The relationship with Jordan and Michael himself and the shoes is still incredibly high in the marketplace. But the fact is that today's kid really needed to be connected to a story. When that happens, when the product is right, we still see lineups and we still see Launch Reservation apps that are ready to blow up with the amount of activity. Even though we saw some slowdown in some key models, we saw some great successes with things like the 6 Rings, the Son of Mars, the Spizike, the Dub Zero – all very, very positive. So it's the right story, the right product, the right connectivity with the customer that makes all the difference. And brand Jordan is one of the great brands that we work with. And I know that Larry and the team at Jordan are working hard to make that connectivity with the customer real every time they launch a product."[33]

---

32   "Foot Locker's (FL) CEO Dick Johnson On Q2 2017 Results – Earnings Call Transcript". 2017. *Seeking Alpha*. https://seekingalpha.com/article/4100368-foot-lockers-fl-ceo-dick-johnson-q2-2017-results-earnings-call-transcript?part=single.

33   Ibid.

Wait a second. Two months before those remarks, Nike reported Jordan sales that were up 13% for the year!

How can this be the case when a behemoth retailer was referencing Jordan brand as one cause of a year-over-year sales decline?

The reality is that the results of a Foot Locker or a Finish Line would actually be more aptly considered as leading indicators for brand heat. When sneakers of a brand sit stagnant on store shelves at large discounts, it indicates that said brand would have difficulty introducing new inventory to the wholesaler, and therefore *future* financial results for the manufacturer would be challenged.

Generally speaking, the *current* financial results, those reported the same quarter that sneakers are sitting, would be less impacted. Once a manufacturer has sold sneaker inventory to a wholesaler, that wholesaler then becomes responsible for driving sales to the end-consumer while the manufacturer, in this case Nike, is able to recognize the revenue from the sale to the wholesaler.

This concept is the difference between *sell-in*, when a brand sells *into* a wholesaler, and *sell-through*, when the retailer successfully sells *through* to an end consumer. Slow sales or discounted sales at the wholesaler are of little immediate financial consequence to the manufacturer itself. However, that does not mean that such a slowdown should not be of grave concern to the manufacturer.

While Nike does not report a breakdown of sales by brand on a quarter to quarter basis, they do so at year-end, and we now know that Jordan Brand wholesale equivalent sales declined by 8% in fiscal year 2018 (9% independent of currency movements).

From positive 13% growth to an 8% decline! In one year!

At face value, those are startling numbers, and it's fair to suggest that Nike and Jordan executives may be far less than thrilled with the results. Still, even with that being the case, it's important to understand that to a certain extent, a portion of that decline is intentional.

While a wholesaler like Foot Locker communicating slower sell-through of Jordan sneakers isn't of *immediate* financial consequence to Nike, it can have severe and potentially irreparable consequences to the standing of the *brand*. For this reason, we saw the tone of Jordan-focused discussion shift on 2018 earnings calls, with an emphasis on protecting the brand's iconic standing.

Edwards, noting that global appetite for Jordan remains strong, had this to say following the first quarter, "That said, in North America, within the retro side of the business, we are managing the cadence of our launches while bringing to market fresher stories and expressions that drive demand."[34]

---

34 "FY 2018 Q1 Earnings Release Conference Call Transcript". 2017. *Nike, Inc. – Investor Relations.* https://s1.q4cdn.com/806093406/files/ doc_financials/2018/Q1/NIKE-Inc.-Q118-OFFICIAL-Transcript- with-QA.pdf.

Just as Dick Johnson noted, there's a pervasive need to connect with consumers through story in order to fuel product demand. Edwards elaborated further, "this is where we're going to really be managing the balance between scarcity and scale at the same time. So we're taking all the right steps to make sure that Jordan remains a special and coveted brand."[35]

Managing that balance between scarcity and scale is what Jordan Brand did so beautifully with the Space Jam release. Products of a special and coveted brand don't consistently sit on store shelves at significantly reduced prices. Allowing them to do so jeopardizes the perception and therefore the future of that brand.

"Our key launches in Q2 proved yet again that the Jordan Brand is a powerful force starting with the great results we saw from the AJ 32 and the AJ 11. When we connect the right product with the strength of the Jordan's storytelling, the results are incredible," Edwards explained, striking a similar chord a quarter later. ". For instance, the Air Jordan 1 was the most coveted product in The Ten collection, cementing its position as 2017's Shoe of The Year. We also want to keep Jordan icons coveted and special, which is why we are proactively managing the exclusivity of specific iconic styles and color ways in North America."[36]

---

35 Ibid.
36 "FY 2018 Q2 Earnings Release Conference Call Transcript". 2017. *Nike, Inc. – Investor Relations.* https://s1.q4cdn.com/806093406/files/

Storytelling matters in the sneaker economy, whether you're talking about a boutique retailer or a manufacturer like Nike. Storytelling fosters the connection to the consumer, and the connection to the consumer drives demand. When demand outstrips supply at retail, brand heat rises.

"Year-over-year comparisons in North America were also impacted by our quick and deliberate tightening of the distribution of select styles within the Jordan Brand," CFO Andy Campion detailed, reflecting in the subsequent quarter on the brand's continued efforts. "That said, as we enter Q4, we believe Jordan inventories are now clean and we also began reigniting Jordan Brand heat in the marketplace through the launches and activations over the NBA All-Star Weekend."[37]

All of this emphasis on managing exclusivity of iconic styles and ensuring that Jordan remains special and coveted translates mainly to one core initiative: reducing supply in the wholesale market. As mentioned previously, the year-over-year decline in Jordan sales was not a surprise and was, to a degree, intentional. In order to "clean" inventories (i.e. reduce the build-up of slow-selling, discounted inventory), Jordan Brand had to reduce and tighten the supply of sneakers to the wholesale market, with a specific emphasis

---

doc_financials/2018/q2/NIKE-Inc.-Q218-OFFICIAL-Transcript-with-QA-FINAL.pdf.

37 "FY 2018 Q3 Earnings Release Conference Call Transcript". 2018. *Nike, Inc. – Investor Relations.* https://s1.q4cdn.com/806093406/files/doc_events/2018/NIKE-Inc.-Q318-OFFICIAL-Transcript-with-QA-FINAL.pdf.

on reducing supply to "undifferentiated" retailers that aren't viewed as adding value in sell-through.

With these efforts largely behind the company, Campion detailed the 2019 outlook for the brand at the close of fiscal 2018:

"As for the Jordan Brand in North America, we are already back to a pull market, and we expect a return to global growth in FY19. Consumers love the Jordan Brand and their passion for the brand is unwavering. At the same time, we saw an opportunity to recalibrate the supply of select styles across just distribution channels. While that included tightening the supply in some cases, it also included expanding the supply of the hottest, most iconic Jordan styles on the NIKE SNKRS app, which has fast become the leading destination for high heat footwear launches globally. We also leveraged both Jordan and NIKE launches on the SNKRS app to create compelling new consumer experiences that merge digital and physical with our strategic retail partners, for example, through initiatives such as Shock Drop, SNKRS Pass and SNKRS Stash."[38]

Campion refers to a "pull" market. To clarify, when inventories were building at wholesalers and experiencing a slowdown in sell-through, it was the result of the creation

---

38 "FY 2018 Q4 Earnings Release Conference Call Transcript". 2018. *Nike, Inc. – Investor Relations*. https://s1.q4cdn.com/806093406/files/ doc_financials/2018/Q4/NIKE-Inc.-Q418-OFFICIAL-Transcript- with-QA-FINAL.pdf.

of a "push market" in which Nike was pushing supply of Jordan sneakers out to market, rather than allowing consumer demand to pull those sneakers to market. As a result, the brand's standing was endangered, discounting became prevalent, and wholesalers would need to re-evaluate their buying processes. To stem these consequences, Nike tightened supply, allowed those inventories to clear, and placed an increased emphasis on connecting directly to consumers with stories most relevant to them.

With the outlook for fiscal 2019 brighter than it was entering 2018, it seems that Nike and wholesalers alike are finding increased comfort in the management of the Jordan Brand and the balance of supply and demand. Still, the rollercoaster of results, from the Space Jam launch and 13% revenue growth to the deliberate tightening of supply and an 8% sales decline, clearly underscores the notion that, for even a cornerstone of the sneaker economy, balancing scarcity and scale is an incredibly delicate challenge, one that requires attention in perpetuity without recess.

The brand may be finding its way onto steadier footing for the moment – the successful holiday 2018 re-release of the "Concord" Jordan 11 seemingly mirrored that of the Space Jam with a bigger marketing push – but questions on Jumpman's ability to return to its prior standing in the sneaker *economy* persist. Its standing in the sneaker *community* and sneaker *culture*, however, is forever unassailable. Rehabilitation takes time, and patience from the brand, retailers, and consumers alike is essential.

While Michael Jordan may have been borderline impervious to the forces of gravity during his prime, even His Airness and his sneakers are vulnerable to the forces of economics.

CLEANING THE MARKET AND CREATING DEMAND

Stan Smith endorsed Adidas beginning in 1971, after winning his first Grand Slam singles title. He won just one more Slam before retiring in 1985. In spite of that, three decades later, you can't walk three city blocks without laying eyes on his namesake sneaker, the Stan Smith.

Smith's face displayed iconically on the tongue, the sneaker bears a hearty share of responsibility for the Adidas resurgence and market share capture in the United States in recent years. How? How does the sneaker of a highly talented but perhaps not all-time great tennis player from the 1970s not only stand the test of time for decades, but find its way onto millions of feet in an explosive movement of the mid 2010s?!

Not dumb luck. Not a posthumous tribute – Smith is alive, well, and rocking his namesake better than anybody!

No, this was the product of careful, disciplined, diligent planning by Adidas executives. Always remember: the brands know what they're doing.

The importance of pulling the strings on supply is not limited exclusively to the management of limited, hyped releases. In fact, effectively managing supply is just as critical, if not more so, when it comes to the sneakers that you see gracing countless feet on a daily basis, because scarcity is relative, not absolute. It's because of effective supply management that you can't go into a Starbucks today without seeing a pair of Adidas brand's Stan Smiths or Superstars. It was largely those two models, old, reliable, and stylish as ever, that provided the launching pad for a reinvigorated and credible Three Stripes threat to Nike in the United States.

Those sneaker stalwarts, however, haven't always been in demand.

In the late aughts and early 2010s, Adidas found its beloved icon in a somewhat perilous position. Sold mainly via sporting goods stores, Stan Smiths had landed in the bargain bin, often selling at discounted prices and consequently losing broader consumer appeal. As Torben Schumacher, Adidas' vice-president of product told *The Cut*, "We weren't really happy with how it was seen and where it was found. We wanted it to get the respect it deserved and the conversation about it that it deserved and for it to be seen as a commodity item. We thought it needed something bold and drastic to prepare everyone for the story again."[39]

---

39 Schwartzberg, Lauren. 2017. "Stan Smith Knows You Think He's Just A Sneaker". *The Cut*. https://www.thecut.com/2017/02/stan-smith-knows-you-think-hes-just-a-sneaker.html.

And so, with that dissatisfaction came a plan to reset and clean out the market. By 2012, the sneaker had been pulled off shelves entirely. The Stan wasn't set to collect dust in the Adidas archives, though. A plan had already been set in motion to stoke demand as the product grew harder and harder to find.

By the time famed former creative director of Celine, Phoebe Philo, took to the runway wearing Stans following a 2011 show, the wheels of change were already turning to return the sneaker to a higher standing. In 2013, with the sneaker essentially unobtainable, Gisele Bundchen appeared in Stans (and nothing else) for *Vogue*. The influencer efforts grew louder and more lively: A$AP Rocky, Alexander Wang, Ellen Degeneres, Raf Simons, Pharrell and others were soon spotted wearing the suddenly scarce sneaker.

You don't know what you got 'til it's gone. Well the Stan was "gone," and men and women alike yearned for its familiar look once again. This was hardly a surprise to Adidas. As Jon Wexler, Adidas Global Director of Entertainment and Influencer Marketing, told *The Guardian*, "We knew three and a half years before we did step one what would happen."[40]

The Stan Smith was never to be retired, only reserved for a moment when it would be treated with greater appreciation. So, as longing for the familiar silhouette grew, the

---

40 Fox, Imogen. 2015. "How 2015 Was The Year The Stan Smith Went Mass". *The Guardian*. https://www.theguardian.com/fashion/2015/dec/22/2015-stan-smith-went-mass-adidas-sneakers-trainer.

sneaker slowly trickled back into stores in 2014, but ever so selectively, starting with high-end, high-fashion stores but remaining at a familiarly accessible price point. By 2015, the resurgence had officially reached a fever pitch, and the Stan Smith was back.

Arthur Hoeld, GM for Adidas Originals, acknowledged to *Footwear News* that the company had taken the Stan off shelves with an eye towards "predicting a re-emergence of the clean-shoe-silhouette trend."[41] Mission accomplished. Not only did the Stan Smith return to the market to great fanfare, but another iconic, fabled Adidas sneaker, the Superstar, sold over *15 million* pairs in 2015.

"The tremendous success of our Originals business lies in our unique ability to recreate iconic sport moments and bring them to the street. This is exactly what made our famous footwear franchises Stan Smith and Superstar driving forces of sneaker culture in 2015. The Superstar on its own was sold more than 15 million times in 2015 and was by far the best-selling sneaker of the year," Former Adidas CEO Herbert Hainer enthusiastically detailed on the 2015 year-end earnings call. "And while we are going to keep some momentum up for those two franchises in the coming years, we will carefully manage their life cycles to ensure longevity."[42]

---

41 Allaire, Christian. 2014. "Shoe Of The Year: Adidas Stan Smith". *Footwear News*. https://footwearnews.com/2014/influencers/power-players/fnaa-2014-shoe-of-the-year-adidas-stan-smith-388/.

42 "Adidas Ag's (ADDYY) CEO Herbert Hainer On Q4 2015 Results – Earnings Call Transcript". 2016. *Seeking Alpha*. https://seekingalpha.

Even as the success of the two icons was freshly rekindled and sales trends remained on an upwards and accelerating trajectory, the cautious tone on carefully managing availability and image persisted. At every point of the product life cycle, executives are thinking forward to the opposite moment. At the peak of a cycle, they're thinking about managing the trough. At the trough, focus shifts to a strategic return to the peak.

Turning a tanker on the high seas is not done quickly and easily, and Stan Smiths and Superstars are tanker sneaker franchises, absolutely massive institutions of the sneaker world. With great size comes hindered agility.

Adidas has grown well versed in managing the Stan Smith lifecycle; after all, they've been doing it since the 1970s. With the reemergence of an appetite for clean silhouettes, though, came the entry of fresh competitors. From Common Projects to Skechers, models closely resembling the Stan continue to come to market (Adidas successfully won an injunction against a Skechers model that was a bit *too* close to the Adidas stalwart). High-fashion Stan homages litter the market at prices that are multiples of the original. Even Adidas' own Raf Simons Stan, with a perforated "R" instead of three stripes, sold at retail for $300.

It resembles a game of musical chairs: when the music starts again, market participants sell, sell, sell until the music

com/article/3953386-adidas-ags-addyy-ceo-herbert-hainer-q4-2015-results-earnings-call-transcript.

stops. Riding the wave of success that began in 2015, 2016 and 2017 saw releases of every kind and color of Stan Smith imaginable: premium versions, versions set upon the Adidas brand's popular Boost midsole, versions made of the light Primeknit material, tie-dye versions in collaboration with Pharrell.

There are moments for scarcity, and there are moments to stomp on the accelerator. Adidas stomped on the accelerator in 2016, achieving 18% constant currency revenue growth, including 24% topline growth in North America. Those are *outrageous* growth numbers for a mature brand.

Remember though, while the brand's foot was firmly on the accelerator, this was not a joyride bereft of inhibition. Rather, the fast and furious Stan and Superstar sales of 2016 were a controlled, measured movement, the brand's eyes firmly on the road ahead, ready to engage the turn signal and pivot to replace those sales when the cycle turned downward. Okay, enough of the driving analogy.

The point is this: Adidas knows that the music stops, and it has a pretty firm grasp on when it happens.

After the first quarter of 2017, CEO Kasper Rorsted was eager to detail the success of newer franchises, those that the brand expected to fill the gaps created by a lifecycle downturn for the Stan Smiths and Superstars: "If you go to the originals business, we see a growth of 30%, which is very strong growth compared to where we are coming from, and I think the most important message here is that we are seeing a 50% growth in our modern footwear franchises: The NMD, the Tubular and the Shadow and the EQT, which means we are doing exactly as we communicated, building a broader franchising landscape."[43]

"We continued to reiterate that despite a declining growth rate in Superstar and Stan Smith, we were able to offset those by growth in our new franchises. I hope you can see that what we said also came true," Rorsted asserted more explicitly the following quarter. "We continue to see a decline in growth rate in Superstar and in Stan Smith; at the same time we're seeing our newer franchises like NMD, Tubular, and EQT being more than able to offset the declining growth in those franchises. Adidas is more than a white tennis shoe."[44]

It's convenient, perhaps even obligatory, for Adidas to assert that new franchises can maintain the brand momentum that was created in large part by Stans and Superstars, but they weren't alone in that assertion. Even as large retailers were working through significant supply of the icons in their stores, Foot Locker CEO Dick Johnson was quick to support Rorsted's assertion in Foot Locker's own first quarter 2017 call, almost precisely echoing his remarks: "There

---

43 "Adidas's (ADDYY) CEO Kasper Rorsted On Q1 2017 Results – Earnings Call Transcript". 2017. *Seeking Alpha*. https://seekingalpha.com/article/4069286-adidass-addyy-ceo-kasper-rorsted-q1-2017-results-earnings-call-transcript?part=single.

44 "Adidas's (ADDYY) CEO Kasper Rorsted On Q2 2017 Results – Earnings Call Transcript". 2017. *Seeking Alpha*. https://seekingalpha.com/article/4095577-adidass-addyy-ceo-kasper-rorsted-q2-2017-results-earnings-call-transcript?part=single.

is a lot of great stuff coming on from Adidas you know and certainly Superstars and Stan Smiths are in one part of the lifecycle, but when you look at things like Tubular Shadow and Nomads and EQT, you know a lot of Ultraboost products, a lot of Pureboost, we've got AlphaBounce..... So the fact that Superstars and Stan Smiths are part of their downward part of the lifecycle potentially, all of these other things are continuing to fuel the great brand heat."[45]

Even with the tall task of managing the downturn of two industry titans, turning footwear tankers, Adidas still managed to grow revenue 17% on a constant currency basis in 2017. Given lower growth rates for Nike (albeit off a larger base), Adidas continued to stake its claim to greater market share, particularly in the United States where sales growth was 27%. Adidas has stated a goal of 15-20% market share in the United States, a level that it reaches in most other markets around the world. While estimates vary, the general consensus seems to be that today, the brand is somewhere in the ballpark of 10% share.

As we sit at the time of writing, Adidas has for the most part successfully anticipated, managed, and navigated the downturn in the Stan/Superstar product lifecycle. In the second quarter of 2018, the company grew sales 10%

---

45 "Foot Locker's (FL) CEO Ric Johnson On Q1 2017 Results – Earnings Call Transcript". 2017. *Seeking Alpha*. https://seekingalpha.com/article/4074866-foot-lockers-fl-ceo-ric-johnson-q1-2017-results-earnings-call-transcript?part=single.

year-over-year, including 16% growth in North America. Gross margins were up 220 basis points over the prior year. Why does that matter? Well, gross margin is the percentage of revenue that a company nets after subtracting its cost of goods sold, direct costs attributed to the production of goods that were sold during the period. Now, while it can be positively impacted by declining costs in production, it is also commonly aided by selling product at full price, rather than discounting. The company's inventory ended the quarter 2% lower on a constant currency basis than it had a year prior.

Altogether, these facts point to tighter supply in the market, more full-price selling, and fewer items in the bargain bin – recall that the discounted positioning of the Stan Smith was essentially the impetus for the sneaker's disappearance and subsequent resurgence. Whether or not that momentum can continue for the brand is up for debate, particularly as signs of more prevalent discounting begin to appear in the fall of 2018, but sales growth in excess of 15% is exceedingly difficult to maintain as the bar grows ever higher each year.

Today, the Stans are available on the Adidas website in the most iconic colorways at the typical price of $75 ($80 for the most familiar white and green colorway), with a message alongside the product that tells you much of what you need to know about the brand's refusal to see the sneaker relegated to bargain status: "This product is excluded from all promotional discounts and offers." The same message accompanies the original white and black Superstar.

The imperative is clear: these are products to be cherished and valued, not impulse-buy afterthoughts.

Rorsted describes the careful management of the receding Stan Smith and Superstar wave at the midway point of 2018:

"Let me be clear; we have proactively managed those two franchises down...In fact, Stan Smith and Superstar have been managed down for the past 18 months now, which did not get in the way of our continued top line growth. As you know from the numbers we have reported to you, year-to-date and also for 2017. Today Stan and Superstar each only account for a low single-digit percentage of our total sales. Volumes out in the market are very healthy. If anything, there is more demand than what we want to supply right now. As such, Stan and Superstar continue to be leading examples of disciplined life cycle management. You can expect us to handle other maturing franchises similarly prudent."[46]

Hmm, more demand than they want to supply. That sounds familiar. Adidas heard the music beginning to fade and reacted accordingly. Not their first rodeo. On that very same conference call, Rorsted hinted that the brand's collaboration with Kanye West on the Yeezy brand, the other vastly scarcer but still significant driver of the Adidas resurgence, may become more democratic in quarters to come. While

---

46 "Adidas AG ADR (ADDYY) CEO Kasper Rorsted On Q2 2018 Results – Earnings Call Transcript". 2018. *Seeking Alpha*. https://seekingalpha.com/article/4197285-adidas-ag-adr-addyy-ceo-kasper-rorsted-q2-2018-results-earnings-call-transcript?part=single.

some are of the opinion that the Yeezy's brand heat has begun to fade as more colorways and models come to market in less scarce fashion, Rorsted insists "wait to see, but we think we have a good plan." [47]

We're all welcome to our opinions, but doubt the brand's planning at your own peril. Adidas has proven that they know what to do when the music stops and that they know when to crank up the volume after a few moments of quiet. How else does the tennis shoe of a player from the 1970s find its way onto millions of feet in the mid-2010s?

So, what does this lifecycle management mean for the collector?

Well, for the foreseeable future, they're less likely to fall backwards into $40-50 Stan Smiths and Superstars, at least of the OG colorway variety. Additionally, these shoes, by virtue of the fact that they were inexpensive and extremely available, were generally not the type to be kept on ice. No, Stan Smiths and Superstars found their way directly onto feet and directly onto the streets. For the OG models, this may not change dramatically in coming years, but collectors may give a thought to the practice of "rock one, stock one", purchasing two pairs with the intent of wearing one and keeping one tucked safely away in its box over the intermediate term.

Such a practice, though probably unnecessary, or even the simple *fear* of increased future scarcity, would help to

---

47   Ibid.

ensure that demand continues to outpace supply as Adidas curtails the number of pairs it brings to market.

For the one-off Stan Smiths – the ones that either sat atop Boost or were cloaked in Primeknit or both, the special color-ways, the collaborations – those may not come around again with great frequency in the near future. Expect that we may see some secondary market appreciation as few deadstock pairs remain to service any rekindling of demand.

Take the Stan Smith Boost, for example. That sneaker could be acquired for $60 on sale directly from Adidas in the spring of 2016. Pairs were selling on StockX in the spring of 2018 for in excess of double that price. Such a bounce-back in price is not uncommon among discount sneakers, due largely to the high likelihood that such sneakers end up on streets and not in boxes. Why preserve something that didn't hold much value to begin with? When sneakers go to feet, the supply side of the market thins out considerably, and with months passing since the last sale, liquidity is already very thin.

So, those Stan Smiths and Superstars in your closet – the ones you picked up for cheap a few years back – maybe they're getting a little dirty, a little beat. Remember: you may not be able to refresh them as easily as you'd like in the next few years.

Does that make you a little bit uneasy? Maybe that's just the way Adidas wants it.

Stans and Superstars aside, generally, when supply significantly outstrips demand for a sneaker and a brand has sufficient and legitimate reason to believe that said sneaker possesses a design and story that is worthy of greater market standing, the most effective remedy is the intentional constraint of supply. If the sneaker resonates with consumers through its design and story, the creation of scarcity should generate renewed demand, particularly if timed to coincide with a moment in which the design will be most appreciated.

Importantly, there are moments when consumer tastes aren't suited to a certain sneaker, or worse, there are designs and stories that simply aren't strong enough to *ever* warrant meaningful demand. In such cases, pulling the levers of supply will accomplish very little. Scarcity does not *always* beget demand. Scarcity plus a rich story and a compelling design, though, is the quintessential recipe for heat.

There are countless variables at play in the release, re-release, or removal of any sneaker. Appropriately understanding, gauging, and projecting those variables is immensely difficult, as is effectively acting upon that understanding. It's for that reason that the Stan Smiths and Superstars "moment" from 2015 to 2017 was a masterpiece of supply and demand excellence years in the making.

PLUGGING THE GAPS WITH
DIFFERENTIATED SUPPLY

If your view of the sneaker economy includes only Nike and Adidas, you're likely one of two things: a hypebeast or ill-informed.

Let's fix that, because you're missing out not only on cool sneakers with great stories, but also on some really fascinating business practices.

Now, to be fair, Nike is the undisputed sheriff of the sneaker economy. Adidas is the undisputed deputy. There's considerable daylight to a third-place contender, and yet, a variety of brands play a significant role in the collector's economy, often punching far above their respective weights. They don't boast the same direct-to-consumer release hysteria, and many of their sneakers remain widely available days and weeks after their introduction. Still, New Balance, Asics, Saucony, Fila, Diadora, Vans, and others still command attention from their respective niches.

How does Fila, a brand many of us probably remember mainly from Marshalls and T.J. Maxx in the 1990s, stage a comeback and attain significant brand heat in 2018?

How does New Balance, a brand that many knew only for their super chunky, all-white dad shoes, boast countless sneakers selling for multiples of retail on the secondary market?

In a world saturated with Air Maxes and Three Stripe silhouettes, room exists for differentiated competitors to capture pieces, albeit smaller ones, of the collector's wallet. Before delving into how those competitors exploit gaps in the market, it's important to understand the different ways in which sneakers can be released. While there are different subsets of each of the following, we'll simplify it to three key categories: General Releases, Limited Releases, and Quickstrikes.

General releases (GRs) are those sneakers that are produced in large quantities, widely available, and easy to obtain. Limited releases are produced in smaller quantities, grace the shelves of fewer locations, and are unlikely to last as long as GRs on shelves and websites. Finally, while the definition of a quickstrike has evolved through the years (including various subcategories), QS releases are significantly more limited in terms of quantity produced, are acquirable from fewer stores and sites, and often sell-out swiftly – no time to be wasted with QS releases.

The smaller competitors typically live in GR territory, and limited releases are less common and less...well...limited. Quickstrikes are the well-worn territory of Nike and Adidas. For the most part, collectors aren't gluing their eyes to their phones at 10:00a.m. on a Saturday morning to purchase a pair of sneakers directly from New Balance or Asics. As we've discussed, scarcity alone isn't enough to create buzz.

Typically, yes, the smaller brands do not play in the QS arena. However, there is an exception to this rule, and it's this exception that claims significant responsibility for the disproportionately large mind-share of these brands among collectors.

The exception is the much-celebrated collaboration.

The idea is relatively simple: by collaborating with a retailer, often a popular boutique, on everything from the materials to the colors to the laces and the box, a story is created that will hopefully resonate with that boutique's loyal community of consumers and create buzz around a certain model. Essentially, they've outsourced the storytelling and buzz creation to the retailer's team. For smaller brands not bearing the same wealth of resources as the industry giants, the collaboration is a potent and effective means of reaching target audiences, the type of consumers who are frequent sneaker buyers.

The sneaker model serving as the collaborative subject will often be made available as a general release in other, more generic colorways concurrent with or shortly after the debut of the collaboration. While collaborations with Nike and Adidas are in fact quite common, most collectors are more apt to associate New Balance or Asics with collaborations than they are the giants.

For New Balance, a masterful collaborator with the likes of lifestyle brands and retailers Concepts and Kith, the efforts have consistently eroded the stodgy, unhip dad shoe perception of the brand among sneakerheads. It was of little surprise that New Balance elected to introduce its 997S model through collaboration with Ronnie Fieg and the Kith team.

Often, the models highlighted in collaborations are premium products, commanding retail prices in excess of $150 by virtue of the quality of materials used and, in New Balance's case, the manufacturing location (the company's Made in the U.S. or Made in the UK models are popular among sneakerheads). In fact, a fall 2018 New Balance marketing e-mail even hailed the 990, released in 1982, as the first sneaker to carry a then "astronomical" hundred-dollar ticket price. Such premium models can satisfy a sneakerhead niche that seeks higher-brow sneakers perhaps worthy of the new-age office, with the quality construction and materials presenting a neat, professional look. Accordingly, many Asics and New Balance models have been made available in collaboration with J.Crew. One such effort, a multi-pronged collaboration among Asics, J.Crew, and industry stalwart, Packer, was a collection of sneakers boasting suede or leather materials that resembled those of traditional dress shoes.

Puma, which sits somewhere between Nike or Adidas and the rest of the pack on the size spectrum (though closer to the latter than the former), has used collaborations to great success in recent years through its Select division, getting creative in the choice of partners: electronic musical instrument manufacturer Roland, iconic video game developer, SEGA, Seoul-based artist collective, Ader Error, and even Polaroid. Such partnerships, not with retailers, allow the brand to utilize the rich stories and detailed design choices that make collaborations so popular without narrowing the scope of potential customers to just one boutique. The results, though of course not entirely attributable to the Puma Select division, have returned the brand to double-digit topline growth in the Americas in 2018.

Collaborations are but one arrow in the smaller brand's quiver, though. In fact, in some ways, the lack of hype – and all of the headaches that come with it – works in their favor.

These brands are often able to capitalize on demand for on-trend looks at reasonable prices, allowing consumers to escape the well-worn territory of something like the Stan Smith. The perfect example in 2018 is the resurgence of the aforementioned, pre-millennium darling with European roots, Fila.

With increased appetite for the bulkier, nostalgia-laden sneakers of the '90s came a desire to be different while embracing that nostalgia. Senior Sports Industry Advisor at the NPD Group, Matt Powell (essentially the preeminent Sneakonomist – if you've read an article on the sneaker business recently, you've likely seen him quoted), sheds light on the Fila resurgence and the rise of the mid-tier brand: "I think what we're seeing is the phenomenon of kids still wearing jeans, sneakers, and hoodies, but they want different logos on them and different brands so that they stand out and so that they are unique. Not too unique, right? I think I would describe it as I want to be different just like my friends."

With an offering that was considered fresh and unique (by virtue of its absence from the U.S. market), Fila perfectly timed the reintroduction of their robust vault of '90s product with the demand from a nostalgic consumer seeking "new" retros. It was this perfect timing that actually made the Fila Disruptor (think of the chunkiest '90s sneaker you can picture) one of the best-selling surprises of 2018, with Foot Locker CEO Dick Johnson specifically calling out the product as one generating significant heat. After effectively disappearing from the country in the mid-2000s, Fila returned to 21% year-over-year growth in the United States in the second quarter of 2018, numbers that would've seemed almost unfathomable a decade ago.

To some extent, accessibility has played a role in the 2018 rise of not only Fila, but Vans as previously mentioned, and Reebok Classics (though Reebok is of course owned by Adidas). Often available at price points of $100 and well below, these brands are largely removed from the gamification of sneaker acquisition–no lines, no frustrating draws, no seemingly impossible online checkouts. Much like the Stan Smiths and Superstars, the reintroduction of supply was simply well-timed with the emergence of favorable, lifestyle-focused consumer tastes.

In a market where brands are less capable of influencing fashion than has traditionally been the case, the Filas of the world capitalized on consumer trends with scale, variety, and availability. These brands also act more nimbly and are better able to amplify the messaging around on-trend styles. Such was the case with Puma's quickness in serving the consumer's 2018 appetite for chunkier sneakers like the Thunder and the RS-0.

Scarcity and resale buzz is not and has not been as relevant for brands of this tier, nor should it be. Sales volume is critical (duh!), but unlike a Nike or an Adidas, these brands don't have the luxury of making hit products extremely scarce in an effort to generate demand and a sense of urgency for other products. Instead, resource constraints dictate that hit products be available, timely, and accessible.

The sneakers of this brand tier (collaborations excluded) generally find their way to feet. Deadstocking is not necessary and, largely, not fruitful due to the accessibility.

No lines to buy and no robust secondary market demand? It sounds negative, but these brands don't thrive on scarcity and the prospect of resale profiteering, nor does aftermarket activity factor into their projections of demand. Certainly, they do compete against each other and against the industry titans, but they face less competition from their own sneakers of prior seasons and years. In this crazy sneaker economy, not competing against the past successes of your own brand is increasingly becoming a luxury.

While the Fila resurgence and other rising tides are inspiring, those ascensions last only as long as the brand can meet consumer tastes and demand, and the track records for these brands over the years are spottier than those of Nike and Adidas. There's a reason that Fila needed to make a U.S. comeback in the first place.

Still, when the smaller brands have appropriate product to satiate consumer tastes, they're facing a market environment considerably less saturated with their own product. Though the players may change, rise, and fall, the smaller brand will continue to exploit gaps left by the titans of the sneaker industry.

As Powell put it frequently throughout 2018, "small is the new big" as it relates to sport lifestyle footwear.

***

Supply is the one key market variable over which the brands maintain firm, complete control in today's sneaker economy. I know what you're thinking: what about price?! Of course, they set prices today, but the wheels of change are in motion. They still decide the price at which they will initially sell to consumers and the MSRP at which retailers will begin to sell, but as the secondary market matures, free market forces more swiftly influence the prevailing price of a sneaker. As such, introducing the "right" amount of supply at the "right" time is more critical than ever, particularly in the quest to sell at full price rather than at a discount.

For those limited, hyped releases – the quickstrikes meant to leave many participants empty-handed and hungry for the next release – oversupplying means more elastic (price-sensitive) demand, more discounting, and, most importantly, diminished brand stature. For the ever-available icon – the beloved general release – excessive, long-tenured availability will only heighten the price elasticity of demand until that exalted icon becomes a bargain bin cellar dweller.

Economics is after all the study of the allocation of scarce resources, which of course means that Sneakonomics, our nascent course of study, centers on the allocation of scarce sneakers. Just remember, scarcity in the sneaker economy is a highly relative term, and it is an adaptable understanding of scarcity appropriately utilized that makes or breaks the economy's constituents.

TAKEAWAYS FROM THE SNEAKONOMIST:

- An understanding of the balance between supply and demand (and the ramifications of any imbalances) is the foundational building block for an understanding of the sneaker economy at large.
- Sneaker brands use supply as a weapon, often by constraining it, to influence and generate demand.
- Resale premiums have traditionally served as impactful marketing buzz for the brands – a sneaker is "worth" more than the consumer paid for it – creating an urgency to buy product.
- Oversupplying a "scarce" sneaker may have negative consequences that extend beyond that release, weakening urgency to buy and the resale demand backstop for future releases.

- Smaller brands often collaborate with popular boutiques on scarce, special sneakers to generate buzz for their general releases, leveraging the loyal and influential followings of those boutiques.
- Above all, scarcity, while a powerful weapon, is an abstract and relative concept. Haphazard, ill-informed use is destined for failure, because scarcity alone is not a guaranteed harbinger of success.

CHAPTER 5

THE SECONDARY MARKET – HOW CONSUMERS GAINED THE UPPER HAND

"The efficiency, credibility and liquidity of the financial markets have been foundational to the largest economy in the world. We believe this is the right time to extend this fundamental concept to appropriate sectors of the online consumer marketplace. Ironically, the original Detroit Stock Exchange once sat less than a thousand feet from StockX headquarters here in downtown Detroit. It is only fitting that we are going to build

the next iteration of the world's most efficient market invention
almost in the same spot."

—Dan Gilbert, StockX Co-Founder[48]

A piece of breaking news hits the usual publications: one of the biggest companies in the space is going to offer more to the market. With this increase in supply should come a drop in price, and unnervingly, you've been considering offloading your ownership stake for some time now. You're on the road, though, not close to a computer to place your sell order. No matter. You pull your phone out of your pocket and open your trading application.

You survey the bid and ask activity on the market. There is significantly more depth on the ask side – perhaps the news is spreading. It must be; the price has faded a bit since the last time you checked, but a few palatable, perhaps uninformed bids remain on the market. Time is of the essence. You don't want to be the last one stuck on this sinking ship.

With confidence and just a few clicks, you execute your sell order against one of the last remaining bids. A sigh of relief. You've offloaded just in time. Tomorrow, the price will sink like a stone, bids will vanish, and countless others will

48 Burns, Matt. 2016. "Dan Gilbert And Campless Founder Launch A Marketplace For Sneakers". *Techcrunch.* https://techcrunch.com/2016/02/08/dan-gilbert-and-campless-founder-launch-a-marketplace-for-sneakers/.

be left watching their profits erode while you move on to cleverly redeploy your proceeds.

You'd be forgiven if you thought the above was a tale from a trading floor on Wall Street.

Alas, no. That was today's sneaker world at its most sophisticated. The asset was a pair of Nike Air Maxes, not shares of Nike stock. The publications were Sneaker News, Nice Kicks, and Sneaker Bar Detroit. The news was the restocking of pairs at retailers nationwide, not a secondary offering of public equity. The marketplace and the application were StockX, not NYSE and E-Trade respectively.

Sneakers are *not* securities, nor are they really investments, but the robust ecosystem that has grown around the sneaker-collecting hobby? It's sophisticated enough to make you think twice.

Welcome to the secondary market.

While understanding primary market dynamics is of critical import, it is the maturation of the secondary sneaker market that has propelled the sneaker economy to its present heights. In its early days, the secondary market lacked trust, it lacked credibility, and it consequently lacked depth and breadth of selection for the prospective buyer.

Matching the credible seller with the willing customer was, frankly, a crapshoot. Was the buyer entering the right search terms on eBay? Was the seller posting his or her pair on the right online forum? Could the buyer trust the seller to ship on time? To provide the right product? To appropriately describe the condition?

Could the seller trust the buyer to pay swiftly? To utilize legitimate payment methods? To properly read and understand the item description?

Those are a lot of questions. With many questions comes significant friction, and friction is an impediment to efficient market function.

Today, the consumer, which in the case of secondary marketplaces means buyer and seller alike, is the beneficiary of numerous marketplace offerings that have been built upon one core principle: instilling trust and credibility in a previously murky market. Through the rise of consignment services like Flight Club and Stadium Goods, which facilitate the sales process from start to finish on behalf of sellers, and marketplaces like StockX and GOAT, which match sellers with buyers to transact at an agreed upon price, the secondary market has grown to closely resemble the primary retail experience.

Many of the stigmas and frustrations of secondary market shopping have been alleviated or eliminated altogether. As a result, consumers are advantaged by a nearly boundless variety of selection at their disposal for purchase at any given moment, with just as much legitimacy in the experience should they opt to purchase from a secondary seller rather than directly from the brand or a trusted retailer.

Resale is not the seedy enterprise it once was. Well, to be clear, there's still a fair amount of seediness out there, especially depending on your opinion of bot use and back-dooring (which is likely, rightfully, a negative one). That said though, generally, resale has been elevated. It's refined, it's sophisticated, and it's increasingly efficient.

While there remains significant ground to cover, this glow-up has given the sneaker collector unprecedented leverage. Urgency to buy is diminished, the power of voting with the wallet has increased, and consumers are better positioned to dictate the prevailing price of a sneaker via free market forces.

Let's examine how we've arrived in this friendly consumer moment and what it means for today's collector.

RESALE: AN ENTERPRISE ENDEAVOR

Connotations of sneaker resale are diverse, often inaccurate, and typically anything but glamorous. Allow me to attempt the recreation of the image likely manifested by the average person when considering the sneaker resale "market."

An individual arrives at an ungodly hour of the morning to wait an unfathomably long time in an unfathomably long line for the latest combination of leather and rubber bearing a Nike swoosh. Upon matriculating to the front of that unfathomably long line, the individual purchases one pair of sneakers in one size for a retail price somewhere between $100-$200. Said individual returns to his or her home where he or she posts the sneakers on eBay and watches as bidding commences.

Days later, the sneakers are purchased at a tidy profit to the reseller of somewhere between $100-200 by either an unlucky individual too far back in that unfathomably long line, a lazier participant, someone with discretionary income to burn, or a combination of all of the above.

We'll call that the outsider's understanding of the resale market. Not entirely inaccurate, but also far from comprehensive and perhaps quite dated. Let's graduate to a slightly more informed view, perhaps that of a casual or novice sneaker collector.

In this case, the prospective reseller's efforts are a bit more diverse. He or she scours the Instagram profiles of dozens of boutique sneaker retailers in the days leading up to a release, seeking information on online raffles and in-store raffles for those stores that are local. In order to gain extra entries to each of those raffles, he or she subscribes to the store's newsletter and follows the store's social media accounts. Visits are paid to the local stores to the same end.

With the boutiques sufficiently covered, the reseller turns to the e-commerce landscape to score a pair or pairs at the exact moment that the sneaker is slated to release (often, but not always, 10a.m. EST on a Saturday morning). Most commonly, using a Nike release as an example, this effort would mean mashing the purchase button on the SNKRS app the second the clock ticks from 9:59 to 10:00 to get "in-line".

Depending on the release, it may also mean using multiple browser tabs to attempt acquisition from the higher-tier boutiques and potentially the Foot Lockers and Finish Lines of the world. For what it's worth though, inventory at the latter likely means more availability and lower premium.

Finally, the reseller may also choose to confront the realities of the unfathomably long line as a last-ditch effort. The spoils of his or her efforts are then listed either on StockX, GOAT, or eBay depending on where the prices and buying activity are strongest.

The above is by no means an unfair characterization. Rather, it's probably somewhat in line with reality for many sneaker enthusiasts. In fact, if you remove the last piece about listing the spoils, what I've essentially done is describe the buying process for any well-informed collector desperately seeking a "must-cop" pair of sneakers.

For a collector seeking a couple hundred dollars' worth of profit every now and again, testing his or her market knowledge and putting it to good use, the above would more or less be the process employed.

Still, the number used (somewhat casually) in estimates since 2015 is $1 billion in sneaker resales annually, which seems to have originated from *The Financial Times*. That's a massive, and in 2018, likely low estimate, which speaks to why the two aforementioned resale perceptions aren't exhaustive descriptions of the market: it's difficult to imagine an army of swashbuckling individual resale hobbyists moving multiple *billion* dollars in product annually.

In a May 2018 article from *The New York Times*, it was noted that a number of resale platforms achieved nine-figure gross merchandise volume (meaning the total value of goods sold via the platform) in 2017. For example, StockX CEO, Josh Luber, revealed that StockX was clearing $2 million in GMV daily (annualizes to well in excess of $700 million).[49] The StockX run-rate has since reached $1 billion annually. While not all of this gross merchandise volume is sneaker-related (many platforms sell watches, apparel, and select other limited items), it's possible to chart a path to resale market sales of *billions* rather than a billion, but not without understanding that there are enterprise players involved.

No, for many, resale is not a hobby at all. Rather, it's an occupation, and a lucrative one at that. There is a plethora of ways to divest of sneakers, but what separates the enterprise level reseller from the hobbyist is the proven and consistent ability to acquire inventory, *especially* at retail or otherwise favorable prices. Anybody can move significant volume, but doing so profitably is another story altogether. That economical procurement of inventory is the seller's secret sauce, and it's the reason that consignment platforms like Flight Club and Stadium Goods seek to make the rest of the process seamless.

---

49 Shapiro, Bee. 2018. "How Much Is That Sneaker In The Window?". *New York Times.*

Those platforms handle everything from A to Z, including the marketplace function, fulfillment, and customer service. They handle all the customer touch points so that the sellers can focus purely on their core competency: acquiring product. By simply sending the product to the consignment platform, the seller has alleviated vast logistical burden, leaving Flight Club or Stadium Goods to handle the rest. For enterprise level sellers moving thousands of pairs annually, the removal of this burden is essential.

So, what is the seller's secret sauce? Well, it varies.

In many cases and in the cases of the most enterprise level sellers, it's quite literally a secret, leveraging connections to parties with access to significant inventory of limited releases. These parties are referred to as "sneaker plugs." When resellers can demonstrate the ability to take on inventory in bulk, they build trust and relationships with these plugs.

This practice is something that Benjamin Kapelushnick, also referred to as Benjamin Kickz and 'The Sneaker Don', credited for his success in an interview with *The Cut*, "I started buying by the hundreds. When I posted it, everyone was like, Damn, he has a lot, so I showed it to other people, other plugs, and they were like, Okay, if he has the money to buy this, he can buy from us too. And then I bought more and more and more."[50] Oh, by the way, Kapelushnick is still

---

50 Schwartzberg, Lauren. 2016. "This 16-Year-Old Has Made Millions Selling Rare Sneakers". *The Cut*. https://www.thecut.com/2016/08/benjamin-kickz-sneaker-don.html.

in his teens, and his site, Sneaker Don, clears $1 million in sales annually, further evidence that the sneaker collecting economy is awash with opportunity for those entrepreneurial and hungry enough.

It takes unrelenting hard work and a little bit of luck to build the connections necessary to choose the "plug" route. Others, much to the ire of diehard collectors, embrace the old adage 'work smart, not hard' and avail themselves of 'bots', computer programs which automate iterative processes like adding items to carts and inputting account information. Bots have many enemies, namely anybody who has ever tried to purchase a pair of sneakers online by moving them into the cart and completing the purchase process in thirty seconds only to find that they've sold out.

In yet another derivative of the sneaker collectors' economy, savvy programmers now sell access to bots for anywhere from fifty bucks to multiple thousands of dollars, offering eager collectors or resellers the opportunity to utilize multiple accounts and deceive "real-person" tests, which seek to ascertain that the purchaser is not a bot but a live human customer.

Frustrating? Yes. Often infuriating? You bet. Unfair? Ehhh, not from a market perspective.

Bot-users are exploiting a market inefficiency that retailers and brands alike are making efforts to rectify in hopes of ensuring that lasting, loyal relationships are built with the end consumer. Seemingly, however, the consumers themselves are not willing to arbitrage the inefficiency away, and as a result, it's difficult not to kindly label the bot-users' efforts as somewhat entrepreneurial.

Allow me to explain the meaning of "arbitraging the inefficiency away." In financial markets, arbitrage opportunities arise when market participants can exploit price differences in identical or highly similar assets, typically buying the lower priced asset and selling the higher priced asset to turn a risk-free profit. Now, in financial markets, these opportunities disappear very quickly. When the opportunity presents itself, participants buy the lower priced asset, increasing demand for it and thereby raising its price, and sell the higher priced asset, increasing supply for sale and thereby reducing its price. The gap in price consequently closes.

Let's address the inefficiency that creates the arbitrage opportunity in this particular case. Think of the expense of the bot in this manner: if a one-time fee was paid for the bot, that fee can then be amortized, or divided by, the number of successful sneaker purchases and added to the cost of each purchase. For the sake of analysis, let's say a reseller pays $1,000 for bot access. That reseller then uses that bot to successfully acquire 20 pairs of highly sought-after sneakers that sell for double their retail price of $200 (for simplicity, we'll say the 2x resale value is after transaction fees). The reseller has paid a total of $5,000 for the 20 pairs of sneakers (20 pairs x $200 = $4,000, plus the $1,000 bot expense) and is subsequently able to turn around sell them for $8,000, or a $3,000 profit.

While it's not necessarily a "risk-free" proposition (a key characteristic of arbitrage), as the reseller must be confident in the resale market for the sneakers purchased, it's fairly lucrative business swiftly attained.

So, how would this advantage, this inefficiency, disappear?

There are several ways that this could happen. First, if all participants were willing to spend the money to utilize bots, in the short-term the increased demand for bots could increase prices for the bots and erode resale profits. Alternatively, the increased demand could cause the market to flood with bot users. With more participants using the bots, the advantage of using them, higher probability of successful acquisition, would decrease. The follow-on effect from that outcome would be a bot arms race of sorts, in which prices for the most sophisticated and effective bots rise ever higher, further eroding profits. Alternatively, if the increased demand caused a commensurate influx of bot supply at more reasonable prices, collectors might avail themselves of their services, increasing their own likelihood of acquisition and therefore reducing demand in the secondary market. Essentially, all of these outcomes rely on a tremendous increase in demand for the services of bots.

That tremendous increase in demand, however, is purely theoretical and unlikely to unfold in reality. Why? Not all participants are resellers and not all participants are willing to pay for the heightened probability of acquiring sneakers that are already over $150. Many participants would sooner pay for a t-shirt reading 'F*ck Your Bot!' (another offshoot of the sneaker economy!) than join the ranks of the 'cheaters'.

So, while bots move inventory in bulk from retailers and directly from manufacturers, if those parties prefer to reach real consumers and build relationships of lifetime value, the elimination of this inefficiency will need to result from their own efforts. Why would they prefer real consumers if the financial implication from that transaction is the same, human or robot? Remember, more than ever, success in sneaker retail is driven by differentiation through the creation of meaningful, relevant experiences for consumers, often fueled by storytelling.

Bots do not differentiate. They acquire by any means necessary, wherever possible. The immediate financial success is not guaranteed to be sustainable. At least for the time being though, bots continue to drive meaningful inventory acquisition for a subset of resellers.

Regardless of the means of acquisition, plug or bot, resale is a big business with enterprise-level sellers, not a cottage industry of rogue individuals selling a pair or two online. For the marketplaces serving as intermediary between reseller and end-consumer, relationships and a moat of supply are critical competitive advantages.

It's part of the reason that industry spectators are wrong to assume that all marketplaces and intermediaries are competing for the same piece of the same pie. There is seller overlap, of course, and there will continue to be, but enterprise-level resale exists, and it's served by intermediaries in more sophisticated ways. Managing and efficiently liquidating inventory is a full-time job, one embraced with enthusiasm by today's major consignment players.

With great inventory comes great responsibility, but that responsibility means opportunity. That opportunity, seized by Stadium Goods and Flight Club, ultimately provides the end-consumer, the next buyer of a pair of sneakers winding its way through the secondary market, with a legitimate, worry-free means of acquiring a long-desired target from a credible source. So, the supply side of the market grows on...

MARKETPLACES: ELEVATION FROM EBAY TO E-TRADE

In the early 2010s, plans were set in motion that would change the secondary sneaker market forever and for better. Inevitable though it may have been, with the proliferation of e-commerce technology and data analytics, two parties embraced the vast resale marketplace opportunity and, through tireless effort and a few lucky breaks, sit at the pinnacle of the industry today. Both efforts were born from the major problems plaguing the space: lack of trust & authenticity and lack of reliable market information.

In 2012, Josh Luber, an IBM data consultant at the time, founded Campless, a site developed to provide consumers with robust, current data on sneaker resale activity, compiling the transaction logs through eBay's public API. For the first time, secondary market participants had convenient access to reliable data on the prices being fetched on eBay for their precious assets or coveted targets. Campless was purely a data company, and by equipping the public with a framework by which they could understand the value of their sneakers, it was introducing structure and reason to a market that previously had very little of either. A market with better-informed participants runs more efficiently than one in which the informational disparities are significant.

One year later, in 2013, Jordan re-released the Jordan 5 in the nostalgia-laden "Grape" colorway. The Grape 5s are as nineties a sneaker as you can imagine. They are so nineties that Jordan released a special Fresh Prince themed version in the fall of 2018. Following that 2013 release, however, Daishin Sugano knew he simply had to acquire them, a childhood favorite. So, he did what anybody would do at the time. He took to eBay. On eBay, he located the sneakers, ordered them, paid, and was rewarded for his efforts by a fake pair arriving at his doorstep days later.

He confided in his friend, Eddy Lu, and they set out to solve the industry's authentication issue. GOAT was founded in July of 2015.

Months later, Campless announced an investment from Detroit Venture Partners, spearheaded by Quicken Loans founder and Cleveland Cavaliers owner, Dan Gilbert. In conjunction with that announcement, Campless launched a new tool, Collections, which would allow users to build their collection and track its value over time on the site, as if the collection was a portfolio.

By winter of 2016, Campless was no more.

Whereas Campless had initially linked to eBay product listings from its site, earning revenue as an eBay affiliate and through data sales to market research organizations, it was set to become an eBay competitor in the world of limited releases. Campless had become StockX, the stock market of things, where buyers and sellers of limited release goods would be connected and armed with price and volume metrics, real time bid and offer data, and historical trends.

These two marketplaces of today and tomorrow, GOAT and StockX, have solved or dramatically reduced much of the friction that characterized the forum and eBay days of resale. One of the lowest hanging fruits was trust and authenticity.

Transacting with a stranger is an awkward experience. You see your counterpart's username and feedback and create bizarre projections of whom you imagine them to be. You hope that they'll ship swiftly. You hope that they've been honest about the product. You hope that they'll honor the transaction.

You can hope all that you want, but there was very little that you could do to ascertain that the internet stranger across the country or world was a stand-up guy. GOAT and StockX realized, separately, that by inserting themselves into the middle of the transaction, acting as the accountable facilitator, the buyer and seller would never need to dance that awkward tango...they never even needed to speak.

Here's how it works. The seller lists a product at the desired price, and a buyer willing to transact at that price purchases the sneakers. Conversely, a buyer lists an offer for a product, and a seller willing to sell at that offer price sells the sneakers. The buyer is charged immediately. The seller ships the sneakers directly to StockX or GOAT via a label printed from the site, and the marketplace verifies that the sneakers are authentic, that they have not been worn (StockX participants transact only in "deadstock" product), and that they are the correct item in the correct size.

Once all of those boxes have been checked, the sneakers are shipped from the marketplace warehouse to the buyer. The seller is paid the funds due to them: the transaction price less a selling fee levied by the marketplace (9.5% for entry-level sellers). The buyer receives the sneakers with the assurance that they have been inspected by individuals who have significant experience authenticating product. Better yet, in the event things go astray, the buyer or seller has a customer service team to turn to, rather than needing to confront the mysterious stranger directly.

By inserting a more trustworthy middle-man into the process, the marketplaces had largely vaporized the industry's trust issue.

Trust and authenticity were far from the only issues handicapping the efficiency of the market, however. The resale market suffered from meaningful optics issues. To put it plainly, listings on eBay and forums simply did not look as inviting as those that you would see on a retailer's or brand's website. Simply *finding* the correct version of a product was an exasperating chore.

Go on eBay today and query for any sneaker. You will almost certainly see a result in your travels with a listing title that looks like this: "NEW JORDAN 11 NIKE AIR MAX YEEZY 350 V2 ADIDAS VERY RARE DEADSTOCK". To put it plainly, that is not confidence inspiring for a buyer, and we're not even past the listing title yet! Then, you get into the user-generated photos and descriptions. Very rarely do the descriptions reassure. In fact, I'd say there's only downside most of the time. The photos, of course, are total wild cards. Most forum and eBay listers are not professional photographers, nor have they mastered that pesky point-and-shoot iPhone camera.

StockX and GOAT realized that, if you're verifying the authenticity of the sneakers anyway, why do you need user-generated descriptions and photos at all? If the sneakers are deadstock and they are the correct item, that user-generated content is completely irrelevant. This realization allowed the marketplaces, in their own ways, to create interfaces that are far more comparable visually to top-notch retail sites than their predecessors are. The interfaces are clean, simple, and intuitive. The impediments to clicking the buy button have been removed, because let's be honest, viewing a user-generated listing is akin to interfacing with the digital version of the sketchiest used car salesman intent on convincing you *not* to buy anything.

Matt Cohen, Vice President of Business Development at GOAT, elaborates on this ambitious effort to create an experience more analogous to high-end retail:

"We strive to create that retail-like experience in a shopping app. When you walk into a store, you see that shoe that you want in your size at the lowest price, and that's what we try to do at GOAT. That goes down to our packaging. When you walk into a high-end shopping mall or department store, you walk out and that package is wrapped in tissue paper with a stiffener, and there's a focus on the customer experience and journey. We do that at GOAT as well. Every package is personally hand-wrapped. Every card of authentication is signed by the team that's authenticating the shoe."

The marketplace experience today does not feel dramatically different from purchasing directly from a brand or retailer. The core difference is that the consumer is a more active participant in the secondary market, whereas the primary market experience is more passive. That active participation, fueled by the availability of substantial data, has turned the secondary sneaker marketplaces into bustling hubs of transacting activity. While the liquidity, the depth of bids and offers for any given pair of sneakers on StockX, doesn't necessarily stack up against the financial markets, where billions of company shares trade daily, Luber's vision for a stock market of things has largely been realized.

"The best part about this is we didn't make this up," Luber explains. "All we did was we took the stock market, which has been the most efficient form of commerce for hundreds of years and pointed it from these commodities to those commodities."

It's the cataloging and presentation of data that could bring us to this point faster than was previously thought possible. StockX users are presented with historical pricing data (where did the sneaker sell most recently and where has it been?), highest bid and lowest offer data (where is this sneaker most likely to trade next?), and the list of active bids and offers (which way is the price most likely to move?). The market dynamic is most impressive in the case of a sneaker that has been released recently, was released in quantities that aren't dramatically limited, and is highly sought-after.

The best example is a sneaker that many consider to be the sneaker of 2018, the Air Max 97/1, designed by Sean Wotherspoon. View this sneaker on StockX and you will find a deep list of both asks (ranging from the low $600s to $1,500 but concentrated in the $600s) and bids (ranging from $25 to $620 but concentrated in the high $500s and low $600s). You'll see a list of recent sales that detail the frequency (multiple times daily) with which the sneaker sells and the fairly narrow band of prices in which it does so.

Most impressively, you'll see a historical price chart which shows a dip in resale price in early June of 2018. Why? The sneaker restocked on the Nike SNKRS application, allowing more buyers to acquire the shoes for their retail price ($160) in the primary market. The secondary market digested that information, reacted accordingly to the greater supply through lower price, and rebounded slowly over time as more sneakers found their way onto feet and off the market.

It's incredible to see a sneaker market function so effectively.

Not all sneakers function quite as efficiently, though, which is why transparency is so important. Armed with historical data and bid-ask transparency, buyers and sellers can transact via what's referred to in financial markets as a "market order": for a buyer, buying at the lowest available ask, or for a seller, selling at the highest active bid. Alternatively, they can set their respective bid or ask wherever they feel comfortable. This practice is the equivalent of a "limit order" in the financial markets, whereby a buyer would place an order to buy shares at or below a certain price. If the buyer places a limit order at $100 when the market is at $110, and the market moves to $100, the buyer's order will be executed at $100. If the market moves in the other direction, the buyer's order will simply go unexecuted and they are left to consider potentially entering a new order. On StockX, that bid is active until it is either cancelled or expires (within 30 days).

However, placing a bid or ask obligates that buyer or seller to transact should a counterparty wish to execute at that level. The buyer will be charged immediately. The seller will have two business days to ship or risk greater future selling fees on the platform (or potentially the revocation of selling privileges).

The beauty of this system, using the buyer as an example, is that the consumer is empowered to examine the market for any sneaker and act accordingly. If there is a sneaker that you want, you can take a look at the list of bids and asks for that sneaker in your size. If there are vastly more asks than there are bids, you can confidently assume that those asks are more likely to come down in price than they are to go up. Why? There's more supply than there is demand.

The ideal scenario (for the buyer) is one in which there are many asks and no bids to speak of. In such a scenario, the prospective buyer can initiate a bid at what he or she considers to be a fair price and wait for those asks to come closer to that level or for that bid to be hit. Excessively low-balling (i.e. launching a bid of $50 for a sneaker that last sold for $200) will do very little, but setting a fair bid will entice sellers motivated by liquidity to act more quickly and more favorably than would otherwise be expected.

What does it mean to be motivated by liquidity? The seller knows that they do not want this sneaker in their possession any longer and they want to convert the sneaker's value to cash as quickly as possible. Essentially, whether they need the funds or they believe that the sneaker's value is a sinking ship, they want out and they want out fast. Not in a few months, not in a few weeks, but in a day or two. When a seller becomes motivated by liquidity to sell, a buyer who sets a bid at a price where he would be happy and comfortable purchasing stands to benefit.

The same can be true in reverse for a seller hoping to exploit the desperation of a buyer in a case where there is little supply. Set a fair price (higher than the current bids) and wait for the buyer to come to you. Now, because of the proliferation of supply, however, these scenarios are rarer.

The fact that the secondary markets are functioning in a manner today that can even be loosely compared to the financial markets is awe-inspiring and would have been unfathomable a decade ago, and the future prospects are equally as astounding.

Sneakers have become an asset, traded like any other. Luber envisions a future for the sneaker trade in which participants wouldn't even need take possession of their portfolios: "This is oil futures and frozen pork, true commodities. We don't do this at scale yet, but we will. We absolutely will. We'll probably have to go register with the CFTC and become a commodities exchange, and we'll do that. That's fine. We have to go through that process."

Eventually, the continued shift towards acceptance of sneakers as a true asset would lead to a custodian model for StockX and presumably, for others, which would even more closely resemble the futures market, where market participants rarely ever actually take possession of the contract's underlying asset.

"I can hold your Yeezy 350 'Zebra', and you can still do everything that you would otherwise do it. You can accept the highest bid, you can place an ask, you can sell it, you can have it returned to you," Luber explains. "That's the only difference between this and oil futures, right? Because if you're buying oil futures, those barrels really do sit in a warehouse and no one ever takes possession. The only difference here [in the custodial model] is you can keep trading it and the digital ownership keeps trading and changing, and then at some point someone's like, 'I would like to own those Yeezys, please send them to me.' But until that happens, this is oil futures. All we're doing is changing the digital ownership of that asset, and we're the custodian – it's sitting in my warehouse in Detroit or wherever it is."

A secondary market that bears the same clean-looks and worry-free transacting as a primary retailer was a fantasy a decade ago, but thanks to Josh Luber, Dan Gilbert, Daishin Sugano, Eddy Lu, and countless others, that's where we are now. And where we're headed? Truly sophisticated trading of sneakers as an asset.

They've set a blueprint for secondary market transacting in deadstock, limited release goods that extends far beyond sneakers. However, can the same strides be made for products that have been bought and, you know, *actually used*?

USED SNEAKERS: LESS SMELL, MORE SUPPLY

Used sneakers, at first blush, don't sound appealing.

Smell? Likely.

Dirt? Probably.

Scuffs? Count on it.

That was the reality of buying used sneakers for many years. In the wild west of sneaker resale, collectors scoured web forums, message boards, and eBay, seeking a cut-rate price on a sought-after sneaker. The price was *probably* going to be lower than that of a deadstock, or brand-new, never worn, model, but *certainly*? No, even that wasn't *certain*.

Prospective buyers assumed the worst as they zoomed in diligently on poorly lit eBay photos, desperately seeking the answer to an impossible question: can I tell what these are going to smell like just by looking at them? Yikes.

Yes, exploring the world of used sneakers was not for the faint of heart. Fortunately, thanks to a number of industry entrants and, more generally, advances in technology, transacting in this world is not nearly as perilous today as it was in those swashbuckling days of the early 2000s. We should all be thankful that this is the case, because the sneaker economy is far more robust when the market for used sneakers runs more efficiently, a meaningful boon for buyers and sellers alike.

Let's imagine a world where market participants are only comfortable transacting in deadstock sneakers. From the buyer's perspective, the supply of a coveted sneaker peaks at the date of release. Supply then drops dramatically and immediately as a significant portion of lucky acquirers does the unthinkable and actually puts them on their feet. Afterwards, supply steadily tapers lower as those who bought and stocked initially sell their pairs to prospective wearers. Every single time a sneaker finds its way onto a foot, and that foot finds its way onto pavement (commonly referred to as "undeadstocking" or being taken "off ice"), the supply of that sneaker has decreased by one pair.

Good luck finding your grails at a reasonable price years after release in that world. Worse yet, accessibility for those who can't afford deadstock pairs all but disappears.

From a seller's perspective, this dynamic isn't the worst thing in the world. Decreasing supply of course means more attractive prices to the seller who has remained disciplined and kept pairs on ice. However, the ramifications are not exclusively positive. First, discipline is now critical. One moment of weakness, one mishap while trying them on for fun and those sneakers now have zero value. This is fairly obvious, but there are more nuanced ramifications. Less supply means fewer transactions, and fewer transactions means less market information. Each model would be more thinly traded, meaning that more time elapses between transactions as fewer pairs are brought to market. The seller, consequently, is less informed on the appropriate value of his or her asset. Comparable transactions on which pricing can be based are few and far between.

The seller runs the risk, then, of bringing the sneakers to market at a price well below the highest willingness to pay, the maximum price at which a consumer would definitely buy the product. Now, knowing that demand likely exceeds supply of the asset, the seller can set the price high and gradually lower it until he or she meets the consumer's willingness to pay. However, if the seller is seeking immediate liquidity for the asset, this process can be time consuming and costly. All of these factors contribute to a market in which there may be little continuity in pricing.

So, while obviously advantaged in this scenario, sellers too can be detrimentally impacted by less efficient markets.

While the disappearance of a market for used sneakers theoretically impacts buyers and sellers alike, we can concretely point to lost business for secondary marketplaces currently operating in the space. An advantage to the marketplace model is the ability of the marketplace to generate a commission (often in the ballpark of 10% of the selling price) on the same pair of sneakers on multiple occasions. For simplicity's sake, let's say that deadstock sneakers generally change hands two times in a marketplace network. For a $200 sneaker, two sales on the network at that price would mean almost $40 in commission to the marketplace. If, after the second sale, that sneaker is taken off ice and out of circulation, commissions on that pair have been exhausted, and there's one less potential seller contributing to the depth of the market.

This scenario is purely theoretical. There will always be some appetite for used sneakers. The reality in years past, however, was that significant friction existed in the market for used sneakers, and this friction meant milder versions of the consequences detailed above for all parties. Just as importantly, a lack of trust and a lack of confidence in buying or selling plagued this market.

Matt Cohen, Vice President of Business Development at GOAT, details the uncomfortable past of transacting:

"Before GOAT existed, you sold on eBay, public forums, message boards, or Facebook groups. And there was just tons of friction no matter which platform you sold on. You had to take photos of all of your different shoes for eBay and upload them to your computer, and there was no standardized listing form. And then there's this trust and safety issue. You don't know if the shoes are real. You don't know if the buyer or seller is going to defraud you. Not only are you worried about who you're buying from or who you're selling to, but you're worried about how used that shoe is. You're worried about the photo the seller is taking. Is he or she masking some worn effect?"

Without standardization of listings and clear ratings of sneaker condition, it's virtually impossible to buy with confidence. You can't buy with confidence because you don't have sufficient and reliable information.

If a deadstock version of the sneaker is selling for $200, and you find a used version listed at $160 on eBay, can you really feel comfortable that its condition is 80% as good as the deadstock version? And what does that even mean?! Cohen elaborates on the clunkiness and awkwardness of imperfect product listings and descriptions: "There's this joke, the traditional sneaker grading way, it was VVVVVNDS which *obviously* means very veryveryveryvery near deadstock. What does that actually mean? We used to joke that more Vs meant more worn."

How can a market operate efficiently when the value of a sneaker is based on the rating of its condition, and that condition is based on the number of Vs included in the description, and that number of Vs may or may not be inversely related to how new it actually is?! If I sound exasperated, it's because the market for used sneakers was (and in many ways, still is) exasperating.

Aside from the obvious issue (buyers and/or sellers having unsatisfactory experiences), the unreliability of data creates broader market problems. The efficiency of the market relies upon robust and accurate data. If sneakers that are, in reality, quite used and in poor condition sell for 80% of the most recently reported deadstock value due to either a misleading description or misleading photos, that price may poorly inform future transactions. The bar for sales of this sneaker has been set artificially high.

So how do participants combat this problem? One marketplace participant, GOAT, has taken it upon itself to bring credibility and integrity to the used sneaker marketplace.

To start, the company has introduced rigor around the process of sneaker photography, going so far as to reject certain photos for the following reasons (from the GOAT website):

- Both sneakers are not shown in a full, clear view.
- Both sneakers are not fully visible within the frame of the photo.
- Low lighting.
- Sneaker details (e.g., SKU, size, etc.) are not fully readable in box/ tag photo.
- Non-sneaker photos. Other objects or distracting patterns or items are in the photo with the shoes.
- Personal information shown in photos.

Photographs aside, once a sneaker successfully sells on GOAT, the seller then ships the sneakers directly to the GOAT warehouse, where the sneakers are inspected to confirm authenticity then they are relayed on to the buyer. Only once authenticity is verified does the seller receive payment for the sale of sneakers. Conversely, GOAT assumes responsibility for collecting payment from the buyer, eliminating fraud risk to the seller. These practices, minimum requisite qualifications in the marketplace for deadstock sneakers, are less common in the used space.

Cohen explains GOAT's willingness to operate in used transactions:

"We've taken the stance where we're fully dedicated to sneakers," explains Cohen with regards to GOAT's willingness to operate in the used space. "The used sneaker marketplace has always been a big part of the culture. We didn't grow up in an era where there were hundreds of retros coming out every year. When I was younger and wanted to buy a pair of True Blue Jordan 3s in size 13 that hadn't released in four years, I wasn't finding a deadstock pair. Used sneakers always represented a massive business opportunity and a significant part of sneaker culture. I think it's a difficult business, and that's why people shy away from it, but GOAT actually embraces that challenge. So, we launched with used sneakers because we really valued that part of the sneaker industry. We know there's a kid out there just entering the sneaker market, who really wants a coveted pair of shoes, but maybe can't afford it. We thought 'We want to give this person the opportunity to buy those shoes, and hope that they will return to buy new shoes.' We continue to feel strongly about reducing that barrier to entry."

GOAT hasn't left the elevation of used resale to improved photography and authenticity verification alone. Rather, the marketplace has embarked on a new service, GOAT Clean, which can be likened to the detailing of a used car before sale. Through GOAT Clean, used sneakers are shipped to GOAT where the shoes are scrubbed, the laces rinsed, the insoles washed, lint removed, and creases smoothed. With the sneaker improved to the extent of its potential, GOAT then strives to render the days of VVVVVNDS a laughable tale of the past via a proprietary grading system.

"When you think about collectibles, there is always a predetermined grading system used. Whether it be baseball cards, art, coins, diamonds, you name it, a grading system helps inform the value of a product, and ensures that the buyer knows exactly what they're getting," Cohen explains. "We have generated tons of data on shoes and every single shoe that sells comes to our warehouse first. In order to build our own grading system, we evaluated over 50,000 used. We first looked at photos and graded those photos, and then graded them when they came into our warehouse. We built a 25-point grading system for internal purposes, and then focused on developing a digestible grade for the consumer. The possible grades were 'like new', 'excellent', 'very good', and 'good'. Four very clear, distinct, and understandable grading categories."

The GOAT website details this system:

- Like New: Minimal to no signs of wear.
- Excellent: Slight wear on tread with minimal creasing.
- Very Good: Gentle wear with some creasing, scratches, and/or slight discoloration.
- Good: Moderate wear with visible creasing, scuffing, and/or discoloration.

Keep in mind, this isn't the seller assigning a grade to the sneaker. GOAT, based on a data set that is among the most extensive in the industry, is applying rigor to the grading process. Yes, it's in GOAT's interest to ensure that sneakers sell for the highest price possible given that the company takes a commission on the final sale price. However, just as importantly, it's also in GOAT's interest to ensure that the buyer has a comfortable and satisfactory experience, so it would be irresponsible to assume grade inflation in favor of the seller. Ideally, the GOAT Clean experience results in more positive outcomes for buyer and seller alike.

"Through the GOAT Clean program, we're providing more value for our sellers and buyers alike. The average GOAT Clean sneaker sells at a premium, compared to the same shoe in a used setting due to customer satisfaction being higher," details Cohen. "If for some reason you don't like your shoe from GOAT Clean, we take it back. GOAT Clean eliminates many common concerns of buying used sneakers, like shoe quality and smell, while simultaneously increasing the value of the used shoe."

To the extent that this process, in which great rigor is applied, takes hold, buyers and sellers will be the beneficiaries of more extensive and reliable data throughout the sneaker economy. Those parties will have a clearer indication of how a sneaker that is truly "like new" should sell relative to a deadstock or "very good" condition sneaker. While the guesswork is not entirely eliminated, the friction dissipates significantly. No longer will we have to regress the amount of Vs in VVVVVNDS against the actual condition of a sneaker to find some degree of reliability.

For GOAT or for any marketplace, engaging consumers in *efficient* transacting of used sneakers, while a cumbersome task, can have meaningful returns in the long-run due to a concept that Cohen describes as the circular economy: "Our buyers become sellers, our sellers become buyers, and different things happen in different courses of people's lives. We want to create that circular pattern, whether it's getting that aspirational buyer in the door by buying a used pair of shoes in a great experience, or that buyer then becomes a seller because he's not into that shoe anymore, and that seller becomes a buyer again because they sold that pair of shoes. It's the circular economy. It's hard but that's why we love the challenge."

By engaging used transactors, a marketplace keeps a sneaker in circulation for additional sales, which means additional commission. While those commissions may be on decreasing sales prices, in theory, 10% of $150 and 10% of $120 certainly beats the alternative: zero commission because the sneaker is out of circulation. Furthermore, the person who bought those used sneakers, they may return to sell that pair on your network. Better yet, if the experience was a positive one, they may return to the network as a buyer of deadstock sneakers.

Ideally, you've created a scenario in which the dollars are never truly leaving your marketplace. Someone buys a pair of sneakers, later sells them, invests the proceeds in another pair, and the cycle persists. For the marketplace, the lifetime value, or profit the marketplace can expect to realize over the course of the relationship, of both the sneaker and the buyer or seller increases dramatically.

Importantly though, the marketplace is only rewarded with this flywheel effect and circular economy if there is confidence that the satisfaction of both buyers and sellers can be ensured. Ensuring satisfaction in used sneaker transacting is an extraordinarily tall task. So, while GOAT has confronted the challenge with enthusiasm, it's understandable that other industry players focus solely on providing the cleanest, deepest, and most efficient market of deadstock sneakers possible, awaiting the arrival of a third-party, industry standard grading system, akin to the PSA system for baseball cards.

Still, any effort to bring trust, safety, and reliability to a market that was once so inefficient is meaningful progress for the efficiency of the sneaker market on the whole. To the extent that the breadth and depth of supply can be reliably extended and transactions can produce accurate data, the market will function in a manner that is far healthier for both buyer and seller. As we of course know, greater breadth and depth of *legitimate* supply favors the consumer.

Plus, those recently acquired sneakers probably won't smell as often. Clutch.

✳✳✳

In summation, we've reached a point at which the difference between primary and secondary marketplaces is quickly evaporating and sneakers are quickly becoming less a shoe and more an asset. Consignment services are effectively, legitimately, and efficiently facilitating the sales process for enterprise sellers. Secondary marketplaces boast e-commerce platforms as cleanly designed as those of well-known retailers and brands (if not more sophisticated). The proliferation of reliable and timely data is fueling the treatment of sneakers as less shoe, more asset. Friction has dramatically dissipated on the secondary market, supply has grown rapidly, and with those forces has come an era of unprecedented consumer choice. In short, it's a tremendous time to be in the sneaker economy, and an even better time to be a collector.

As we've discussed, scarcity is purely relative. Scarce though certain new releases may be, those releases or close substitutes of those releases are never far out of reach. In fact, that reach is only as long as the current distance between your hand and your phone. Unfathomably long times spent in unfathomably long lines are a thing of the past. The future is here, and the consumer's gain is another participant's loss. But which participant? The secondary seller, sure, but what if the wounds are seeping into the primary market as lines between secondary and primary blur? Those lines are blurring, and those wounds are seeping. The secondary market has grown too vast to ignore.

StockX recently raised $44mm in a round led by GV (formerly Google Ventures) and Battery Ventures, and boasts previous investment from not only Detroit Venture Partners and co-founder Dan Gilbert, but from several high-profile individuals including Eminem, Joe Haden, and Mark Wahlberg. GOAT raised $25mm in funding in 2017, merged with Flight Club in 2018, and raised an additional $60mm from Index Ventures. Stadium Goods kicked off 2017 by raising $4.6mm from Forerunner Ventures, The Chernin Group, and Mark Cuban among others. In 2018, it was announced that LVMH Luxury Ventures would take a stake in the company, though terms were not disclosed. Finally, luxury retail platform Farfetch closed out 2018 by announcing its intent to acquire Stadium Goods outright for $250mm in cash and stock.

The secondary market players are well funded and on a trajectory for tremendous growth. They may not have only changed the game, they may soon dictate how the game is played.

TAKEAWAYS FROM THE SNEAKONOMIST

- Sneaker resale is not a cottage industry or a micro-business. It can be those things, but enterprise-level sellers have grown a market in which *billions* of dollars in product are transacted annually.

- Secondary marketplaces have introduced trust, authenticity, and confidence to a market that was previously murky, inefficient, and fraught with scams.

- The era of user-generated sneaker listings has ended, replaced by clean secondary market interfaces resembling best-in-class e-commerce sites, further blurring the lines between primary retail and secondary resale.

- The capture and presentation of robust secondary market data, including historic transactions and current bids or asks, has further enhanced participants' ability to transact with confidence, while simultaneously furthering the perception and acceptance of sneakers as an asset.

- All of these advances have led to a vast proliferation of secondary market supply, significantly broadening the selection available and increasing the ability of end-consumers to dictate the price they're willing to pay.

- The secondary sneaker market has captured the attention of the investment community at large, and the amount of funding flooding the space will lead to a more dramatic acceleration of growth and maturation in the next five years than the previous. We'll explore the ramifications of that growth and maturation later.

CHAPTER 6

SO MANY SNEAKERS, SO FEW ON FEET – HAVE SNEAKERS BECOME A BUBBLE?

———

"The Greater Fool is actually an economic term. It's a patsy. For the rest of us to profit, we need a greater fool, someone who will buy long and sell short. Most people spend their lives trying not to be the greater fool; we toss in the hot potato, we dive for his seat when the music stops. The greater fool is someone with the perfect blend of self-delusion and ego to think that

he can succeed where others have failed. This whole country was made by greater fools."[51]

—The Newsroom, written by Aaron Sorkin

Dot-com stocks. Tulips. Baseball cards. Cryptocurrencies. Sneakers?

It's a dangerous game we play, enraptured by the promise of profits. That frenzied pursuit of financial gain blankets our eyes with rose-colored lenses that alter our perception of the world before us.

Pets.com becomes a blue-chip. Tulips become more than flowers. Homes become impenetrable fortresses of capital preservation. We pretend cryptocurrencies aren't totally freaking confusing.

And sneakers? They're not just neatly stitched and glued compositions of leather and rubber.

Seemingly astronomical values are assigned to these compositions every day. But are they astronomical or are they sustainable? Or are they both?

Here's the inescapable reality of the sneaker economy today: there is *a lot* of supply in the market. The sneaker brands continue to charge forward, mainly to serve that prevailing consumer that still sees sneakers as just...shoes. While the sneakerheads' appetite no doubt looms in their planning,

---

51   *The Newsroom.* "The Greater Fool." 1.10. Directed by Greg Mottola. Written by Aaron Sorkin. HBO, August 26 2012.

the pressure of obligations to shareholders, public or private, and the revenue growth expectations that come with those obligations looms constantly larger.

We know that the brands can take supply of certain models out of the market to influence future demand, but those aforementioned obligations mean that brands can't painlessly deflate the supply on the market as a whole. The conveyor belt that brings robust new supply into the sneaker economy is not slowing down, and it's certainly not going to stop.

If the brands are the conveyor belt bringing baggage from the plane to baggage claim, the secondary market is the baggage carousel, and there's a lot of unclaimed luggage there.

Once pairs reach the market, they're not necessarily finding a new home on feet. Instead, the profiteering aspect of sneaker collecting has created a practice in which sneakers are bought and put on ice, preserved for a resale profit harvest in days, weeks, or months to come. For all intents and purposes, those pairs continue to constitute supply on the sneaker market, accessible to any consumer that uses eBay, StockX, GOAT, or other resale emporiums of repute.

Supply of sneakers purchased for their utilitarian purpose of protecting the soles of your feet is digested by the market and correspondingly reduced. Participants in the economy of sneakerheads, however, are less concerned with that utilitarian purpose and more concerned with maintaining a pristine collection, whether for resale or simply aesthetics.

Consequently, the sneaker economy is replete with supply – not only that coming online with each new season but also supply of brand-new sneakers released over the course of the last decade or even before. As primary and secondary markets converge, consumers are faced with unprecedented breadth and depth of selection. So many sneakers, only so many feet. While multiples of retail price will likely always be attainable on hyper limited, hyper popular releases, on the whole, it's fair to ask the question: are we going to reach a tipping point of supply that will lead to a broad deflation of resale prices?

Is the sneaker market a bubble? And if it is, what happens when it pops?

THE ANATOMY OF A BUBBLE – NOT THE NIKE AIR KIND

So, what exactly is a bubble? How do we spot one? How does it burst? Let's peel back the layers to get a better understanding of how we might assess the current market for sneakers.

An asset bubble is characterized by a swift rise in prices that is unsupported by underlying fundamentals, which include demand for the asset itself. The rise is self-perpetuating, as speculators inspired by that sharp increase take to the market en masse, inflating prices to levels that become unsustainable due to the lack of commensurately strong fundamentals.

Often, typically last in the door among these speculators are ill-informed parties that are blissfully unaware of the associated risks. Exceedingly overcome by the prospect of newfound riches promised by the unrelenting upward charge of the asset's price, they buy now and ask questions later. The arrival of this class of speculator is a reliable sign that the bursting of the bubble is near.

It's worth noting that supply shortages, or the perception thereof, have also been known to contribute to the formation of bubbles. Hmm, I can think of a certain asset whose buyers are motivated consistently by scarcity – whether illusion or reality.

Important in the examination of bubbles is a theory dubbed the Greater Fool Theory. The idea is that the buyer of an asset need not necessarily worry over the intrinsic value; they can simply buy the asset and flip it to a greater fool who is willing to pay a higher price at a later date. In ignoring intrinsic value and embracing the belief that foolish demand will persist, participants contribute to the formation of a bubble. Eventually, the wide availability of greater fools dissipates as the prospect of profits grows more uncertain. As that trusty pool of greater fools dries up, prices fall precipitously, whether to the intrinsic value of the asset or otherwise.

In any case, the bubble pops.

One of the oldest examples of a bubble comes from the Netherlands in the 1630s, after tulips were introduced to the country. Due to their rarity and the lack of ease with which sought-after patterns could be grown, the value of the flower began to rise rapidly. Seen as a luxury product and somewhat of a status symbol, collected alongside paintings and other valuables, the subjective assessment of value inflated. People became increasingly willing to pay elevated prices, due in part to the comfort of knowing that somebody else would likely be willing to pay even more.

People began buying not for the bulb itself, but for the prospect of selling at a higher price. There were records, though rare, of tulips being sold for as much as an estate or annual wages. As sellers became increasingly motivated to realize their profits though, whether the result of supply concerns or otherwise, the pool of greater fools dried up and the bubble popped. The greatest fools were those stuck with the flowers as the bubble burst, with most participants having bought and sold a bulb at a profit without ever physically possessing it above soil.

Assessments of value can be subjective, indeed, but when they become magnificently out of touch with reality, it's only a matter of time until that disconnect is rationalized. That's when the clock strikes midnight and a tulip becomes a flower once more. There are countless examples similar in nature, but perhaps more sophisticated and less laughable by today's standards.

In the 1990s until just after the turn of the millennium, share prices of technology stocks broadly skyrocketed, as investors, first institutional and then mainstream, became enamored with the possibilities of internet-centric businesses. In many cases, rich initial public offerings didn't require attractive products or services, just a catchy domain name. Investor measures of value shifted away from traditional mainstays like price-to-earnings and price-to-sales ratios, which made the stocks look expensive and unattractive, to a focus on page views and clicks.

The latter stages of that decade were characterized by fast money. IPOs generated huge first day pops in price, fortunes were made by the rise of the NASDAQ index (on paper at least), and countless companies sprouted with long term plans for innovation and success that could be characterized as suspect at best. Yet, there were consistently greater fools eager to join the ranks of those profiting.

Eventually, market participants sobered up to the less than stellar underlying fundamentals of their golden geese, and the downturn unfolded swiftly starting in March of 2000. Those paper fortunes were all but erased. When the damage was done, the NASDAQ troughed at 1,108.49 in October of 2002, down from its March of 2000 peak of 5,132.52.

For those keeping score at home, that's a precipitous drop of SEVENTY EIGHT percent!

But bubbles aren't limited to the ridiculous or the intangible. In fact, assets don't get much more solid than American homes, and we still found out that their prices could prove anything but.

At its core, the housing bubble of the mid 2000s was fueled by an unshakable belief that the price of housing in the United States had always gone up and would therefore continue to go up in perpetuity. Now, homebuyers aren't generally considered fools, but you can see that the Greater Fool Theory still applied here. Catalyzing the expansion of the bubble was the bank practice of loaning money to unqualified "subprime" borrowers, and then often packaging those loans and selling them to investors. As long as the homes collateralizing the loans increased in value, all would be okay.

All was not okay.

Not only did the Greater Fool Theory apply to the homes themselves, it applied to the loans that allowed the homes to be purchased. As it turned out, the proliferation of easy lending to parties unable to repay was unsustainable, as was the rise of housing prices caused by it. Housing prices tumbled, borrowers defaulted on their mortgages, and investors were left holding the bag. Bubble burst.

All right, so how do we apply all of this to the sneaker market? Tulips, stocks, houses, even baseball cards – how do these lessons shape our understanding of sneakers?

Well, let's think about what we know:

- Many buyers, though a fraction of the overall market, aren't buying sneakers for the sneakers themselves but for the prospect of profit. They do so with the belief that someone who values them more will come along to buy them at a greater price. They buy and sell without the sneakers ever touching their foot or even leaving the box.

- The value of any pair of sneakers is largely subjective. In other words, the value isn't really based on underlying fundamentals. There are no cash flows, and one can effectively protect the soles of their feet for far less than hundreds of dollars. Demand is based on subjective assessments of various factors: style, exclusivity, and hype among them.

- Scarcity (or the fear of scarcity) often begets demand. Demand begets higher prices. Higher prices often beget higher prices.

As we'll address in greater detail, there's reason to believe that it's becoming increasingly difficult to find greater fools in the sneaker market. The market is currently replete with great fools, making ill-informed purchase decisions motivated by the prospect of profits that are unlikely to come. They saw resellers attain unfathomable riches from sneakers. They saw the success stories of the well-informed and well-equipped, and so they dove in. But if they can't acquire the Off-White Nikes or the rare Yeezys at retail, lacking either the luck, connections, or savvy to do so, they're having trouble consistently finding a greater fool for their poorly chosen inventory.

Matt Powell of the NPD Group sheds light on the impact of profiteering efforts and, in the process, touches upon the application of the Greater Fool Theory to sneakers:

"The other phenomenon that really drove the rise of Jordan over the last five years or so was the resale market and people profiteering as opposed to really coveting the product. It was more about being able to flip it for some multiple than it was 'I love this shoe, I gotta have this shoe'. Now, the end buyer, to some extent, was that person who coveted the product, but you also just had people who were simply trading in the product because they thought they could make a quick buck. And of course, that's a Ponzi scheme at the end of the game, because if you're the last guy buying, you're screwed. And if the supply gets to be too great, you're screwed."

When you're reliant upon the existence of a greater fool, you'd be well served by a keen sense for sudden increases in supply, suddenly weakening hype, or some combination of both. Otherwise, you're the one left holding the proverbial bag, or in this case, shoe box. In some cases, navigating those shifts is turning out to be more trouble than it's worth. "Look, we're even starting to see this happen with Yeezy," Powell explains. "I had people telling me on a recent release that kids are coming back and returning Yeezy's because they couldn't get the multiple that they thought they should get. So rather than resell it for 10 bucks over MSRP, they just got their money out."

Are there elements of a bubble here? Certainly. Are we likely to see this dramatic, widespread pop? Not necessarily.

Why not? Well, consider, for example, why baseball cards "popped." When the monopoly on MLB licensed cards was eradicated, competitors flooded the market, eager to capitalize on demand and generate revenues that had eluded them for the preceding decades. They paid no real mind to the balance of supply and demand and the ramifications that excessive supply would have on the market for cards in the years to follow.

People often excitedly and skeptically pose the question to StockX CEO, Josh Luber: could sneakers crash like baseball cards? His response highlights an important difference. "No, there are biased actors sitting in the middle of this that understand how to leverage scarcity and we have transparency into it," he explains. "We didn't have that in baseball cards."

Now, say what you will about the brands. Say that they don't always correctly understand, project, or act upon the balance between supply and demand. But do not suggest that they aren't constantly thinking about both the short and long-term ramifications of any imbalances. Yes, quarterly results create pressure to think about the near term, perhaps disproportionately so, but Nike and Adidas are well aware of the long-term damage that can be caused by a flood of supply and other missteps.

To expect that they'll foster circumstances in which an out-and-out *pop* is possible may be misguided. The stakes are simply too high, both now and in the future. Moreover, as covered previously, the availability of actionable market data provides further buffer against a shock nosedive.

But to an extent and as we'll discuss, we are seeing some evidence of broader price deflation, both at retail and in the resale market, as brands, retailers, and resellers alike discount to move product. Not *all* product, though. If we were to picture sneaker market prices on a histogram, it's the growing, fat middle of the curve (think $150-$250) that will ultimately shift to the left, towards lower values. Moreover, greater supply of those relatively obtainable releases in the middle will increasingly encourage demand for the rare jewels of the industry, as collectors pursue perceived quality rather than quantity, particularly in the face of overflowing closets. These jewels are the sneaker economy's true veblen goods, goods for which demand increases as price increases. A shift toward these status symbols will further widen the divide in value between the hyper limited, hyper popular releases and the rest of the pack.

As we'll discuss later, that shift is exacerbated by the more frequent sourcing of demand from new, wealthy demographics ready to flex, in addition to the matriculation of a sneaker-buying youth into more powerful income-generating phases of their careers. For those gems, the sneakers with stories that resonate effectively with consumers and are seemingly impossible to acquire, the dearth of supply and increasingly lustful demand will continue to perpetuate commensurately high secondary market prices. Trends come and go, but this recipe is unlikely to lose potency.

That favorable supply and demand imbalance isn't easily achieved though. Consequently, for most models falling into the "rest of the pack" category, price deflation is likely to ensue as end-buyer demand struggles to keep pace with the arrival of new supply. We'll explore in greater detail how and why that deflation is manifested.

The fools always get less foolish eventually, and soon they'll know exactly what belongs in "the pack." The price levels at which the end-user of a pair of sneakers purchase will need to drop. I believe that this process is already in motion. With that process should come a thinning of supply over time, both in terms of the volume on the secondary market and the volume coming to market as the biased actors right the ship.

They're not tulips. They're not Dot-Com stocks. We haven't gotten *that* carried away. Still though, Nike Air isn't the only thing in the sneaker economy that *resembles* a bubble.

HOW SECONDARY MARKETS ARE
CHANGING PRIMARY BEHAVIOR

Do you know how lucky we are to be consumers in the present era?

To understand our great fortune, you have to recall how much freaking *harder* things used to be. Even in the internet era, deal-seeking for sneaker collectors was a major chore. Without real sneaker media, there was no credible way to know if a product was going to sell out. Without a reliable secondary market, there were no certain second chances.

You could cross your fingers and hope that a product would eventually reach clearance racks. But how would you know when that happened? That news was acquired mostly on a "pull" basis. If one was daring enough in the absence of solid information and credible resale participants to allow the release date to pass in hopes that the sneaker would later be discounted, the consumer would have to (gasp!) visit either the store or website to find out. Absolute best-case scenario: the retailer sends an e-mail blast alerting customers to the initiation of a broader store sale.

On its own, that reality doesn't sound all that bad. In contrast to today, though, my God it's exhausting to even think about. Today, we as consumers are armed with more accurate and more plentiful information than ever before. Social media accounts, like Kicks Under Cost or Kicks Deals, deliver attractive and timely deals right to the palms of our hands. We learn of new discounts almost immediately, and we can make a journey from discovery to purchase in less than sixty seconds.

It's cushy for the consumer, but the benefits are felt more broadly. Leftover inventory is more efficiently matched with willing wallets. When sales are initiated and an attractive deal hits the market, action becomes a time-sensitive matter. Sneakers still sit on shelves, both virtual and physical, but due to the perpetuation of timely information, once the level of discounting meets the broader consumer's willingness to pay, supply moves quickly.

It's not all boon for retailer and brand in this era, though. In fact, complexity is rising, particularly with regard to the process of discounting.

While robust information is increasingly available in the sneaker economy, not all market participants make effective use of that information. Some novice resellers will purchase product in the primary market at the time of release, only to be consumed by a sinking feeling as they realize hours or days after release that the product remains widely available at retailers all over the internet. Those "ask" prices that they posted on StockX at a hearty premium to the retail price suddenly seem foolish.

Before long, reality sets in: not only are these sneakers not going to fetch a premium, the reseller may not even recover retail value. The investment thesis has failed, and the return will suffer. In order to narrow the bid-ask spread, the gap between the highest bid on the market and the lowest ask, the seller is going to need to lower the asking price. With adequate supply remaining in the market at retail price, a ceiling (albeit temporary in nature) has been placed on bids.

Because of a miscalculation of the supply-demand dynamic prior to release, these resellers actually perpetuate the imbalance. Demand trailed supply to begin with, and the foolish reseller is actually keeping supply levels elevated by buying but not consuming. Some sellers, realizing the folly of their ways, will cut bait as quickly as possible to minimize losses, fearing further market declines and front-running discounts in the primary market. These parties are motivated by liquidity, seizing on whatever demand exists and offloading the unwanted inventory before it becomes more difficult to move.

In just days or in some cases even hours, a sneaker that some mistakenly believed to be a hot commodity is essentially on clearance on the secondary market.

GOAT unveiled new functionality in December of 2018 that highlighted sneakers selling below their retail price on the marketplace. Those prices are displayed prominently in bold red text. The subtext, of course, is that these sneakers are "on sale." In the secondary markets, though, it's not a "sale" – it's simply the market-dictated value, more rapidly discovered by forces of supply and demand. The call-to-action of the "Under Retail" tag, subtle and effective marketing, is clear: come shop here; the sneakers and the experience are the same, but our prices are lower.

Savvy consumers no longer have to patiently wait weeks or months for a product to be discounted by the manufacturer or by retailers. Instead, a tactically sound participant in the secondary markets can identify situations in which liquidity-starved resellers have been caught flat-footed by lingering inventory, launch a bid at a satisfactory level, and wait for the market to come to them.

Meanwhile, retailers and the sneaker brands themselves are now competing against the secondary markets, where minimum selling prices don't apply. Offloading inventory that was already slow-moving would now seem to be a Sisyphean task at full retail price. Remember though, while information is now far more readily available, the sneaker market is anything but efficient.

Market efficiency refers to the extent to which market prices reflect all relevant, available information. Referring primarily to the stock markets, in the 1960s, economist Eugene Fama developed the Efficient Market Hypothesis (EMH), in which he argued that it's impossible for investors to consistently outperform the market, as asset prices fully reflect all available information. Essentially, the idea is that, with the market reflecting all available information, an investor cannot repeatedly exploit informational advantages by, for example, purchasing a stock at a price while in possession of information indicating that the stock should be valued at a higher price. Under EMH, that advantageous information is already priced into the stock.

Fama later developed three forms of efficient markets: weak form, in which information on past price movements can't be used in an advantageous fashion, semi-strong form, in which prices adjust very quickly to new public information, and strong-form, in which market prices reflect all information regardless of whether it's public or private.

Now, sneakers are not really financial assets, and they don't behave like equities, but with marketplaces like StockX treating the secondary sneaker market like a stock exchange, it's interesting to apply traditional market concepts to sneakers. Even on its best day, the sneaker market can't even truly be considered weak-form efficient. The reality is that experienced, shrewd participants can absolutely leverage knowledge of prior price behavior to better inform their buying and selling decisions.

The fact that retailers and brands end up putting sneakers on sale weeks after they've traded at a discount on the secondary markets is evidence of this reality. Over those weeks, some consumers are still buying at full retail price despite the availability at lower prices in the secondary market. On the flip side, it's not at all uncommon to see sneakers selling for a premium on the secondary market when they're actually still available from various retail outlets.

Information and data that allows consumers to buy at the best possible price is out there and readily available to anybody seeking it. Although not everybody seeks it, and consequently, the market is replete with, well, suckers who enjoy paying more than they have to.

The suckers won't remain suckers forever, well at least most of them. The perpetuation of accurate, timely information is not going to slow. It's going to be produced more rapidly and digested more broadly. As that happens, retailers and brands aren't going to be able to wait as long to discount if they intend to bring similar levels of supply to market. Inventory simply won't move when supply exists at better prices on the secondary market, and, importantly, when more participants are aware of those prices.

It actually gets *more* complicated though, because not only are the brands competing against the secondary markets to sell current product, they're competing against vast supply of their very *own* product from prior years.

While resale is not a new concept, so sophisticated has the resale experience become, so retail-like in nature, that customers are no longer faced with a simple binary choice between buying and not buying a new Jordan release. They're free to choose between the new Jordan release and pretty much every single other Jordan that's *ever* been released. Instead of seeing a new Jordan releasing and thinking that it may be the only worthwhile opportunity to acquire a new pair for a little while, a customer can take inspiration from that upcoming release, open up StockX or GOAT, and buy a pair in their favorite colorway from 2014. The pair will be authenticity verified, it will come in its original box and packaging, and there will be nary a scuff on the outsole. You can even anticipate for most pairs that the price will have been suppressed down to levels not egregiously dissimilar from current retail, as the extraordinary breadth of resale supply and bountiful consumer choice tilts the scales in the buyer's favor.

So really, what's the difference between buying the new release at retail and picking up a predecessor on the secondary market?

There really isn't one, and if there is, it's rapidly disappearing. That's a tricky problem for brands to navigate.

That being the case, how do the brands and the retailers adjust as market efficiency increases and the plethora of choice on the secondary markets removes the urgency to purchase?

In the short term, one would expect that discounting would become swifter, more drastic, and less incremental, all positive shifts for the consumer and largely detrimental to the retailer and brands. As we've covered at length though, brands don't like to see their products sitting in the market at deep discounts. It's bad for brand heat and inhibits broader ability to sell-through at full or premium prices. We saw it with Jordan Brand, we saw it with Stan Smiths, and we'll see it again.

What StockX is lending to the consumer product space though is the opportunity to make pricing more variable in an effort to more quickly and efficiently satiate demand and exhaust supply. Should the primary market embrace such an opportunity, the financial impact may be meaningful.

"So, it's the end of summer, and all board shorts are 40% off on Nike.com. But what if you understood demand? What's the real holy grail value [of StockX]? It's understanding true consumer demand because you have bids," says Josh Luber. "If you understood demand, maybe some people would bid 10 percent off and some people would bid 20 percent off, right? And you could step down the discounts that you're giving on board shorts because you would use variable pricing. Nobody ever uses variable pricing in consumer goods, because theoretically variable pricing is better *except* if you don't know demand, right? So, in the supply and demand world, in the supply and demand equation, we know supply. Brands choose however much they make of whatever widget they're going to sell, but the demand is a forecast. It's an estimation, it's a percentage of last year, it's not true demand. So, if you knew true demand to create variable pricing around the discounting process for board shorts, then you should be able to maximize the amount of revenue."

If you're going to eventually end up at 40% off anyways, why not satiate demand at every price level as quickly as possible, without missing out on sales at higher prices in getting there? That's what clear indications of demand (bids) offer retailers and brands. It's solving such a problem that Luber believes will bring the secondary marketplace model into the arena of broader sneaker retail: "From a business problem standpoint, now all of a sudden I'm out of the $1 billion or $2 billion resale market and I'm in the $90 billion retail market. If you could save a couple points on the millions of dollars that go to close-outs in every category in every season of every brand – holy sh*t, that is a way, way sexy business problem and opportunity. From a brand and timing standpoint, that's probably nowhere in the immediate roadmap and ultimately that probably is like a white label solution that lives on Nike.com or something. Who knows? But that's exactly the value of the model and the bigger idea."

A better, clearer understanding of demand mitigates the need for drastic discounting, but that need is also mitigated by speed. Speed is and will continue to be everything in the modern sneaker world. Consumer tastes change quickly, and brands and retailers alike have to adjust accordingly. Better understanding of the consumer, fueled by digital engagement, and faster, more agile manufacturing will contribute to a more efficient go-to-market approach and better-balanced supply and demand.

It's difficult to see, however, new releases coming to market with the same frequency of cadence and with the same depth of supply in the future, particularly in the case of retro releases, for which there are many secondary market alternatives. Do the brands dramatically reduce supply? They can try, but remember, the large brands are publicly-traded companies with obligations to shareholders. A dramatic reduction in supply, in a vacuum, means lower sales and commensurately weakened equity performance. Well, as they pull the lever down on supply, the brands can try to pull the price lever higher, hoping that increased scarcity can command higher prices.

Obviously, there's some merit in this approach. The most limited releases go for healthy premiums *immediately* on the secondary market. In theory, the brand has left money on the table with its pricing. Why not capture some of this premium at the outset, rather than allow it to line only resale pockets? Surely, the demand for the coveted limited releases is price inelastic enough to allow more premium pricing.

The problem, however, is that demand is not dependent on scarcity alone. Scarcity certainly helps, but at the end of the day, design and story matter deeply. In reality, there are only so many retro sneakers with rich enough stories and designs to command such a premium and create sufficient hype, and consistently innovating with new designs that inspire the same fervor is anything but simple. Still, for the sake of brand heat, it may make sense to treat a select number of releases annually as truly premium releases. As long as there's scarcity, there will be a place for resale, but as resale becomes a more meaningful competitor to the brands and retailers, shifting the premium pricing, or the *value*, forward in the supply chain from reseller to retailer and brand may be a competitive necessity. We'll discuss how that's done in a bit.

And what about heading in the other direction? More supply at palatable prices that won't require steep discounting to move? Sales growth may be resolute in the short term, but margins would thin, and in many ways the can would just be kicked down the road, as the problem in question is really one of broad supply saturation to begin with.

There seems to be a third option emerging in the market-place, one in which a product is simultaneously scarce and obtainable. That option is manifested in Nike's treatment of the "Anniversary" Air Max 1 in the OG white and red colorway. The sneaker was released in highly limited quantities in March of 2017, generating secondary market prices approaching $500. It was later restocked in September of 2017 in less limited quantities and has restocked through many retailers a number of times since. The sneakers don't sit for long, and they don't often get discounted, but Nike still satiates demand in spurts, The secondary market price hovers right around the retail price of $140. While such a practice may grow increasingly predictable over time, it ensures that greater quantities are sold without diluting the brand or the iconic image of the sneaker.

Nike has discovered another, similar way to create a perception of scarcity for products that turned out to be fairly obtainable – highlighted by the releases of Jordan icons like the Black Cement Jordan 3 and the Concord Jordan 11. Nike conducted surprise releases of these sneakers on the SNKRS app weeks in advance of their official release. These surprise releases were limited in quantity and sold out in very short order. News of the instantaneous sell-out spread, and those with the bitter taste of defeat in their mouths suddenly had increased urgency to buy on the official release date. The releases of both sneakers were, of course, immensely successful. That may have been the case absent the surprise pre-release, but it never hurts to force the consumer to question if they'll have difficulty acquiring at retail price.

It is clear that something has to give to better balance supply and demand in both the primary and the secondary market at prices that are palatable to both brand and consumer alike. This isn't just about discounting. It's about the wheels of change churning toward industry pricing that is far more variable. Until that happens though, leverage rests increasingly with the consumer, particularly the savvy, astute, well-informed market participant, as resellers (especially the suckers), retailers, and brands alike battle the increasingly frightening reality of saturation.

Cheers 'em while ya got 'em, because surely the "clearance" market won't last. The suckers will suck less, and prices will correct with greater speed. All the while, the lines between primary and secondary markets will continue to blur...

SECONDARY MARKETS, PRIMARY MARKETS — WHAT'S THE DIFFERENCE?

Why exactly should primary and secondary market be segregated to begin with? Why should we even use those terms today?

The experience in buying sneakers via GOAT or StockX is no different in reality from buying a pair of sneakers via Nike SNKRS or Foot Locker's website. Frequenting Stadium Goods or Flight Club is certainly no less satisfactory an experience than that on offer from most traditional retailers and boutiques. It's the product offering and prices, though, that differ, and they do so quite dramatically.

While sneaker brands and retailers have undoubtedly benefited from the prevalence of resale via the implicit demand backstop that it provides, we've also detailed the ways in which the broad proliferation of supply on the secondary market can have detrimental impacts on players further up the supply chain. Not to mention, the benefits provided by the resale market are beginning to wane, as the consumer grows wiser.

"People are smarter now to know that that hysteria doesn't apply to every sneaker," explains StockX CEO Josh Luber. "It used to be that hysteria could feed sales of other sneakers that weren't going to be as limited. Now, that's not the case. They know that, at the end of the day, they can always come back to StockX and see what the value is and act accordingly."

"The halo hypothesis works to some extent in a physical retail store. 10 years ago, you rush to the store to get something, see it's sold out, and maybe buy something else. But that certainly doesn't work online, and it doesn't even work in brick-and-mortar anymore because that customer that wants an Off White Jordan 1 doesn't say 'I didn't get that Off White Jordan 1 for $200, maybe I'll go buy the Jordan Trunner.' It's just not the same thing, especially when you have an unlimited breadth of choice online. "

With the positive impacts of the halo hypothesis losing potency, brands and retailers must increasingly turn their attention to alternative retail constructs. One such idea is the sneaker IPO, a concept whose merits Luber has long touted.

In the same way that shares of a company are initially offered on a stock exchange and continue to trade there, sneaker brands could sell their products directly onto a marketplace like StockX. There are a number of ways in which that works. One such method is a Dutch auction, hailed by Luber for its ability to allow brands to capture higher prices while still ensuring that the sneaker doesn't crater in value, but actually has room to appreciate post release. In a Dutch auction, bidders place bids based on the amount that they are willing to pay. The product is then allocated, starting with the highest bid and moving downward, until supply is exhausted. Here's the key, though: each successful bidder pays the price of the lowest successful bid.

So, let's say that there were 100 pairs being auctioned off, and you were the highest bidder at $1,000. The last successful bid was for $500. Rather than paying the $1,000 that you were willing to pay, you would pay $500. Theoretically, as a result, the product has been released at a higher price than typical retail price, netting greater revenues for Nike or whoever might be releasing the shoe, but lower than the highest prices at which demand exists. If for example, Nike offered such an auction only to loyal Nike+ customers, it fosters greater brand loyalty, but also ensures that there will be further demand from non-members at higher prices to prop up the secondary market.

Targeting in such a focused manner would essentially allow Nike to choose their product "underwriters," according to Luber. In an initial public offering of stock, the company offering equity hires banks to sell the shares to institutional investors. Essentially, the underwriter acts as an intermediary in bringing the equity onto the market, offering advice and expertise in pricing and positioning along the way.

In the case of the sneaker IPO, the winning bidders can either take delivery of their products or turn right around and sell them to willing bidders on the open market. Just like that, the product has released and begun trading, all in one arena.

StockX has executed such a sneaker listing before, collaborating with Nike to offer 46 pairs of Lebron 14s, which sold for an average of roughly $6,000. Seven of the 46 winners turned right around and resold at a profit of roughly $1,500.

It's part of the long-term vision for StockX to not only act as a secondary market but to work directly with brands and retailers, offering an exchange that facilitates the immediate trading of consumer goods and blurs the lines between primary and secondary markets. The stock market function of the secondary marketplace creates a foundation on which to build a better mousetrap for releasing limited items.

From the brand's perspective, whether they partner with StockX or develop their own mechanism, it's not difficult to see how such a method of bringing product to market could be beneficial. If a minimum bid price is set, the worst-case scenario is essentially the current status quo, in which unpopular product sits and is eventually discounted. Let's take that off the table though, since the focus for the auction release method would be more limited product. By selling directly to the consumer through an auction process, the brand is capturing a healthy portion of that resale premium it previously missed out on, and the product is allocated to those that value it most highly. This means that limited releases, which traditionally have been sources of buzz rather than huge sources of revenue due to the low quantities in which they are sold, bring in multiples of the revenue that they would have otherwise captured, all without necessitating guesswork around a palatable price.

But there's so much more value that brands and retailers are leaving on the table in hesitating to collaborate with the secondary marketplaces. Perhaps more valuable than any resale premium is the treasure chest of *data* possessed by these players.

Luber describes the lost opportunity: "Today, you go to the Nike SNKRS app, and you want to buy a sneaker, but it's sold out. Well now you're on your own, right? You're totally out of that ecosystem. Nike doesn't know where they went. You as a consumer, you're not falling for the halo strategy. You're not going to navigate and buy a Trunner. You're like 'I'm going to bounce out. Maybe I go to eBay, maybe I'll go to StockX, maybe I asked my friend.' But you totally leave that environment."

Once discerning consumers fail to acquire a product via SNKRS or otherwise, they typically leave that ecosystem and search for the product elsewhere. They're not sticking around to buy a substitute. And once they're gone, they're taking valuable data with them. What price were they willing to pay for the product? What bid did they place? What offer prices were too rich for their tastes? Who was ready to pay $1,000? What other sneakers did they start following as a result?

Nike, Adidas, Foot Locker, JD Sports...they don't have the answers to those questions, but StockX does.

"They have some product page. They're getting some 10, 20, 50x multiple of people that are coming to that product page trying to buy something, and they can't buy it," explains Luber, describing the wasted value when demand exceeds supply on retailer websites. "That other 49x is just having a crappy experience and [the retailers] get no value out of them."

All of those unanswered or partially answered questions a retailer or a brand asks when a customer leaves its ecosystem *could* be answered. They *can* be answered.

We can look to the market for tickets to sporting events. Primary and secondary markets used to be totally bifurcated. Teams and leagues had disdain for resellers and for the secondary market. Today, the StubHub logo graces the uniforms of the Philadelphia 76ers. The company and team partnered to launch a new marketplace in which primary and secondary market inventory are combined, and available seats are not designated as "primary" or "secondary."

Sixers CEO, Scott O'Neill, detailed the launch in a press release: "We're excited to launch a groundbreaking ticketing marketplace with StubHub that for the first time, seamlessly integrates and makes available primary and secondary seats in one marketplace, on one seating map, with one blended pricing purchase process. This game-changing platform will provide Sixers fans unparalleled access to available seats with a world-class, fan-friendly mobile experience. Equally exciting to fan-centric thinking is the data capture, pricing opportunity, and revenue upside. With StubHub and Spectra as our partners in this venture, we have front row seats to what will be a seismic shift in the business."[52]

StubHub also has an official partnership with Major League Baseball, which includes exclusive ticketing integration on MLB.com and promotional signage for the company on outfield walls and behind home plate. A key piece of that partnership: the sharing of data.

The integration of secondary ticketing markets with primary has not only created a vastly better fan experience, but the clubs and leagues are no longer losing data on the fan that missed out when tickets initially went on sale. There's sharing of financial value, absolutely, and that's hugely meaningful, but there's also marketing value, the value provided by data,

---

52 "Sixers & Stubhub Launch Revolutionary New Ticketing Platform | Philadelphia 76ers". 2016. *Philadelphia 76ers*. https://www.nba. com/sixers/news/sixers-stubhub-launch-revolutionary-new-ticketing-platform.

and the legitimacy provided to the secondary market by the explicit backing of the league and the teams.

For the secondary sneaker marketplace, the benefits of those blurring lines could be numerous. For example, if the initial auction is conducted on the marketplace, the marketplace could presumably take a commission on the initial sale, it benefits from the data provided by the primary auction, and the sneaker begins its life within the confines of that marketplace's ecosystem. The latter point is critical, both reputationally and economically. In the current model, the consumer turned reseller has vast optionality on potential listing destinations, but if the sneaker started on StockX, friction is minimized by a system in which you need not take delivery, need not create a new listing, and need not handle any logistics whatsoever to sell it. If it truly becomes like day or commodities or futures trading as Luber envisions, then the marketplace extracts commission with increased frequency.

But why not go this route if you're a brand? Well, by nature, not all products can be limited. To be successful in growing or maintaining revenue, more often than not, brands have to sell product in mass quantity as well. Traditionally, limited releases have acted as one tool to generate buzz that feeds the sales of these large-scale products. At present, while the system certainly isn't perfect, consumers who want limited products successfully acquire or fail to acquire products on the basis of some combination of luck, speed, and connections or lack thereof. No doubt, frustration still abounds. In the auction-based system described above, however, consumers would miss out solely on the basis of price. That's a difficult way to inspire broad-based brand loyalty, as customers become disenchanted by a shift that caters to the upper economic classes.

There is absolutely room for the auction style to be used in the creation and nurturing of an ultra-premium customer segment. For truly luxury product, like the aforementioned Lebron 14s, which came in a box made out of authentic Cleveland Cavaliers hardwood court and were accompanied by an authentic championship ring, or the Shinola watch that IPO'd on the StockX platform, products that are clearly premium goods intended for buyers of means, the auction style makes tremendous sense. The brand can reap greater profits and learn exactly who is willing to pay thousands of dollars for sneakers.

An alternative consideration would be to release a highly limited sneaker in two phases. The first phase would be the Dutch auction method, where a quantity is sold to the highest-bidding, loyal customers weeks in advance of a broader, more open release. That second phase would resemble the current system, in which the sneaker is priced at traditional levels and the ability to acquire is largely based on luck. If there is a belief that the sneaker should sell on the secondary market for multiples of traditional retail price, then the brand can capture some of that highly priced demand from their most sticky, high-paying customers. Simultaneously, the general public still has an opportunity, albeit with extremely slim odds, to acquire the pair for a more traditional price. Demand still exceeds supply and secondary market prices still heartily exceed retail, but the brand captures more revenue on the release while also gathering more data on what their customers are willing to pay and for what product.

The marketplace concept need not offer a better solution for limited releases alone, though. Perhaps it can be leveraged to release less limited product, by rendering supply the variable component of the release rather than price. Such a method of IPO is known as a Fixed Price Offering. Essentially, the brand would reveal its intent to release a product at a certain price, and the marketplace could be used to better understand the volume of demand at that price through firm, binding bids. While consumers may be reticent to order a product that they have to wait an extended period of time to receive, innovations in manufacturing (as will be discussed later) are shortening the time from design to market, so this problem may be mitigated.

Once the pre-bidding period is concluded and the product is brought to market, no additional pairs are sold at retail. Consequently, the brands accurately match the demand in the market, avoiding excess supply that is susceptible to discounting. Additionally, pairs are no longer bought at retail and listed on the resale market where they essentially become competitors to the brand's remaining inventory on the primary market. Because the demand has been fully satisfied, the brand need not worry about leaving resale premium on the table in the short term – those who wanted them at retail price acquired them. As we've detailed at length, striking the appropriate balance between supply and demand is extremely difficult. If brands could leverage the marketplaces to better address demand, that would seem a worthwhile endeavor. Again, lead times are the major obstacle to this effort, but we are not far from a future in which that friction is meaningfully reduced or even eliminated.

While the blurring of lines between retail and resale continues to accelerate, there remains clear bifurcation between the two. Still, there is opportunity to work with or learn from the marketplace mechanisms created by secondary market players that may be of great benefit to brands in the primary market. With secondary markets encroaching on the turf of the primary market, primary players need to learn to play by a new set of rules.

According to Luber, those new rules are to be dictated by pure market forces: "Our shorthand for the revolution is that MSRP is dead. Retail price is dead for certain products. Certain products, supply and demand is the way you should determine how much this sells for, a true market value. If you understand supply and demand, you can do that."

***

The rise of the secondary market and the consequent re-circulation of abundant supply can no longer be ignored by primary market players. While the demand backdrop provided by resellers once rendered the secondary market somewhat beneficial to brands and retailers, there is evidence that supply has grown so vast that it cannot be ignored. Behaviors and business practices must be altered to more appropriately manage against the backdrop of a market with unprecedented breadth and depth of offerings and dwindling amounts of greater fools.

The surge of unsophisticated resellers into the market buoyed demand and price levels for a time, but sophistication is rising with better information and greater volume of experience. Traditional methods of bringing product to market may not work with the same efficacy that they once did. Sneakers may not be a bubble, but there are, for lack of a better word, bubblicious (okay, there's definitely a better word, but I couldn't resist) elements at play, which if ignored, will have widespread impact on the sneaker economy.

On the whole, most business participants would agree that they will all be better off if bubbles are confined to the midsole of Nike Air Maxes.

TAKEAWAYS FROM THE SNEAKONOMIST

- Bubbles are generally created when asset values detach from their underlying fundamentals and are driven instead by the belief that a greater fool is willing to purchase the asset at a higher price.

- When the supply of greater fools is exhausted, demand dries up, and sellers looking to crystallize once robust profits en masse are met with precipitously dropping prices.

- The sneaker economy has been replete with greater fools, resellers lacking either accurate information or reliable connections, which has increasingly shifted the supply and demand balance in the end-consumer's favor, as these greater fools are willing to liquidate at discounted prices.

- The sneaker economy is not a bubble in the sense that we should expect a widespread, dramatic pop that craters prices. Scarce, limited products will remain in demand, and brands will continue to manage supply to ensure longevity.

- The broad but mild deflation of prices may persist in the short term, both on the secondary market and through the promotional primary market, as the existence of greater fools with poorly chosen inventory continues to thin out.

- To better satiate demand and extract value, the primary market should look to secondary market mechanisms, which provide clear indications of demand, variable pricing, and crucial customer data.

- The ways in which limited products are released is likely to continue evolving, as the halo effect diminishes, and brands and retailers look to foster both better customer experiences and more fruitful financial results.

PART 3

ADAPTING TO
THE CONSUMER'S
SNEAKER MARKET

CHAPTER 7

FOCUSED SPEED – THE RISING IMPORTANCE OF AGILITY AND PERSONALIZATION

———

"Nike makes some of the best product in the world. I mean, product you lust after, absolutely beautiful, stunning product. But you also make a lot of crap. Just get rid of the crappy stuff and focus on the good stuff."

—Apple CEO Steve Jobs to Mark Parker
upon his elevation to Nike CEO in 2006

Consumers, we're a fickle bunch, and we're getting more fickle every day.

What we like today, we may no longer like tomorrow. So, the Nikes of the world need to shorten the amount of time it takes to design a product we'll lust after, to make more SKUs of that design if popular, and to get it to us – before we change our minds.

We live in an era of fast fashion.

Not just fast-fashion, but consumer-dictated, *extremely* fast fashion. Pressure has been squarely placed on brands and on retailers to keep up with a consumer whose tastes are evolving more quickly than ever. Not only are tastes changing, but consumers also have higher expectations of how quickly brands and retailers should be capable of serving those changing tastes. To an unprecedented extent, brands and retailers are challenged to anticipate rather than react, and when they do react, they must react faster.

These higher stakes amount to many initiatives which are commonly held across the industry but perhaps best articulated by Nike's "Triple Double" growth strategy: 2X Innovation, 2X Speed, and 2X Direct. Brands seek closer connectivity with the customer through direct interaction. These interactions are then leveraged to bring the consumer popular new products with greater speed. When a product is a hit, brands and retailers alike must react to satisfy demand before it inevitably shifts elsewhere.

The pressure is real, and it is unrelenting, but as the saying goes: no pressure, no diamonds.

KEEPING UP WITH THE CONSUMER

The speed with which consumers today are evolving, constantly creating and adopting trends, immensely challenges brands and retailers to respond, and quickly.

"The way I would sum it up is this," Finish Line CEO Sam Sato shared on a September 2017 earnings call, "our consumers, because of today's ability to access trends and events globally, their influencer circle is worldwide, and what that enables the consumer to do is kind of formulate their own kind of self-impression and style and as I said to the earlier question, the speed at which they are evolving in changing the speed of which they are creating and adopting trends is significantly faster and more often than ever. I think that the biggest challenge we have faced and we'll continue to face, both retail and our wholesale brand partners is the speed at which we can evolve and innovate."[53]

This rapid consumer adoption of and subsequent disassociation from trends is forcing brands and retailers to think differently, to think faster. Focus must be directed entirely to speed – omnipresent in the company's operations.

---

53 "The Finish Line's (FINL) CEO Sam Sato On Q2 2018 Results – Earnings Call Transcript". 2017. *Seeking Alpha.* https://seekingalpha.com/article/4108914-finish-lines-finl-ceo-sam-sato-q2-2018-results-earnings-call-transcript?part=single.

Innovation without speed becomes stale before it becomes popular. Popularity without speedy capitalization dissipates before the financial fruits can be fully harvested.

Voxel8, based in Somerville, MA, focuses on assisting the footwear brands in their pursuit of greater speed through the technologically advanced production of sneaker uppers. CEO Travis Busbee describes the three-pronged pursuit of sneaker manufacturers today: "One is elimination of tooling, two is automation of processes, and three is dramatic reduction in the time to market. Many of these things are related."

The brands are working to eliminate a traditional supply chain construct in which it takes 12-18 months to bring a product from design sketch to shelf. Such lead times necessitate projecting demand a year or *years* in advance. Today, brands must move ever closer to the consumer to render their servicing of demand less a projection and more a real-time dialogue, particularly as consumer tastes become a faster moving target.

Nike CEO, Mark Parker, described the 2X Speed initiative at the company's 2017 Investor Day: "In 2X Speed, we're investing in digital end to end to serve this insatiable consumer demand for new and fresh products."

"To use a sports analogy," continued Parker, "you can't run an uptempo offense if only half your plays are designed for speed. So we're building new capabilities and analytics to deliver personalized products in real time, and we're engaging with more partners, company-wide, to move faster against our goals. In our supply chain, we've joined forces with leading robotics and automation companies, and we're serving millions of athletes and sports fans faster through manufacturing bases that are closer to our North American consumer. 2X Speed is really all about delivering the right product in the moment, 100% of the time."[54]

In theory, it sounds great, and the number of buzzwords that can be employed to make it sound even better is essentially infinite. But how do they make 2X Speed meaningful to the consumer?

The Express Lane initiative, described by former Nike President, Trevor Edwards, at the same investor day brings 2X Speed to life in a more tangible way: "And there's no better way – no better example of how we're accelerating speed than our Express Lane. Express Lane is where we are building the muscle to maximize consumer demand in real-time through 3 capabilities."

"The first is Create. Delivering new products and moving from design to shelf in less than 6 months. Express Lane's second capability is Update. Through Update, we're adding and amplifying dimensions of our product line through new materials, colors, prints on popular existing models and styles based on real-time consumer insights, shrinking the process down to less than 90 days. And the final capability

54 "Nike Investor Day 2017". 2017. *Nike.* https://s1.q4cdn.com/806093406/
    files/doc_events/2017/10/updtd/NIKE-Inc.-2017-Investor-Day-Tran-
    script-With-Q-A-FINAL.pdf.

is Fulfill, which is about being in stock on the product that our consumers love when they want it, whether it's the ability to scale new innovations faster or always being in stock on our favorites, we're accelerating this model to be as fast as 2 days."[55]

***

Indeed, such a practice is certainly not exclusive to Nike. Take for example, the Speedfactory developed by Adidas. With one in Germany and one in Atlanta, Adidas has developed a factory built on digital tenets of automation and robotics, aimed at quickly producing more inventory of items flying off shelves or quickly creating limited runs of personalized product.

"We have ambition to have 50% of our sales [from] under what we call speed programs," Adidas executive Gil Steyaert told *Business Insider.* "That means that product which would be reproduced or created in the season [is] for the same season." The intent, as Steyaert puts it, is to embrace "the fast fashion model where we can bring product closer to the consumer."[56]

---

55 Ibid.
56 Green, Dennis. 2018. "Adidas Just Opened A Futuristic New Factory
    — And It Will Dramatically Change How Shoes Are Sold". *Business
    Insider.* https://www.businessinsider.com/adidas-high-tech-speed-
    factory-begins-production-2018-4.

For Adidas, speed is not just about the production of new product, particularly in North America, where explosive growth in recent years has stressed the company's existing infrastructure. Importantly, speed means ensuring products are reaching customers faster, which has required substantial North American infrastructure investment in order to alleviate margin pressures incurred from the inability to quickly match product to demanding consumer.

"What we're seeing is that footwear companies, especially the big ones like Nike and Adidas, are really investing heavily and trying to revolutionize their supply chain," explains Busbee. "Really, they want to do this in a few ways. One is they want to be able to prototype their shoes much faster and, ultimately, when they get a design sketch, they don't want to wait many weeks to get the first prototypes back from Asia. They want to be able to test those ideas immediately and tweak it multiple times in the same day to create a physical product, and then get that product into wear testing as rapidly as possible, get real feedback from consumer groups. Then the second thing they want to do is be able to translate these prototypes into production much more quickly than they have been able to do in the past."

Where this rapid prototyping and production takes place is just as important as the production enhancements themselves, as brands seek the development of a supply chain that can respond to real measures of demand, rather than relying on projections. "They would also like to be able to do this with minimal tooling and labor such that they can utilize manufacturing that's much closer to their customers so that they're not wasting three weeks of their time having their products sitting on a boat," continues Busbee. "They would like to, through the elimination of tooling, introduce much smaller batches of product to market-test it in key cities, which could include places like London, New York, LA, Tokyo, Shanghai, Paris, some of the key sneakerhead testing grounds."

All of the investment, though extensive, remains in fairly early stages, and retailers remain challenged by the need to move faster.

"But our industry still does move too slow," shared Foot Locker CEO Dick Johnson during a March 2018 conference call. "I think that our vendor partners are certainly addressing that with their efforts around speed. Their developmental cycles are shortening. Their ability to produce product is getting quicker. And we've sort of started to understand that as well that the big bets that we place have to be bets that are going to disappear on a much quicker product lifecycle."[57]

Footwear retail has long been characterized by big bets. When those bets are misplaced or consumer interest wanes faster than anticipated, retailers are pained with excess

---

57 "Foot Locker's (FL) CEO Richard Johnson On Q4 2017 Results – Earnings Call Transcript". 2018. *Seeking Alpha*. https://seekingalpha. com/article/4152868-foot-lockers-fl-ceo-richard-johnson-q4-2017- results-earnings-call-transcript.

inventory, which needs to move at discounted price levels. Because of the speed with which today's consumer moves, those bets must either be reduced in size or the confidence in them must be of a higher degree.

There also must be delineation between what constitutes a seasonal "bet," a flavor of the month, and a consistent winner.

"We're certainly trying to adapt to the way our consumer moves and the way that our vendors move product into the marketplace," Johnson explained in May 2018. "There are some things that you continue to buy very much the way that you've always bought: a white Air Force One for example, which [has] great marketability and is very consistent. There is a pattern with how we buy that. When you think about some of the excitement that comes in and pops and then goes away quickly, we do buy as aggressively as we can but we know that we're going to be out of that. We've talked for a long time about how the peak of product receptivity of our consumers is much, much faster from the old days of seed to scale. We need to see the scale quicker and we're working with our vendor partners to do that."[58]

From design to storefront to discount rack, the product lifecycle is growing shorter than ever to accommodate a consumer that is evolving with tremendous speed. It's nicer to be

---

58 "Foot Locker, Inc. (FL) CEO Dick Johnson On Q1 2018 Results –
   Earnings Call Transcript". 2018. *Seeking Alpha*. https://seekingalpha.
   com/article/4177373-foot-locker-inc-fl-ceo-dick-johnson-q1-2018-
   results-earnings-call-transcript.

on the consumer side of the equation, because the pressure that we are imparting on the brands and retailers which serve us is immense.

HUMANIZING THE CONSUMER

The industry can focus on speed with limitless tenacity, but speed without understanding is meaningless. Therefore, when companies speak of growing closer to the consumer, they aren't referring simply to bringing them product faster. They are also referring to engaging the customer more directly in an effort to better understand wants and project demand accordingly, the importance of which cannot be overstated.

"One of the greatest opportunities in this shift is about digital, which lets us serve our consumers more personally. And while some might be scared or see this as a moment of apprehension, we see this opportunity to serve the powered consumer as a tremendous opportunity," expresses Mark Parker. "Nothing is more exciting to us. Because brands that listen and connect, win, and we are well served in that journey. How about this? Nearly 3 out [of] 4 consumers say they expect brands to proactively understand their unique needs and their expectations. And if you're too slow, there's a downside. Half of consumers say they will likely switch brands if someone doesn't anticipate their needs."[59]

---

59 "Nike Investor Day 2017". 2017. *Nike*.

The stakes couldn't be higher.

The only way to proactively understand needs, to anticipate them, is to interact with the consumer. It's for this reason Nike (most vocally) and Adidas are investing in their own direct-to-consumer channels in an effort to better control the relationship between brand and consumer. It's not for the warm-and-fuzzy coziness, but for the tangible and dramatic impact on results.

"Getting closer to the consumer allows us to generate a more reliable demand signal, which has 2 major benefits," according to Trevor Edwards. "It leads to better full-price sell-through, which leads to fewer markdowns, returns and higher gross margins as well as optimized inventory. All this adds up to consistent quality, long-term growth. The difference between getting the demand signal right versus wrong, as you know, can be hundreds and millions of dollars in revenue and significant margin upside."[60]

Nike is already incredibly good at projecting demand and controlling inventory. Today's consumer, however, requires them to be better at it. So today, the brand aims to more accurately target consumers with products they want and care about, informing those decisions through user-generated data captured from Nike.com and Nike application interactions.

---

60 Ibid.

"The strategic shifts towards the new models of access, exclusives and Express Lane are all part of a member-first, member-centric vision for NIKE Direct," articulates Nike Direct President, Heidi O'Neill. "Powering this vision are the investments we're making in personalization capabilities. These include a single member profile, proprietary algorithms, and machine learning. These capabilities enable us to better understand the needs of each individual member and build assortments and buys that meet those needs. It's a virtuous circle. As more members generate more data, we're positioned to serve up even smarter and more personalized experiences for each and every member."[61]

With more data, Nike can more effectively provide Nike+ members with access to exclusive product or opportunities to reserve product that matters to the consumer. By more accurately targeting consumers with desired product, these Nike+ members become more likely to spend in greater volume than non-members.

***

For the sneaker collector, most critical to their relationship with the Nike brand is the SNKRS application.

"I think we at Nike take an approach where we really seek to understand the psychology of the sneaker fanatic,"

---

61   Ibid.

Ron Faris, General Manager of Nike's digital studio and the SNKRS application told *Highsnobiety*.

In fact, there is thoughtful psychology that goes into improving the app. "And one of the things we learned early on was that for many of the most fanatical sneakerheads, how they cop the shoe is almost as important as the shoe itself."[62]

Increasingly, through the power of geolocation, augmented reality, and other technological advances, Nike is finding ways with SNKRS to better ensure that coveted products end up in the hands of those who treasure them most. For example, fans at a Kendrick Lamar concert were given the opportunity to purchase his signature Nike Cortez through the application while at the arena. SNKRS Stash releases take consumers on a physical scavenger hunt to unlock the opportunity to buy. The SNKRS team strives to ensure releases are more an experience and less a crapshoot, though overcoming the feeling of the latter is a tall task. Creating a system that inherently feels fair and just, rather than impossible, remains top of mind.

"As the app grows in scale," continued Faris, "and it's seen a lot of growth over the last year, there's a lot of heavy lifting that needs to be done to try to keep the app fair. And that's something that we tend to obsess [over] right now. As more and more people come to the app, we can't treat everyone the

---

62 Danforth, Chris. 2018. "Nike's SNKRS App Is Making Sneaker Releases Fun Again". *Highsnobiety*. https://www.highsnobiety. com/p/nike-snkrs-ron-farris-interview/.

same. We can't treat the person that comes and enters their first draw, as a new user, the same as someone who's joined and perhaps lost 10 draws. We have to kind of recognize a lot of members for their engagement in the app."[63]

At the very least, it will be a humanization of the process that needs to take place in order for consumers to feel treated fairly by draws for the most limited product. That humanization requires action to accomplish the following goals:

- Provide the consumer with increased transparency
- Provide the consumer with the comfort of knowing, if he or she lost, it wasn't because someone made thousands of bot generated entries
- Leverage purchasing history, app interaction data (what sneakers did the user "like" or try for previously), and demographic data to funnel highly limited product to a loyal customer before bots get a chance

These are the types of steps that will need to be taken to ensure consumers don't abandon a system viewed as flawed. Those consumers need to be kept around should a resale bubble burst and the demand backstop disappear.

The release of products isn't the only thing which requires personalization, however. The future consumer will increasingly demand personalized product, served in a hurry. This is part of the aim with the Adidas Speedfactory, Steyaert tells

---

63   Ibid.

Business Insider, "Speedfactory is able to customize the shoe indefinitely while being in an automated engineering process. We can actually tune the shoe to the customization that the consumer wants to have. That's the goal: full customization, but without compromise on speed."[64]

The shift toward increased personalization extends across the industry. Busbee'sVoxel8 offers manufacturers the ability to personalize at a low cost. The company's technologies enable "the ability to totally digitally define and fabricate the shape of the mechanical structures, the material properties of the mechanical structures and the color of the mechanical structures on top of any textile without labor, tooling, or adhesives," says Busbee. "So that really opens the door to create smaller batches of shoes, have many more colorways, and offer full personalization to an individual at costs that are competitive with existing manufacturing processes."

Whether personalizing product, experience, offers, or otherwise, it's clear that closeness to consumer is top of mind for industry participants. To better project demand, inform supply, sell at full price, tighten inventories, and control the story told to the consumer, brands are striving to interact with us more than ever. Better results for them, better products and experiences for us.

Maybe it can be warm and fuzzy after all.

---

64 Green, Dennis. 2018. "Adidas Just Opened A Futuristic New Factory — And It Will Dramatically Change How Shoes Are Sold". *Business Insider.*

ITERATE, REACT, REITERATE

Designing a massively popular product is anything but easy. With the demanding time constraints imposed by today's consumer, it's becoming more difficult.

"I feel for the material and color and designers these days because I didn't know this until I started the YouTube channel and started buying all the shoes, but the level to which the entire community around shoes thinks that they can design shoes," says former Nike engineer, Tiffany Beers.

Beers, sheds light on just how difficult the design process can be, despite how vehemently the armchair designers littering the internet today argue otherwise. "These brands are competing with each other internally. Now they're competing with everyone outside who thinks they can just be a designer. If it was so simple to design shoes, there would be more shoe brands out there. There wouldn't be the big three. There wouldn't be the big five. Figuring out how to design a shoe in a way that is actually manufacturable and at a right price is a very complex equation that I wish people would have more respect for."

Beers has welcomed the opportunity to educate the armchair designer through her YouTube channel, where she reviews sneakers from a design and engineering perspective, a welcome reprieve from the sneaker YouTube's proclivity for saying "these are super dope."

This perspective forces us to think about the painful trade-offs between comfort and aesthetics, between performance and cost, between complexity and simplicity and speed of manufacturing. For example, the Nike Element React 87, a favorite of consumers in 2018, was not a favorite of Beers. While impressed by the aesthetics, she found the upper materials to be irritating in contrast to the supreme comfort of the React foam midsole.

Watching and listening to Beers, it becomes evident: the design and engineering process is so much more complex, intricate, and demanding than we have appreciated to date. It should come as no surprise, then, that introducing new hit product is very challenging.

***

There's a reason that we see the same retro models released again and again and again – because people buy them, and importantly, because brands *know* people will buy them.

Saturation may be looming for many models, particularly as boxes pile up in sneakerhead homes, but until recently, retros have effectively been a risk-free strategy. Still, brands today feel the pressure to innovate – to create the icons of tomorrow, and when they sense they might have one in the making, they quickly rush to satiate demand for it.

Nike CEO Mark Parker described the "edit-to-amplify" strategy at the 2017 investor day: "Starting this January, we're putting 25% fewer styles into the marketplace. Editing down to fewer styles creates the space to amplify. Amplifying means more choices of the products that consumers already love. This strategy comes to life through our power franchises, our most premium products that define our brand right now and in the future with defined expectations for sell-through and consumer perception."[65]

The strategy is particularly interesting when viewed through the lens of the advice given to Parker by Steve Jobs.

Today more than ever, when Nike identifies a new product that consumers lust over, it devotes significant focus to that product. Such dedication is evidenced through recent releases of the Nike VaporMax and the Nike Air 270, commercial successes quickly followed with vast iterations on color and materials. While that "OG" colorway of a new silhouette may be a quick sell-out, you can rest assured that most new hits will be released in seemingly limitless arrays as the brand hastens to capitalize.

More and more frequently, brands are marrying the certainty of selling retro models with the rush to grow new technologies into icons; they do so through "hybrid" models. For example, Nike puts an iconic Air Max 97 or Air Max 95 upper on a VaporMax midsole. Or Adidas, leveraging the tremendous success of its Boost midsole and the dependability of its icons, puts Stan Smith and Superstar uppers onto Boost.

The strategy also makes sense given certain manufacturing constraints for retro sneakers. While brands have

---

65   Nike Investor Day 2017". 2017. *Nike.*

made dramatic technological advances in the production of midsoles and modern uppers, producing retros is not so simple, mainly due to the complexity of the design and the tooling required to manufacture it. "I would say that there are manufacturing optimizations that can be used to shorten the lead time on retro sneakers, but also there's an element of needing to design sneakers that are suitable for manufacturing processes that are fast," says Busbee.

Given the investment made in tooling for these retro models, for purposes relating to economies of scale, it makes sense to produce the retro uppers in great quantity to amortize that cost over a larger number of pairs. While demand may not call for that quantity of sneakers on the original midsole at any given moment, the uppers can be more swiftly re-purposed onto new, technologically advanced midsoles.

In one fell swoop, the brands are finding new ways to sell the icons and introducing more customers to an impressive technology.

Given the difficulty of designing a hit, Beers endorses the hybrid strategy, but questions the future implications: "When you find a model or a midsole that seems to resonate with a lot of people, why not? Why not build on top of that? Now for the collector, I mean how many combinations of shoes do you really want to collect? I think people are getting to a saturation point on some level."

These are important, thought-provoking questions:

- With some retro fatigue setting in, these hybrid models offer fresh life in the moment, but for how long?
- If and when the exhaustion sets in, does it come at the expense of just the retro or at the expense of the newer technology as well?
- Does the amplification strategy of essentially saturating the market with product until demand is exhausted make sense?

There are only so many ways you can sell (and own for that matter) the Silver Bullet colorway of the Air Max 97. A consumer can only own so many VaporMax sneakers. The amplification and hybrid strategies make sense for immediate financial gain and quick capitalization, but if the goal is to create new icons that can be re-released as retros to eagerly awaiting demand, brands should proceed with caution.

That caution may be best exemplified in the release of the extremely popular Nike Element React 87. Significant buzz was generated for the release of the two original colorways. Afterwards, the cadence of follow-on releases for new colorways was slower and seemingly more measured, in stark contrast to the unrelenting conveyor belt bringing VaporMax and Air 270 product to market. If the approach is a barbelled one, with some hit products devoted to mass-market adoption and others restrained to avoid saturation, it becomes additionally important to choose carefully the big bets.

In any case, the popular retro sneakers of the 1980s and 1990s have by this point found their way to the closets of many sneakerheads. While the ranks of the sneaker collector are growing, an already vast supply of retros cannot grow in perpetuity. Stay tuned to better understand what the future might bring.

***

Everything moves faster in 2019. It moves faster and it's more complicated, particularly as technology renders our lives easier in many ways, but more complex in others. With an inundation of social media activity, our likes, dislikes, passions, fears, and tastes are shaped faster and more imperceptibly than ever. Where fashion used to dictate to us what we liked, the script is flipping. We have high expectations, and we want them met swiftly. It is the enormous task of the brands and retailers, then, to get to know us better while learning how to serve us faster in the background. Failure at this task is, of course, not an option.

They may be best served by the advice of Ferris Bueller: "Life moves pretty fast. If you don't stop and look around once in a while, you could miss it."

TAKEAWAYS FROM THE SNEAKONOMIST

- Everything moves faster today, including consumer tastes, popular trends, social media sentiment, and as a consequence, demand.

- We as consumers believe we must be served and served now, or else we often turn our attention – and our wallets – elsewhere.

- Brands and retailers must invest to better understand the consumer and more closely interact with the consumer in order to avoid being caught flat-footed with surplus inventory, widespread discounting, and missed opportunities.

- That close interaction must also result in more humanization of consumers to prevent the disenchantment that comes with frequently striking out on limited product.

- Designing new hits is a challenge, so when success becomes apparent, brands must act quickly to ensure they capitalize fully, while also taking care to avoid dilutive activity.

- Designing new hits, while challenging, is paramount to future success, given the inevitable saturation of retro models, which have been successful to date.

CHAPTER 8

DIFFERENTIATED RETAIL – HOW RETAILERS REMAIN RELEVANT

———

"It's really now about entertaining you guys. You can buy the product anywhere now. The internet has made the landscape really wide. That was actually a scary thing for us a couple of years ago. For me personally, it was almost like an identity crisis. Oh sh*t, if we can't captivate our audience here on Long Island, how can we captivate a global audience?" —Bernie Gross, Art Director at Extra Butter

Sneaker retailers, large and small, both wholesale and boutique, have their hands full in 2019.

Sneaker brands are focused with increased intensity on more frequently selling product directly to their consumers. Through personalized offerings, customization, and digital engagement, they're bypassing the wholesale channel more often and reaping the benefits of superior profits.

Where does that leave retailers? Upstream without a paddle? Left out in the cold fighting for scraps?

For some, the answer to those questions will be an unequivocal *yes*. However, retailers that can differentiate and add value still have much to offer the sneaker economy, with both brand and consumer as beneficiaries.

A retailer's failure to convey a sneaker's story or to engage the consumer in a manner which is *additive* to the sneaker brand's own efforts offers the brand little incentive to funnel further product its way. Continued provision of product means not only lower profits to the brand on the sneakers that were allocated to the undifferentiated retailer, but also weaker long-term relationships with the retailer's patrons as well. Were those patrons reached either by the brand directly or by a differentiated retailer, loyalty and therefore lifetime value would be bolstered.

A retailer *can* still differentiate in the internet age, even when products are relatively homogeneous, sites look similar, and a lower price is just a Google search away. As it turns out though, that differentiation may be better found *offline*.

BRICK AND MORTAR: ALIVE AND
WELL...WITH A CAVEAT

Across America, shopping malls are shuttering, replaced by gyms, condominiums, or, in the direst of circumstances, completely abandoned. The death of physical retail is widely discussed, particularly as the 'Amazonification' of retail persists. Shopping excursions today are not excursions at all but instead quests to answer, "how many Google Chrome tabs is *too* many?"

Yet, in the world of sneakers, differentiated brick-and-mortar persists – and thrives – as a valuable storytelling asset.

To be clear, the sneaker world is not immune to the evolving retail landscape. Longtime footwear retail behemoth, Foot Locker, has felt the sting of declining mall appetites. In 2018, the retailer is in the midst of repositioning its footprint (pun absolutely intended) off-mall towards more differentiated stores. In some cases, these outposts are referred to as "power stores," or key locations in which Foot Locker can create memorable experiences for customers.

CFO Lauren Peters elaborated on the persistent desire for in-store experience in the face of mall decline. "We're about 15% off-mall in the U.S. today, 85% mall," she explained on the company's 4Q 2017 earnings call. "But as you look back at our store closure, opening cadence by geography, we've been net closers in the U.S. for quite some time as we have been trimming the underperformers in the fleet. So, we find ourselves at this place where we still had good traffic in what would be lower rated malls in the U.S. But clearly, the customers still want to shop in store. If the mall goes away, he's still going to want to shop in his neighborhood. So that's off-mall strategy, to find that property and the format mix that works."[66]

In 2018, Foot Locker expected to close 120 stores, and the company has been a net closer for several years. However, as the thinning of the herd continues and underperforming stores are shuttered, the company is taking a more targeted, focused approach to new store openings, planning to open just 40 over the course of the year.[67]

"Across some of our key geographies, we will begin testing Power Stores, a new retail concept to inspire, build community and provide a seamless shopping experience for our customer," detailed CEO Dick Johnson on a November 2017 conference call. "This concept is all about community with a hyper-local approach. We believe the design and programming of the space will provide inspiration to our customers through premium product and experiences presented in unexpected ways."[68]

---

66 "Foot Locker's (FL) CEO Richard Johnson On Q4 2017 Results – Earnings Call Transcript". 2018. *Seeking Alpha*.
67 "Foot Locker, Inc. (FL) CEO Dick Johnson On Q1 2018 Results – Earnings Call Transcript". 2018. *Seeking Alpha*. https://seekingalpha. com/article/4177373-foot-locker-inc-fl-ceo-dick-johnson-q1-2018-results-earnings-call-transcript.
68 "Foot Locker (FL) Q3 2017 Results – Earnings Call Transcript". 2017. *Seeking Alpha*. https://seekingalpha.com/article/4126064-foot-lock-er-fl-q3-2017-results-earnings-call-transcript.

Johnson later notes the mall format doesn't necessarily provide the flexibility for Foot Locker to be able to create the requisite consumer experiences. Within the confines of the mall, Foot Locker struggles to create the "shop-within-a-shop" displays that better tell each specific brand's stories.

In a world where we can buy anything with just a few clicks, it's the experience that has become critical to consumers. It's not enough to have the Gatorade Jordan 6 sitting on your shelves, especially if you want to sell it at full price. Instead, Foot Locker transformed that launch into an *experience*, housing an interactive "Be Like Mike" display in its flagship Los Angeles store. The Power Stores specifically feature not only technologically advanced and sleek product displays, but also local artist collaborations, gaming zones, sneaker cleanings, and even a barbershop as is the case in the Hong Kong location. The idea is that the product itself is not the sole reason for consumers to visit.

Differentiation in that regard is critical to retail success. Nike has made it a mission to lead the wholesale marketplace in its entirety toward greater differentiation. Those that cannot differentiate will be left behind, replaced by not only those retailers who can but also by Nike's own digital efforts. As Andy Campion noted on Nike's fourth quarter earnings call for its 2018 fiscal year, "Digital continues to reshape the consumer experience and to some extent disrupt the more undifferentiated, multibrand, wholesale dimensions of the marketplace."[69]

Many may assume Foot Locker fits neatly into the undifferentiated, multibrand wholesale bucket and is therefore doomed to fade meekly into the background as Nike pursues digital conquest. Fortunately, for Foot Locker, this is not at all the case. Partners are indeed a large part of Nike's differentiation efforts, and those partners do not have to go it alone.

"We're working with our key partners to help differentiate them in their respective positions. Those conversations are ongoing with most strategic partners," explained Mark Parker on the 3Q 2018 earnings call. "We've aligned on the role that they play in serving our consumers from Dick's to Foot Locker to Nordstrom, and this is not only physical retail but it's how physical and digital interact. And then, we have other digital partners which are obviously key to this transformation. Zalando and TMall, ASOS and even Instagram for example. So this is a multi-year journey for us, and I'd say we're making great progress in shaping that marketplace and I think we'll continue to elevate our own direct business, but we will also help to differentiate and elevate our key wholesale partners along the way."[70]

---

69 "FY 2018 Q4 Earnings Release Conference Call Transcript". 2018. *Nike, Inc. – Investor Relations.*
70 "FY 2018 Q3 Earnings Release Conference Call Transcript". 2018. *Nike, Inc. – Investor Relations.*

Indeed, Foot Locker has differentiated its experiences in many cases with Nike acting as a partner. For example, the two companies collaborated on "Sneakeasy" pop-up shops in NYC, Boston, and other cities. The Sneakeasy featured a curated selection of coveted product, including not yet released sneakers, which were then dispensed to consumers via containers resembling safety deposit boxes. The sneaker boxes themselves were gold foil styled, complete with a notary type stamp.

In discussing the fourth quarter results, Parker further explained how the partner-related differentiation efforts take shape more generally to drive results: "We're also piloting and scaling NIKE Consumer Experiences with key wholesale partners. For example, the NIKE Certified Athletes program turned selected Foot Locker associates into NIKE experts and after showing stronger early results, Foot Locker will scale the program across North America in Q1. And with JD Group in EMEA, we launched both a physical and digital concept to celebrate Air Max storytelling called Undisputed Air, driving triple-digit growth of NIKE Air products in JD versus last year."[71]

For American readers unfamiliar, JD Group is a popular European sports fashion retailer which, in June of 2018, acquired a retailer with which you are likely very familiar: Finish Line. On the company's last independent earnings

---

71 "FY 2018 Q4 Earnings Release Conference Call Transcript". 2018. *Nike, Inc. – Investor Relations*.

call, Finish Line CEO Sam Sato highlighted the company's refocused efforts to better differentiate.

"As we look forward, you can expect Finish Line to continue to build engagement experiences that enhance our relationship with the customer," said Sato. "At the same time, we continue to make strategic brand investments designed to build an emotional connection to our consumer and positioned Finish Line as the destination for the latest and greatest sneakers....Our efforts with the Nike brand included a pinnacle retail expression in our flagship doors supported by local events, best-in-class digital storytelling and unique asset creation through Finish Line influencers in Chicago and New York."[72]

Nike's increased focus on profitable, direct-to-consumer sales need not spell the end for brick-and-mortar wholesale or large wholesale generally. However, the message is quite clear: get differentiated, get on board, or get left behind.

The necessity of differentiation is a reality well understood by the sneaker world's successful boutiques. All of which were, at one point or another, scrappy underdogs trying to offer a different value proposition than the mega-retailers of the world. It's no coincidence the most successful players are

---

72 "The Finish Line's (FINL) CEO Sam Sato On Q3 2018 Results – Earnings Call Transcript". 2017. *Seeking Alpha*. https://seekingalpha.com/article/4133328-finish-lines-finl-ceo-sam-sato-q3-2018-results-earnings-call-transcript.

those that create highly differentiated experiences and tell the most colorful stories.

Bernie Gross of New York based Extra Butter explains how the retailer took a progressive but practical approach to standing out: "We sat down and said, 'what is our challenge, what is our void?'. We realized we're not really in the business of retail because we're being handed these products that everyone wants. It's really about how we bring that product to market."

"I've come to terms, and my partners alike – we're really in the business of entertainment now," continues Gross. "How do you add an experience and social currency for your consumer? They want something that goes with the product. It's not even about the transaction. If it is about the transaction, you can easily just do that online. It's the reason why Amazon is where it's at. And yes, we have the SNKRS app and we have the Adidas confirmed app – there are platforms that facilitate that. I think there's a reason why boutiques are still so important to brands like Nike and Adidas because they know we can bring something extra. It comes down to the activation. It comes down to small nuances in how we take care of customers in-store, even facilitating online."

Within a retail store's four walls, experience can be controlled and enhanced, but it's difficult to differentiate online. As consumers gain access to greater amounts of higher-quality information, the market becomes more efficient. They seek the lowest price until the lowest-priced inventory has been depleted, then they're on to the next lowest-priced retailer. With the help of a unique, experiential storefront however, retailers can build relationships that are more meaningful. The retailer becomes more than a URL, more than just shelves with the same pieces of leather and rubber as everyone else.

That tangibility, the ability to interact physically, still matters in the sneaker retail space. In fact, it was only when Nice Kicks founder, Matt Halfhill, opened a retail store to accompany his popular blog that brands began taking him more seriously.

"When I started the blog in 2006, of course I had always had the dream of having a retail store, but I began wanting that more and more the more I worked on the blog," says Halfhill. "The reason was the brands didn't believe in the idea of blogs or digital media for many years. I don't even think some brands could grasp what a blog was until I opened the retail store. It was like, 'Oh this blog thing's legit, you have a brick-and-mortar store!' Oh, so the millions of people we talked to a month weren't legit, but if I make a brick and mortar store, *now* you believe me?!"

Of course, when the Nice Kicks retail store opened, we weren't quite as far along digitally as we are today, but Halfhill's core learning holds water. Any entrant in the sneaker retail space is taken more seriously by brands and consumers alike once they've demonstrated an ability to create compelling experiences. These experiences might come in the form of events or they may simply be inherent to the store's aesthetics; we'll describe examples of each type shortly. While brands *can* be built online, a physical, tangible representation can accelerate a consumer's connection to that brand.

In Matt Halfhill's case, a retail space was an opportunity to physically manifest the online brand of Nice Kicks. "A lot of people said, 'Oh, you did it in reverse order. You did a blog first, and then you built a store'," he explains. "I never set out to start a store to begin with, but the store just happened because the site became so much of a brand online that I wanted to create an offline representation of it. The idea of the store was not really to sell products, more so to create an atmosphere and create an experience for people to understand what Nice Kicks represents."

"While I can see and visualize a lot of stuff online, there are things that, when taken offline, you get a better understanding of, and that's what the purpose of the retail space was. We called it the Nice Kicks *space* or retail *space*. We never called it a retail store or retail shop. I always felt that with retail shops and retail stores, you're expected to buy something. We were never pressing people to do that. I kind of had this attitude that I wanted people to leave with something even if they bought nothing, and that meant they had a good experience, or a good conversation, or they saw a product displayed a certain way that made them think about it in a different light."

Halfhill strikes a critical chord. In a digital world, brick-and-mortar retail stores, or *spaces*, serve a purpose beyond solely revenue generation. Ideally, as echoed by Bernie Gross, the retail space provides opportunities to connect with the consumer outside the confines of the transaction. In Extra Butter's case, free movie screenings, discussion panels, and other events unrelated to product launches offer some of the most valuable opportunities to stand out. These events are the moments to nurture truly personal relationships between customer & customer and customer & retailer that, in aggregate, comprise a community.

Retail spaces also serve as valuable branding tools which can influence and shape future digital interaction. Ideally, the brick-and-mortar store will tell the same story as the digital presence and the reciprocal will be true as well – the channels will act cohesively to provide a differentiated retail *identity*. This concept is applicable in the resale market as well.

The brick-and-mortar locations of Flight Club and Stadium Goods are among the most iconic and impressive in the sneaker industry. Not only are those locations meaningful revenue drivers, but they present the resale players the opportunity to strengthen their brands and communicate their identities. Offering a backdrop for social media content and shows like *Sneaker Shopping*, these venues are not just stores but must-visit sneakerhead tourist destinations.

The brick-and-mortar space provides an opportunity to understand the consignment player's staggering breadth of selection in a very tangible way. Sure, anyone can simply visit their website and navigate through the vast inventory, but physically seeing the selection under one roof – walls lined with highly sought-after, highly popular sneakers – is a meaningful experience. In store, Stadium Goods and Flight Club both provide a sophisticated, comfortable experience with knowledgeable staff, replicated online via clean interfaces and product pages replete with rich story detail.

In a podcast interview on *The 20 Minute VC* following GOAT's merger with Flight Club, GOAT co-founder and CEO, Eddy Lu, struck a similar chord on the value of a brick and mortar location: "With GOAT, we were 100% digital before the merger, but we knew that we wanted to become omnichannel in the future. Sneakers are a very tactile experience. People want to feel the shoe, wear the shoe, even smell the sneaker that they're buying. It's one of the few commerce categories that I think actually makes sense to have physical retail stores."[73]

Lu also dispelled concerns regarding the margin implications of a physical store. "While there's store overhead," he explained, "if the store is in a class A location, it's no different than spending money on Facebook marketing. Instead of spending it on digital ads, you're spending it on rent and having a physical showcase for your product."[74]

---

73 Stebbings, Harry. 2018. "GOAT's Eddy Lu On Pivoting From Failing Social Dining App To The World's Largest Sneaker Marketplace, How The Best Founders Pick Their Investors & Why It Is Better To Be Hated Than Unknown". Podcast. *The Twenty Minute VC*.

74 Ibid.

Lu and the GOAT team had the luxury of bringing aboard a company with a blue-chip brick and mortar retail pedigree in Flight Club, so the learning curve eased dramatically, which highlights the logic behind the merger.

Now, for Matt Halfhill and Nice Kicks, the challenge was bringing an online brand *offline* to tell stories. Having achieved this goal, Halfhill sold the retail side of the Nice Kicks business in 2014 to refocus his efforts more centrally on his penchant for written storytelling and the company's roots in sneaker media. For other successful boutiques in the sneaker space, however, they must do the reverse: they must find ways to manifest their unique brick-and-mortar presence in their online identities.

Take for example Boston-based boutique, Bodega. Bodega offers one of the most unique, coolest in-store experiences in sneaker retail. The store is located in Boston's Back Bay, but don't expect to find any inviting, loud signs drawing you inside. Rather, upon arrival at Bodega, you'll be greeted by a storefront which resembles its namesake: a local, neighborhood bodega with various convenience store essentials lining the shelves. Only by approaching the Snapple vending machine, which automatically slides open, does one gain entry into the larger retail space where the latest in streetwear awaits.

Now, the first time I ever visited Bodega, I had already been tipped off on the means of entry. Even with that being the case, I timidly walked up to the Snapple machine with all of the conviction of Harry Potter approaching platform nine and three quarters his first year at Hogwarts. As the vending machine door abruptly yielded without warning, I flinched.

This was not the behavior of a casual regular. This, my friends, was the behavior of a square.

Cut me some slack – I've never entered a store through a vending machine before! And unless you've been to Bodega, neither have you. It's a hidden in plain sight retail experience unlike any other.

Bodega sets the tone for its entire brand with the literal front door of its establishment. It's a community establishment first and foremost – like your neighborhood bodega – harboring and reflecting the culture of its patrons.

Bodega strives to be additive to that culture, to more tightly knit the fabric of its community, and to reflect the spirit and vitality of that community. It's because of these drives that Bodega is an attractive partner to the Nikes of the world; it's able to offer an authentic connection to the streetwear community. It's for this same reason Bodega could survive and succeed without the Goliath sneaker brands. The boutique, and frankly larger retailers to the same extent if not more so, are subject to the whims of those brands. Only by creating an authentic, living connection to the community it serves and adding value to that community can a retailer somewhat insulate itself from those whims.

Bodega forges that connection through its in-store experience and through the events that it holds with its community of patrons. It's more than a store. It's a living reflection of culture.

How do you take that community approach and transfer it onto a smartphone? How do you create an online identity that is uniquely Bodega?

Co-founder Oliver Mak admits, "It took us a long time to figure out how to bring the store's personality online." Sure enough though, the Bodega team found a way to create an online presence, which could not be mistaken for any other store's. "If you look at our social media," Mak elaborates, "we take our pictures, crumple them, distress them." Bodega's social media posts take on a distinct aesthetic, often with product photographs resembling the distressed pages of a 1980s or 1990s sportswear magazine or the coupon booklet from a Sunday newspaper. It's consistent and, more importantly, uniquely identifiable as Bodega content.

Bodega infuses culture into everything it does, and the online representation of the brand is no different. Models are often members of the Bodega community; the store held an open call in the summer of 2018 for interested applicants. These models are often authentically captured in settings squarely in the neighborhood of the retail location or otherwise in Boston (or Los Angeles, where Bodega opened a second location). Bodega is authentic in its reflection of and contributions to the culture of the community it serves, an effort that is spearheaded by the differentiated retail experience. That authentic connection is of immense value to partners farther up the chain.

Differentiated retail comes in many different forms. As the Nikes of the world intensify their direct-to-consumer efforts, undifferentiated players will inevitably fall by the wayside. Those that can differentiate and connect to consumers through their storytelling and through the experiences they provide, however, have a real value proposition to offer consumers and brands alike. That reality applies to boutiques and former mall stalwarts alike.

Tales of physical retail's demise have *not* been greatly exaggerated. Rather, they've been misguided.

Undifferentiated retail faces an inevitable decline. All it takes, though, is a visit to Extra Butter on one of their movie nights or a trip through the Snapple machine at Bodega to see the brightest and most creative minds in sneaker retail produce brick-and-mortar experiences that are anything but undifferentiated.

HOMOGENEOUS PRODUCT, HETEROGENEOUS EXPERIENCES

The products lining retail sneaker shelves worldwide are fairly homogeneous. That's a reality of the industry.

Sure, some retailers are Tier Zero Nike partners, meaning they receive allocations of the most exclusive Nike sneakers and product. To attain that status, these retailers have thoroughly demonstrated their ability to differentiate. As undifferentiated retailers fall by the wayside and the herd thins, product homogeneity is bound to persist.

So how did those retailers of repute earn distinction despite an undifferentiated product set?

If truly and meaningfully differentiating the sneaker product set is somewhat beyond their control, they must look to the *experience* they provide their customers. To develop a better understanding of what a differentiated experience looks like in practice, let's consider how Extra Butter makes the most of limited releases.

Of course, the sneaker community has long been notorious for the fervor surrounding any truly limited release. While the advent of secondary marketplaces, online raffles, and mobile applications have somewhat mitigated the chaos, the scarcest, hyped releases continue to draw a frenzied crowd. With resellers providing reinforced demand for retailers, limited releases are certain to sell out within hours and without issue.

While they might make for a nice day of sales, those releases often do little to foster deeper customer relationships that extend beyond the transaction, *unless* the retailer is willing to think creatively and invest accordingly.

Perhaps no releases in recent years have been better guarantees to sell out than the Off-White & Nike collaborations of 2017 and 2018. While we'll discuss the collaboration in greater detail later on, for the time being, it's important to understand a few things:

- The Off-White Nikes, designed by shooting star Virgil Abloh, bear a very distinct aesthetic, with text labeling various parts of the sneaker like "AIR" or "SHOELACES".
- Virgil's take on the Air Jordan 1 in the original "Chicago" colorway graced an impossible number of famous feet leading up to their release, including athletes, musical icons, and other figures of import.
- The frenzy created by the unique aesthetic and unprecedented social media attention contributed to sustained, four-figure secondary market prices.
- Again, retailers were *guaranteed* to sell out any allocation they were fortunate enough to receive.

As resale prices for the "Chicago" Off-White Air Jordan 1 rose beyond $2,000, news of additional future colorways emerged, with a white and university blue version to hit stores just months after the original's release. While not expected to test the secondary market levels of its predecessor, there was little doubt the follow-up offering would command similar attention and demand. Those fortunate retailers would again have the opportunity to swiftly deplete their inventory.

Extra Butter was one such retailer, but Bernie Gross and team were not content to reap the spoils and move on. They viewed the release as an opportunity.

To dampen the chaos typically associated with line-ups, Extra Butter conducted an online raffle through which the winners would secure a spot in line the day of launch to purchase the sneakers. Winners were provided with specific half hour increments during which they could come to collect their treasured prize. It sounds simple enough, but they weren't about to line up in front of the Extra Butter they were used to seeing on a daily basis.

Instead, Extra Butter had invested out of pocket to mark the entrance with signage mimicking the text used by Virgil Abloh on the sneaker, only instead of "SHOELACES," "AIR," and "Beaverton Oregon," theirs read "MARQUEE SIGN," "DOOR," and "Rockville, NY." Once inside, winners were met with a super-sized Nike sneaker box in which they could take pictures with their latest acquisition.

Despite the fact that Jordan did not fund this activation, according to Bernie Gross, by the end of the weekend, Extra Butter was the retailer on the lips of the brand. "The build-out, the graphics, that was all just saying this is on us to provide something special. We were the only New York account that actually did a line-up. Everyone else just went straight to raffle it online. It spoke volumes to who we are as a retailer. Jordan is still talking about us."

In an industry where retailers are selling similar assortments of product, standing out is a challenge. It can be difficult to look beyond the significant immediate windfalls of a release like the Off-White Jordan 1 and see them as opportunities to deepen relationships. Those that differentiate, even when it doesn't seem necessary, will find themselves vastly more likely to secure increasingly elusive consumer loyalty and vendor mindshare.

The sneaker landscape often seems so large but is, at its core, comprised of many tightly knit communities. Such a structure necessitates demonstrations of gratitude and loyalty to the consumer in order to receive the reciprocal. In the same regard, strong vendor relationships require a display of creativity and value-add from the retailer.

"Technology has enabled consumers to become less reliant on solely their local retailers," says Gross. "It's all about where to buy the product and where to find it fastest and earliest. Hopefully, they're at least engaged enough to have the curiosity to check in on us. From a vendor point of view, they're always going to start to have us higher on their list of go-to accounts when they're ready to do a full-on partnership and activation."

Gross cited the Nike x Atmos Animal Pack and the Nike ACG collection as examples of the fruits of their differentiated efforts over the years, as Extra Butter partnered with the Swoosh on both initiatives. The trepidation and fear concerning the widening and maturation of the internet landscape that once plagued Gross and team has been somewhat assuaged by Nike's strategic desire to conduct hyperlocal, tailored activations with Tier Zero accounts. A place on that activation shortlist, however, requires the ability to differentiate. Differentiation may not come cheap, but as with any investment conducted with savvy and conviction, the potential for lasting returns is meaningful.

For Extra Butter, that effort to provide release experiences isn't limited to Nike and to Off-White. Visit the retailer's Instagram profile, and you'll see creative releases highlighted for Reeboks and Pumas as well – opportunities to be imaginative where others are not.

It would be relatively easy to become complacent once a retailer has reached the status with a brand that grants them access to coveted releases. Those highly limited releases are unquestionably going to sell out, and the retailer is going to do a healthy chunk of business no matter who acquires the shoes on that day – reseller or collector. Focusing simply on that day, however, is not a recipe for long-term success, nor is it the formula that propelled the retailer to such heights in the first place.

As Copdate founder, Andrew Raisman, puts it: "The guys that got to the top of the food chain didn't get there by being complacent and predictable."

Avoiding complacency is exactly where Raisman and Copdate come into play. Copdate, which we'll discuss alongside other ancillary sneaker services later, essentially offers release day expertise to retailers. The application facilitates either a reservation system or a more sophisticated, less hackable raffle system, depending on the choice of the retailer.

Whether through proprietary efforts or through the assistance of a third party, the stakes are such that retailers must invest the time and funds to ensure they are innovating on behalf of the consumer. While in the very short-term it feels like limited releases are a low ROI area, it is precisely because those moments offer large, captive audiences a compelling opportunity to achieve high ROI and improved customer lifetime value.

One day, those retailers who rest on their laurels could very well rest upon crippling unsold inventory.

***

Importantly, there are exceptions to the rule of homogeneous product offerings. Perhaps the most important is the previously discussed collaboration between brand and retailer. With collaborations, generally, a sneaker brand will identify a retailer which it views as providing an additive, differentiated connection with consumers and approach said retailer to develop a story around a sneaker model that the brand is either looking to launch or draw more attention to. It's a mutually beneficial endeavor: the brand generates increased buzz for a strategically important product and the retailer receives an opportunity to develop a reputation with brands as an effective storyteller and with consumers as a creative force.

Take for example Cambridge, MA based retailer, Concepts, which also boasts locations in New York and Dubai. For many, Concepts is the preeminent collaborator in the sneaker industry, successfully devising stories and, well, concepts, around sneakers with Nike, New Balance, Asics, Adidas, and others. In fact, many Concepts collaborations are viewed as some of the most widely adored sneakers on the market. This reputation enables Concepts to cultivate relationships with sneaker brands and consumers that are anything but cold and transactional. Such is the strength of the retailer's storytelling capability that Adidas went so far as not only to collaborate with Concepts on a pair of sneakers but also on an *entire retail store*, located on Boston's heavily trafficked Newbury Street.

Pascha Naderi-Nejad, Senior Director of Originals at Adidas, elaborated on the partnership in a statement: "This partnership symbolizes yet another level of our commitment to offering a diverse and multi-faceted portfolio of unique, retail experiences for our fans. Our co-designed and curated boutique with Concepts is a perfect example of this, uniting two partners in the development of a new retail identity that is authentically laser focused on the consumer experience."[75]

Now, this is an extreme example, but the learning from it cannot be understated: even a goliath sneaker brand like Adidas looks to retailers to enhance the brand's storytelling and to better engage the consumer through unique experiences.

---

75 Ofiaza, Renz. 2017. "Adidas & Concepts Open Exclusive Boutique In Boston". *Highsnobiety.* https://www.highsnobiety.com/2017/08/25/adidas-concepts-store/.

Concepts creative director, Deon Point, explained the retailer's value proposition for brand partners to *Footwear News*: "When we started doing our own pop-ups for any collaboration we did, we fully immersed ourselves in the story and made sure it wasn't something people walked away from and forgot. For that reason, we believe Adidas recognizes us as the best storytellers in the boutique channel and appreciated what we could do for them."[76]

In many cases, collaborations with sneaker brands themselves may not even be a cash cow for the retailer. There are rare cases where the retailer's reputation for collaborations allows it to bring the sneaker to market in meaningful scale so that the monetary gain is substantial. Often, though, collaborations serve to generate buzz and as such are released in limited quantities. That being the case, the monetary return on the time, energy, resources, and staff needed to develop a successful collaboration from the retailer's point of view is not extraordinarily attractive. As with the Extra Butter release experiences, though, the collaboration is a hugely important investment.

To engender loyalty with brand and consumer alike, a retailer must differentiate at every opportunity.

---

76 Verry, Peter. 2017. "What Sneaker Fans Can Expect From Adidas' Co-Branded Store With Concepts". *Footwear News*. https://footwearnews.com/2017/focus/athletic-outdoor/adidas-concepts-store-boston-410840/.

Collaborations offer perhaps the most valuable opportunity to do so, given the rare chance to break free from the shackles of homogeneous product and offer something not seen on shelves across the sneaker world – something truly unique. Those that seize such opportunities, like KITH or Concepts, find themselves with not only a competitive position far closer to vendors of import, but also an elevated status for their own brands.

HYPER-LOCALITY IN A FLATTENING WORLD

As we'll touch upon shortly, the sneaker world, like most industries, is flattening with greater rapidity each day. Geographic borders are increasingly meaningless and product thousands of miles away is available at the click of a finger. Yet there remains tremendous value to be added on a hyper-local level by retailers with their fingers on the pulse of their respective communities.

As we now know, personalization provides a significant competitive advantage in the sterile world of e-commerce. It's the reason Nike utilizes the SNKRS application to provide targeted release experiences in specific cities and geographic areas or to fans of a specific artist, athlete, or team. Similarly, it's the reason Nike is pursuing a concept dubbed "Nike Live", as explained by Mark Parker on the company's Q1 2019 earnings call: "The premise behind the concept is to create a live and ever-changing experience. We're testing a number of new features, including product assortments that update frequently based on what's trending with the local consumer; a service that allows consumers to reserve an item on our apps and then pick it up curbside or in the store from a personal smart locker."[77] Tested initially in Nike's Los Angeles Melrose store, the Nike Live concept will next make its way to the critical New York City and Shanghai locales.

Different locales, different communities, can have vastly different tastes. Foot Locker has arrived at this recognition and is responding through the new "power store" concept and through the select stores, which are being opened and not closed today. "As we see the mall starting to deteriorate, we know that even though the mall goes downhill, the customer doesn't leave that neighborhood and wants to be served," explained CEO Dick Johnson on the 2017 fourth quarter earnings call. "So we're testing some off-mall power stores. We're testing some off-mall formats that we see as great opportunities to stay very relevant and hyper-local to that customer, while we try to connect with them digitally, obviously."[78]

The aim is to connect on the community level to cultivate the roots of a relationship that grows, thrives, and evolves further in the digital realm. It's extraordinarily fascinating

---

77 "FY 2019 Q1 Earnings Release Conference Call Transcript". 2018. *Nike, Inc. – Investor Relations.* https://s1.q4cdn.com/806093406/files/doc_financials/2019/Q1/NIKE-Inc.-Q119-OFFICIAL-Transcript-with-QA-FINAL.pdf.

78 "Foot Locker's (FL) CEO Richard Johnson On Q4 2017 Results – Earnings Call Transcript". 2018. *Seeking Alpha.*

that the mammoth brands and retailers of the industry are devoting attention to this idea of hyper-locality as a means of creating an opportunity to truly connect and offer relevant experiences.

Why is that so fascinating? Because it's something that has been achieved by boutique retailers in abundance.

Improved digital targeting, Nike Live, power stores – these are all strong concepts and ideas in theory. In practice, it's going to take time for them to make a tangible impact on results, because cultivating a community relationship and ingraining oneself deeply within its culture does not happen overnight. Furthermore, and this is critical, it must happen *authentically*, if the results are to be optimal. This authenticity, frankly, is more difficult for large corporations to achieve in contrast to the Bodegas and Extra Butters of the world, which take a sincere interest in becoming a part of the fabric of the community at street level.

The reality is that despite the flattening of the world perpetuated by e-commerce, thinking and acting locally is still a highly valuable means of fostering deeper, stickier relationships with a higher propensity for brand loyalty. Brick and click starts at ground zero. Shortcuts are few and far between. For that reason, those retailers, both within the sneaker economy and in consumer retail more broadly, which can build and demonstrate a sturdy bond with their respective communities will continue to play a vital role over the long term.

***

Retailers in the sneaker economy have far more to do than simply move product through to the end consumer. Such a singular focus would run that retailer out of business in a hurry. The responsibilities of the retailer, at least the one that will persist into the future, are diverse and demanding. The retailer wears several hats: storyteller, purveyor of experiences, cultural contributor, and in summation, *creator*.

Yes, they are indeed tasked with selling the product created by the brands, but that does not mean that their own creative capacities may lie dormant. Those that are successful layer creation onto those products through their storytelling, through their accompanying experiences, and through their understanding of their customer. There's a clear addition of value. They achieve differentiation *through* creation.

TAKEAWAYS FROM THE SNEAKONOMIST

- In an e-commerce environment that empowers sneaker brands to more efficiently and cost-effectively reach consumers directly, there's no need for retailers that offer no value-add to the consumer or vendor.
- Product offerings that are fairly homogeneous from store to store make it more difficult for retailers to stand out.
- Retailers *can* stand out and add value, namely by offering their patrons unique and differentiated experiences and through the power of creative storytelling.

- Creating experiences and differentiating requires invest-ment – of time, effort, and money – in order to realize returns in the form of increased customer loyalty and greater vendor trust.
- In a world of cold, transactional e-commerce, authentic connections to a community and its culture are an extremely valuable asset; it's an asset possessed by many of the successful, creative boutiques of the sneaker world.

CHAPTER 9

EXPANDING DEMAND – CROSSING BORDERS AND DEMOGRAPHICS

―――

"The phenomena of the internet is that if you can actually communicate on a global basis, what is viewed as a niche just becomes absolutely massive."[79]

—Danny Rimer, Partner at GOAT Investor Index Ventures, to GQ

The sneaker economy is awash with vast supply. We've established that. We've also established this vast supply may become a problem, but only if unfulfilled by a commensurate

―――――――――

79   Wolf, Cam. 2018. "The $60 Million Sneaker Merger". *GQ.* https://www.gq.com/story/goat-flight-club-sneaker-merger-60-million.

increase in demand. Such an increase, of course, requires a departure from the sneakerhead niche.

The uninformed reseller, the so-called greater fools, have provided a comforting demand backstop to date, but what happens when the fools are no longer foolish?

What of the purist sneaker collector? Logic would dictate that some level of saturation looms on the horizon. It's a frustrating reality: sneaker collectors have only two feet and a finite amount of storage. The brands, retailers, and resale players must compensate for a deceleration in demand from this loyal niche.

New demand must be unearthed, new end-user demand in particular.

It's precisely for this reason the sneaker collector's demographic must expand. The familiar stereotype must be abandoned. Previously underserved or under-targeted parties, those who don't fit neatly into the bucket of hip-hop and sports loving American males between the ages of 18 and 34, represent a meaningful growth runway for the economy as a whole.

There are a lot of feet outside of that stereotype. Consider the executives who are trading their wingtips for high-tops in increasing numbers, as sneakers find their way into luxury fashion and the modern office. Consider women: once tragically overlooked, they are increasingly becoming a focus of the brands, of the retailers, and the marketplaces. Consider the potential presented by crumbling international borders, as the resale market utilizes its vast investment funding to expand globally. These are merely a few growth opportunities, albeit critical in nature, which must be seized upon in order for the sneaker economy to continue to grow and to flourish.

Sneakerheads are no longer solely male. They're no longer bound by age. They're no longer bound by geography. They simply can't be.

Sneakers are an airborne virus, and with renewed and refocused efforts from the sneaker economy's participants to create new demand, nobody can claim immunity.

TRADING LOAFERS FOR LIMITED RELEASES

"Buy what you like."

It's the most popular, novel piece of advice to budding sneaker enthusiasts building their collections. If only it were that simple.

The sneaker world can be overwhelming for those new to the hobby. Sure, I'll just buy what I like...and risk ridicule in the process.

Many a sneaker snob has cringed upon hearing a novice friend boast about their new "Jordans," looking down to find -gasp! – that they haven't acquired a numbered Jordan (for those overwhelmed parties, a numbered Jordan refers to a flagship annual release like the iconic Jordan 1 or 3), but instead something funky called a "Spizike".

What the heck is a "Spizike"?

While most sneakerheads know exactly what a Spizike is – a hybrid of various iconic numbered Jordans – they're not exactly beloved fixtures of the sneaker community. The point is that 'buy what you like' is fantastic advice for those unconcerned with the opinions of others. For the novice collector, however, there is some inherent desire to "flex" as they start out, to buy a conversation piece that others will appreciate.

As a newbie looking to gain the admiration of those in the know, it's difficult to ascertain with confidence just what that statement piece is or what it looks like, and even more difficult still to actually acquire it with confidence once identified. At least, that *used* to be the case. Now though, the sneaker craze is being carefully expanded into territories which may be more familiar to the uninformed.

Resale is no longer the arena of solely the savvy eBay explorer. Consignment players have sought to ensure the hottest releases of the past decade and beyond are not only readily available to those interested, but also highly accessible. They've elevated resale to a sophisticated retail experience in which buyers can confidently purchase, secure in the knowledge they are receiving authentic, curated product from a trusted party. So successful has this shift been that stalwarts of luxury retail like Farfetch have taken notice, developing an interest in playing the secondary sneaker category in earnest. But much like with the green collector, the guidance of seasoned experts is required in order to access the category with legitimacy.

Enter Stadium Goods.

While Farfetch has long sold sneakers on its platform, in April of 2018, it enlisted Stadium Goods to provide a limited, curated selection of inventory. The platform's shortcoming to date had been procurement of the true, premium rarities on the secondary market, and Stadium Goods, with its proprietary treasure trove of supply, proved an ideal partner to plug that gap.

The synergies of the partnership are clear and mutually beneficial. For Stadium Goods, distribution via the Farfetch platform would mean introduction to a sophisticated, globally-diverse customer base willing and eager to spend on high-end product. Stadium Goods reciprocates, offering a tremendous value proposition to Farfetch. Resale is complex in a number of ways: acquiring sufficient supply, curating it appropriately, authenticating it, understanding how it will sell and at what price – these are just a few of the head-scratching matters that have the power to make or break a business. Importantly, when dealing with luxury customers expecting luxury experience, it's best to avoid leaving those matters to chance.

For a newcomer to put its best foot forward in entering the resale sneaker space in earnest, deep industry knowledge is required. That's not an asset easily acquired.

These partnerships allow large retail platforms and Stadium Goods to essentially barter trust for trust. The trust and goodwill earned by Farfetch from its customers, not necessarily traditional sneakerheads, are transferred to the resale sneaker space (to Stadium Goods in particular), and in return, Stadium Goods provides the assurance of authenticity, expert curation, and efficient inventory management. In order to truly realize the enormous potential of the resale market, the marketplaces must discover ways to expand their footprints by engaging previously untapped demographics. Partnerships provide a valuable launch pad to do just that.

Though Farfetch consumers may not know Stadium Goods, they do trust the Farfetch platform. They are, therefore, comfortable purchasing resale sneakers, knowing that the product is, in essence, co-signed by a trusted party.

Resale industry expertise is not an asset easily acquired… unless of course you *literally acquire it*. So floored was Farfetch by the success of the partnership and the growing demand for sneakers as luxury fashion that the company ultimately decided mere partnership wasn't enough. In December of 2018, Farfetch announced the acquisition of Stadium Goods at a valuation of $250 million. While Stadium Goods would continue to operate independently, the acquisition is a firm indication that the surge of sneaker resale into the realm of luxury commerce is only just beginning.

Stadium Goods co-founders John McPheeters and Jed Stiller set out to elevate resale and project an aura of sophisticated retail. If anything could validate the accomplishment of that goal, acquisition by a renowned purveyor of upscale fashion would certainly fit the bill.

The Farfetch partnership and subsequent acquisition is not the only example of increased focus on luxury-centric demographics, though. In the spring of 2018, luxury department store Nordstrom announced its intent to house a Stadium Goods concept store within a new Manhattan-based men's location, as reported by *WWD* among others.[80]

While that Nordstrom location's grand opening ultimately occurred without the store-in-a-store partnership as noted by *Fashionista*[81], the motivation for such a concept is rational in the present moment. With increasing frequency, luxury retailers are citing sneakers as a fast-growing category, noting their newfound appeal both in the office and in social situations. Stadium Goods, among others, offers the opportunity to line shelves with the rarest and most coveted of sneakers. A few years back, though, even the idea of a high-end retailer of repute embracing sneaker resale would have been difficult to imagine. Whether that combination ultimately comes to fruition or not, the concept itself is further evidence that sneaker resale's unyielding infiltration of luxury retail is gaining momentum.

80 Hughes, Aria. 2018. "Stadium Goods To Open Concept Space Inside Nordstrom". *WWD*. https://wwd.com/menswear-news/mens-retail-business/stadium-goods-to-open-store-inside-nordstrom-1202633799/.

81 Street, Mikelle. 2018. "Nordstrom's First Standalone Men's Store Is Banking On 'High Heat' Product And Prime Customer Service For Success". *Fashionista*. https://fashionista.com/2018/04/nordstrom-mens-store-nyc.

Consequently, the typical sneaker consumer needs to be prepared to see the most hyped and hot-selling sneakers popping up on shelves in unexpected places. In many cases, those sneakers will be positioned as premium, luxury product – high-priced statement pieces that may serve as gateways to broader sneaker consumption. We're going to see Off-White Jordans on unexpected feet, like those of a hedge funder, which were previously adorned with dapper, polished wingtips.

Matt Cohen of GOAT elaborates on this demographic shift: "I actually think that the industry tailwind behind us is that less and less people are wearing brown shoes, more and more people are wearing sneakers. Tech CEOS are now expressing and flossing through the use of highly coveted sneakers." That being the case, the Yeezy-wearing Jack Dorseys of the world may be less the exception and more the rule, particularly as a younger generation comes into greater business responsibility.

The elevation of sneaker wear is not confined to the resale market's infiltration of high-end retail. Take for example J.Crew, which lines its shelves with high-quality, office-friendly models from the likes of New Balance, Asics, and others. The preppy retailer has taken a shine to the powers of collaboration as mentioned previously, once teaming with popular sneaker retailer and longtime industry mainstay, Packer Shoes, and Asics to release a pack of four Gel-Lyte IIIs: one in oxblood leather, one in navy buck, one in white buck, and one in charcoal suede. These are premium looks, created in tandem with an extremely reputable and culturally in-touch sneaker retailer, fit to replace a loafer or traditional oxford shoe without seeming particularly out of place. This is but one example, but traditional retailers and sneaker-head-endorsed companies are frequently collaborating to bring incremental buyers into the fold on a mutually beneficial basis.

On a similar note, it begs the question of whether the tech community's obsession with Allbirds, which reside wholly outside of the sneakerhead niche, may serve as an *additional* gateway to broader acceptance of and interest in sneakers as modern office attire. The direct-to-consumer purveyor of monochromatic wool runners, a design that does little to capture the fancy of sneaker diehards, recently attained a valuation of $1.4 *billion.*

However, what does the introduction of this new demographic – let's call it the upscale, professional demographic – mean for the sneaker economy at large?

Generally speaking, unlocking a new demographic of course means increased demand in the short-to-intermediate term. Whether that demand would be sustained long term or if it would be a passing trend is unclear. Still, we could anticipate a mild increase in resale price for the most popular, coveted pairs, particularly those just weeks out of retail – those with no slack in supply. Many incremental buyers from this demographic are used to paying premium prices for footwear and may be less inclined to shy away from surging secondary market values. It's additionally fair to expect that those incremental buyers intend to wear their sneakers and would therefore reduce deadstock supply. Getting more sneakers out of their boxes and onto feet (after all, that is their purpose) is rarely a bad thing, but it may mean higher prices for those hoping to score these pairs (deadstock) 1-2 years down the road. Such behavior would further exacerbate the elevation in value of the market's jewels over the rest of the pack.

Despair not though, incumbent sneakerheads. More consumers do not necessarily mean more competition at retail. For those who troll the sneaker blogs and Instagram for hours on end, enter countless raffles, and slam the "Buy" button on SNKRS at exactly 10:00am, acquisition at retail is unlikely to grow significantly more difficult (could it really get that much harder anyways?!) as a result of the introduction of these new demographics.

Rather, a demographic like the Farfetch or Nordstrom customer is simply empowered to buy in the resale market with confidence, replacing Gucci loafers with an off-the-run pair of Yeezys. Should they wish to enter the fray for retail releases, however, that should not be cause for panic. In the short term, acquisition may become marginally more difficult, yes, but remember, brands often want their products to be perceived as scarce but not *impossible* to acquire. Or else why try at all? The brands aren't out to leave unnecessarily large amounts of revenue on the table, just *enough*.

If the competition should grow without a commensurate increase in supply, though, the newbies know not what they face. Their opposition, the seasoned veterans, will be ready, taking the odds-enhancing steps of which novices are blissfully unaware: enabling Apple Touch ID in the SNKRS app, heightening raffle chances by subscribing to newsletters and tagging friends on Instagram, and trolling the sneaker blogs for the full list of retailers offering product. They may not win those raffles, but then again, does anybody?

Incumbent sneakerheads, new kids on the block – all will find common ground in the inevitability of missing out.

LADIES NIGHT IN THE SNEAKONOMY

It's a novel idea, really. Need more demand? Address the HALF of the population that has been overlooked to date.

It's no secret female sneaker enthusiasts have long been underserved by the sneaker economy. Streetwear has traditionally been male-dominated, and while apparel has become less gender-dominant, there has remained a fairly strict bifurcation between men's and women's sneakers. Consequently, women have been left to make the most of a far less than ideal situation.

Rather than foolishly attempt to "mansplain" this unsavory situation, I'll defer to Tora Northman, who details the struggle far better than I ever could in a piece she wrote for

Hypebae, a site driven by a female editorial team focusing on fashion and culture: "Being a woman, there are a lot of options when it comes to copping cool shoes – but when it comes to more exclusive drops, it seems as if the female audience is often excluded. Usually, women tend to have smaller feet than men, (duh) with the average female shoe size being US 5.5 in men's sizing, yet most sneaker releases tend to start at a US 6 or 7 if we're lucky, and sometimes even higher than that. Of course, the release is meant to be exclusive, but does that mean that so many women need to be excluded?"[82]

If women want an exclusive release, they often first have to break out the size conversion chart and figure out where they fall in male sizes. As Northman alludes to, that converted size typically isn't even offered for super limited releases, those that are usually the most desirable. Inclusion requires women to go to great lengths – extra soles, thick socks, and a lot of inconvenience.

In her study, *Sneakers: Fashion, Gender, and Subculture,* a fascinating exploration of the constructs of subcultures generally and of the sneaker subculture specifically, Yuniya Kawamura explores how sneaker subculture became so male-centric:

"A group of sneaker enthusiasts have established a persistent male-dominant community that excludes and

---

82 Northman, Tora. 2018. "How Come Brands Still Aren't Making Sneakers In Women's Sizes?". *HYPEBAE.* https://hypebae. com/2018/8/lack-of-womens-sneaker-sizes-nike-adidas.

alienates girls and women. Gender is visible and present in various ways through objects, places, and words among others. Sneakers represent manhood and masculinity. Material culture of gender creates and recreates gendered beings, and a pair of sneakers that is used in sports is in turn associated with men, and in which women are in the subordinate and secondary position. Boys and young men are the biggest consumers of sneakers. While clothing is becoming unisex and androgynous, shoes remain to be gender-specific in terms of their designs, colors, and sizes. Few realize that there are far more varieties and choices for male sneakers than female sneakers."[83]

Kawamura provides rich historical context on the evolution of footwear and its cultural constructs, and explains how the pursuit and acquisition of the most exclusive and sought-after sneakers became an expedition in male dominance, a quest to reign supreme by wearing Supreme, if you will.

Among the contributing factors to the male skew of sneaker subculture, she suggests, are the roots in athletics and the fascination with technology. "While the pursuit of adornment and self-display has been a female terrain, sneakers that are associated with sports and the incessant use of technology by the enthusiasts make it a male affair."[84]

---

83 Kawamura, Yuniya. 2016. *Sneakers: Fashion, Gender, And Subculture.* 1st ed. Bloomsbury Academic.
84 Ibid.

Northman's anecdotes, and those of countless other female sneaker enthusiasts, suggest that Kawamura's assessment of the sneaker culture holds validity.

Whether intentionally or not, sneaker brands, retailers, and marketplaces have skewed heavily male, a bias that was seemingly irreversible...until recently. Recently, there has been an increased focus and intensified effort by each of these parties to better satiate existing demand and generate new interest, to widen their audiences by better serving the female gender.

These efforts are evidenced by the increasing array of women's exclusive models. In 2018, Nike released a women's exclusive model of the Air Jordan 3, one of the brand's most iconic silhouettes, in partnership with Vogue. Virgil Abloh and Off-White collaborated with Nike on a line of apparel and footwear for Serena Williams. Designer Aleali May recently became the first female collaborator to work with Jordan on a pair of sneakers for men and women: a custom-designed Air Jordan 1. In another milestone, the brand introduced a women's exclusive version of the LeBron 16 in collaboration with Harlem Fashion Row, designed by three African-American women – the first sneaker of a male athlete's signature line designed *for* women *by* women.

Nike, of course, is not alone in these efforts. Adidas, capitalizing on the dad shoe trend, released the highly popular Adidas Falcon exclusively for women in the fall of 2018, with the assistance of an endorsement from Kylie Jenner. The irony of a popular women's exclusive being referred to as a "dad shoe" is certainly not lost on this author, but that has indeed become the accepted vernacular for chunky designs previously revered only by (often dorky) dad-aged men.

Still, while some of these women's exclusives and limited releases catered toward women are a noteworthy step in the right direction, there remains significant work to do. Northman explains: "we don't need more shoes that are pink, glittery and labeled as "women's exclusive" – we really just want what the dudes are getting."[85]

"My point is, that regardless of your gender, size, and background, you should be able to take part of the immense culture that is sneakers. Just because I'm a girl with small feet it shouldn't mean I'll never be able to rock the coolest creps, right? Brands should be recognizing that there is an interest and a huge audience when it comes to women's streetwear, and that most of the time we're more interested in the exclusive men's releases than the women's."[86]

One-off women's exclusives aren't enough to bridge the gap, even as they increase in frequency. This is a reality not lost on the brands. "It's the idea that not one size fits all in the women's market," Julie Igarashi, VP and creative director of Nike Women, told *FootwearNews* at Paris Fashion Week in February of 2018. "Some consumers want a men's shoe, but

---

85 Northman, Tora. 2018. "How Come Brands Still Aren't Making Sneakers In Women's Sizes?". *HYPEBAE*..

86 Ibid.

they want it in their size. In other cases, she wants it for her and by her. So it's exciting to be able to offer that breadth."[87]

Answering this call to action is the responsibility of the brands, and it's a call to action addressed with increasing intensity. Still, in the meantime, resale marketplaces are increasing their focus on providing a better quality of service and offering to the female consumer.

The recently merged GOAT and Flight Club combination is eager to break down the walls of the traditional sneakerhead demographic. "Flight Club has traditionally catered to that original sneaker collector, the sneakerhead: traditionally male dominated, 18-34, loves hip hop and sports. Flight Club is the most internationally recognized sneaker store outside of the big brands. GOAT is a technology disruptor, it's an app. We broke down that barrier of who shops in that setting," says Matt Cohen of GOAT. "It's really reflected in our demographic. Over 50% of our customers don't fall into that traditional sneakerhead demographic. We reach a much wider audience – women are our fastest growing category right now."

Indeed, GOAT's female user base grows at a rate that approximately doubles that of its male users. GOAT hired a new Chief Operating Officer in 2018: Lizzie Francis, whose

---

87 Abel, Katie. 2018. "Why The Women's Sneaker Market Is Finally On The Cusp Of A Revolution". *Footwear News*. https://footwearnews. com/2018/fashion/athletic-outdoor/womens-sneakers-nike-un- laced-paris-fashion-week-selfridges-510156/.

background includes acting as CMO for the Gilt Group and at JustFab.com. That's a background very well-suited to a vastly more inclusive sneaker economy of tomorrow. In the pursuit of growth, businesses of the sneakonomy are evolving their target audiences well beyond the friendly confines of the traditional sneakerhead. That party will always be well served, but for companies with investment dollars to put to good use, the opportunity to better serve women is far too attractive a growth driver to ignore.

As Francis told *TechCrunch*, the time to broaden horizons is now: "There are so many things that are going so well here [at GOAT], but in terms of immediate opportunity, obviously expanding into women is important for the company, and we're seeing some really favorable tailwinds and data points that indicate that it's a great time for us to be doing that. And also, our current customer base is primarily male. I'm sure you know, 85% of consumer spending is controlled by women. So, it feels like now that we have a great platform in place it's actually a great time for us to focus on that female customer that's both a buyer and a seller."[88]

Among the ways that GOAT plans to cater to this female participant–sizing conversion tools for women on the platform. The resale marketplaces can't rewrite history; the supply of yesterday can't be retooled to include more

---

88 Panzarino, Matthew. 2018. "Sneaker Market GOAT Hires COO Lizzie Francis And Makes A Play For Women Sneaker Shoppers". *Techcrunch*.

women's sizes. Still, they can remove much of the headache of best understanding how that supply suits women. As the space continues to evolve, ideally, the need for such tools will largely evaporate. Exclusivity can be a powerful tool for demand – just ask Mark Zuckerberg about the role exclusivity played in the early success of Facebook – but gender exclusivity in the sneaker economy may be not only passé but economically foolish.

While the generation and accommodation of female demand cannot alleviate supply excess where it's most problematic – in the most common men's sizes – it *can* assuage and mitigate future issues. Hyperbolically speaking, just about every release *ever* has been available in men's size 8 to 14. Epic hyperbole aside, if there's budding saturation anywhere, it's there. With female demand in tow, brands could theoretically lean out the introduction of new supply at those common sizes without forgoing meaningful revenue, specifically by shifting supply down the size spectrum in a more *inclusive* manner.

It's the lowest of low-hanging fruit: including the heretofore underserved female half of the world. The reality of most subcultures is that they are strongly intertwined with capitalist enterprise. The capitalist enterprises, which rose from sneaker subculture, must now cast aside the male skew of that subculture in the pursuit of healthy, long-term growth.

It's the right thing for the business. It's the right thing, period.

THE FLATTENING OF THE SNEAKER WORLD

Sneaker resale is swimming in more cash than Scrooge McDuck.

Stadium Goods taken out for $250 million. $15 million to Grailed. $60 million to the merged GOAT and Flight Club. $44 million to StockX. These are significant sums of investment money, all hitting the resale space at roughly the same time, but where does all of that funding go?

With supply moats largely built already, those dollars focus on expanding demand, and in many cases, that means expanding the geographic borders of the resale market.

With most announcements of new investment funding comes some disclosure on the intended use of funds. Every time, international expansion can be found toward the top of the list, and with good reason. There's the obvious of course – increased volume potential. What may be less obvious, however, is the intense voracity of overseas demand, as the scarcity of coveted products is often even more severe than it is in the United States.

It may not be as apparent to the U.S. consumer, since it is well-served by brands and resale marketplaces alike, but there is tremendous demand from Europe and Asia for products unavailable in their markets. Cross-border transacting is a meaningful source of potential business, but the hurdle has always been trust, authenticity, and efficiency. That's where a trusted platform like Stadium Goods comes in. It's difficult for an individual seller to satisfy demand across borders on their own. Facilitation by a trusted third party can make all of the difference when considering a transaction between an American and an Australian or between someone in Europe and someone based in Asia.

Stadium Goods is a terrific case study, as the New York based company has been a pioneer in international sneaker resale, boasting a particularly effective focus on China. By partnering with Tmall Global, Alibaba's cross-border platform, starting in 2016, Stadium Goods capitalized on a tremendous future growth driver very early on. Essentially, the platform allows users to sell directly to Chinese consumers without actually establishing operations there, shipping from the U.S, or storing product with a logistics partner in a Chinese Free Trade Zone. By collaborating with a deeply knowledgeable and supportive partner, Stadium Goods gains access to a massive population with growing disposable income, while leveraging both its own reputation and Alibaba's reputation for authenticity and combating counterfeit goods.

As CEO John McPheters told *Forbes*, "Selling to China was a big early win for us. Our business grew exponentially as a result. The key moment came for us on November 11, 2016, China's Singles' Day Shopping Festival. We had a big spike in sales and millions of people were exposed to our brand and business."[89]

---

89 Zakkour, Michael. 2018. "When Alibaba Met Stadium Goods: The Case For Foreign Smes To Try And Crack Chinese E-Commerce". *Forbes*.

It was noted by Forbes that the company's sales on Singles Day 2017 were more than 10x those of 2016, which provides an indicative snapshot of the explosive growth ripe for cultivation. The company has barely scratched the surface of what's possible in China and its status as a first mover equips Stadium Goods with meaningful brand recognition and a growing customer base. McPheters has even suggested China could one day surpass the United States as the company's largest e-commerce market.[90]

In the wake of Farfetch's acquisition of Stadium Goods, much of the conversation regarding synergies centered around cross-border logistics, with Farfetch's infrastructure poised to further accelerate the company's rapid international expansion. Indeed, in sneaker resale, it's a critical moment to ensure that players are well-positioned, well-funded, and well-prepared to capitalize on surging international demand.

GOAT's investment funding will finance a charge towards Asia and Australia, primarily through application functionality geared toward better serving those markets. Similarly, StockX's top priority for its fresh $44 million is global expansion. The company already ships globally, but next comes the development of marketing, customer service, and operations

---

Com. https://www.forbes.com/sites/michaelzakkour/2018/01/22/when-alibaba-met-stadium-goods-the-case-for-foreign-smes-to-try-and-crack-chinese-e-commerce/#414b5342631c.

90 Milnes, Hilary. 2018. "How Stadium Goods Is Seizing China's Streetwear Opportunity – Digiday". *Digiday*. https://digiday.com/marketing/stadium-goods-seizing-chinas-streetwear-opportunity/.

in Asia and Europe, as well as the ability to transact in currencies beyond USD. Indeed, StockX officially launched its European expansion in October of 2018, announcing a West London authentication center in the process. The opportunity in Asia beckons.

"In some of these countries, we have, a pretty decent customer base where people are tendered on a VPN," Luber told *TechCrunch*. "There are pictures of people that walk around China with a StockX tag hanging off their shoe." *TechCrunch* notes that 15% of StockX sales come from international buyers. That proportion is set to increase dramatically.[91]

The disappearance of borders is by no means exclusive to resale, either. Certainly, resale is where it's most impactful, given the nascence of the market abroad, but importantly, the ease with which we can transact globally is also impacting how sneakers are acquired at retail. For example: it is often the case that limited releases hit shelves in Europe a week or weeks ahead of the United States release date, or perhaps the release is exclusive to Europe.

Not a problem.

Head to a European retailer's website for a crack at them. For a slightly higher price due to currency, tax (VAT), and shipping cost, you have just as good a chance to procure them

---

91 Burns, Matt. 2018. "Detroit's Stockx Raises $44M From GV And Battery To Expand Marketplace Internationally". *Techcrunch*. https://techcrunch.com/2018/09/12/detroits-stockx-raises-44m-from-gv-and-battery-to-expand-marketplace-internationally/.

as someone in those markets does. Sweden-based Sneakersn-stuff ships to most countries globally and offers a wide array of trusted payment options, PayPal and Klarna among them. Germany-based The Good Will Out, Swiss-based Titolo, and UK-based Size? are all examples which function similarly.

There may even be potential profit opportunities at hand. The general pattern of resale prices for highly limited releases is a steady uptrend leading up to the official release, followed by a dip shortly thereafter as sellers flood the market, and a subsequent, gradual recovery from there. In some cases, the economics may work out in a United States-based reseller's favor if they were to get lucky in snagging a pair internation-ally before the domestic release.

As consumers, we're simply not confined to the options within our borders anymore. We can procure supply from anywhere, exhausting all options until we succeed. If we don't succeed at retail, the resale communities are about to grow dramatically larger.

The introduction of international markets would certainly bring additional supply on line. Keep in mind, however, that the primary genesis for geographic expansion, as described by the resale experts, is the massive demand for products sold in the United States. On a net basis, global expansion will better balance supply and demand, particularly over the short-to-intermediate term. International consumers with a higher willingness to pay than their American counterparts, driven by their previous lack of access, will provide support for prices. In the long term, there will be more market depth on both the bid and ask sides.

Recall, in the first chapter, we reminisced about the mid-1990s efforts of Japanese retailers in traveling to the U.S. on "scavenging trips" to procure sought-after styles for lucrative resale back in Japan. No longer nichey, cross-border sneaker trade is a wildly different and vastly more convenient beast today.

With funding in tow, the internet at its disposal, and consumers worldwide eager to buy, the global sneaker economy is on an irreversible path to unbelievable global scale and scope.

***

It is often the case that subcultures are inextricably tied to capitalist urges. Sneaker subculture is no different. That doesn't necessarily have to be a negative relationship, though. Yes, market participants are reaching for bolstered demand to rise to meet abundant supply. But that capitalist yearning for expansion, for growth, for *more* is leading to more inclusion. The sneaker economy is including people of more ages, it's including more women, and it's including people of more nationalities and cultures. Moreover, because of the accompanying ability to communicate on a global basis, all of this inclusion can serve to enrich, embolden, and enliven sneaker culture as stories are shared and more people express their individuality through sneakers. What has been the case in local sneaker culture can be the case globally: that expression of individuality can serve to bring us closer *together*.

Sneakonomic growth is capitalistic, no doubt, but that doesn't mean this growth is devoid of soul and of culture.

TAKEAWAYS FROM THE SNEAKONOMIST

- The proliferation and subsequent preservation of supply has created a need for new sources of demand, not only for the brands and retailers, but for the secondary marketplaces as well.
- This demand must come from previously underserved consumers that fall outside of the confines of the traditional 'sneakerhead' demographic.
- Sneakers are invading traditional high-end retail, reaching the feet of new customers that are swapping out their trusty loafers and oxfords for Jordans and Yeezys for office-wear.
- Women, long overlooked by sneaker culture, are increasingly becoming a focus of the many constituents of the sneaker economy, presenting unparalleled and largely untapped potential for growth.
- International borders are crumbling, as retailers and resale platforms alike expand geographically and enable better service of cross-border sneaker trade.
- For the sneaker economy to continue on a healthy growth trajectory, a consumer constituency far broader than the

stereotypical demographic, where deceleration is inevitable, must be cultivated and nurtured.

PART 4

THE SNEAKER ECONOMY EXPANDS AT THE PERIPHERY

CHAPTER 10

SNEAKER MEDIA – HYPED SHOES AND FAKE NEWS

———

"Sneaker media being a thing! You'd be a joke if you even said it. I visited my old Physics teacher in Canada, and he was like 'What are you doing?'. I said, 'I'm doing stories about sneakers online.' He was laughing, 'What are you, a sneaker journalist?' I wouldn't use that word, journalist, but that was the first time I thought, 'Oh sneaker media! It's a legitimate industry'."

—Matt Halfhill, Founder of Nice Kicks

How did it become so darn hard to outperform as an investor in the stock market? Why did the investing public become increasingly reliant on passive investment products like exchange traded funds and index funds, eschewing in greater numbers the superstar mutual fund and hedge fund managers of eras gone by?

Increased efficiency.

Now, increased efficiency is the product of numerous trends and forces, but at its core, it results from increased coverage and thus the increased proliferation of timely data and information.

Bloomberg, CNBC, even Twitter ensure that breaking market news is spread, digested, and priced in immediately by the investment world. Research departments of banks ensure that vast universes of companies, both their equities and debt, are covered in depth, with institutional investors kept apprised of any compelling investment theses on a daily basis.

In short, information is constantly available and actionable, and any information of an advantageous nature is very quickly acted upon and priced into the market. As a result, the financial markets are considered more efficient. This is a simplistic summary, but it informs how we might think about today's sneaker market in contrast to the sneaker world of old.

When the sneaker world was still the Wild West, the swashbuckling nature of the hobby was largely due to the inability to easily procure reliable and accurate information. Sneaker releases popped up somewhat out of the blue, and if you weren't in line outside the store in time, you were out of luck. Word of mouth and connections were everything. But as the demand for limited sneakers and sneakers more generally grew, so too did the demand for better information, the kind of information that would adequately prepare sneaker-seekers for the hunt ahead.

With that demand for information came the advent of a cottage industry: sneaker media. Today, we as consumers are the beneficiaries of sneaker media. We know when sneakers are to be released. We know where they'll be released. We know what's coming down the pike in six months or a year. Perhaps most importantly, we know how difficult something will be to acquire and where we can expect it to price on the secondary market.

Our attention is drawn constantly to models and colorways that we may have otherwise missed, and we gain introduction to retailers nation and worldwide that have graced their communities with inspiring collaborations for years. The sneaker economy is enormous, but we now have sneaker blogs, sneaker shows, and sneaker podcasts (and one book on sneakonomic growth) there to act as our Sherpas. All the while, the market is growing more efficient, as buyers and sellers alike are armed with better information.

EXTRA! EXTRA! READ ALL ABOUT IT!

In the early 2000s, the closest thing the consumer had to sneaker media was internet forums, like NikeTalk, where like-minded sneaker enthusiasts congregated to exchange opinions and more importantly information: what was dropping, when was it dropping, and which stores had stock. The information was almost entirely crowd-sourced. It was dependent upon word of mouth, willingness to share, and active participation. The demand for such information was apparent, and so it wasn't long until a variety of online sneaker sites were developed to service that interest; by the mid-2000s, Highsnobiety, Kicks on Fire, Hypebeast, and Nice Kicks had made their respective debuts, with Sneaker News following shortly thereafter.

Fast forward to today. Hypebeast raised HK$65 million via initial public offering on Hong Kong's stock exchange. Sneaker News garners in excess of 20 million monthly views, per the company's website. Nice Kicks and KicksOnFire boast roughly 3 million Instagram followers apiece. To put it plainly, the sneaker media business is booming.

Nice Kicks founder Matt Halfhill reflects incredulously on just how far the industry has come: "There are not only a number of outlets that focus on shoes, but there are probably 50-75-100 people where that is their job! Creating content, documenting, telling stories about shoes. That, to me, is incredible."

People, likely in excess of 100 now, have carved full-time *careers*, through affiliate marketing and advertising, out of simply discussing sneakers on the internet. They identified a passion, dedicated themselves to it, bravely inserted themselves into the conversation, and cultivated mass followings. In the process, they've provided us, the consumers, with an invaluable resource: reliable and actionable information. And if you're paying attention – identifying which sneakers are getting a lot of coverage, noticing which posts are generating significant buzz and interaction, monitoring for positive or negative community reactions – you're well equipped to transact intelligently, whether at retail or through the resale markets.

Those running the blogs themselves are armed with data stores of great value, which in turn render them tremendous projectors of a sneaker's success or lack thereof. Says Halfhill, "We can see pretty quickly where [releases] are going to go, but now with all these years of experience, I know from the time I look at the product and when it's going to hit and knowing what else is going on. I've gotten pretty good at knowing which ones to put more behind from the jump."

"With time and experience and testing things out and analyzing the analytics, you can get a really good feel for things, but I also try not to get too lost in the data. I think that there is definitely a lost art of touch and feel and knowing and building an opinion for yourself and trusting that."

Now, there are certain drawbacks to the sneaker media community. At the behest of the brands, certain models receive significant coverage, almost creating an echo chamber or self-fulfilling prophecy of hype. Those models consequently draw the most buzz and inspire the most passionate demand, maybe for the sneaker itself but often simply for the prospect of profits.

Halfhill details how these hype trains can gain steam: "Believe it or not, brands don't show us everything. We see what their big campaigns are – the stuff they're putting a big push behind. There are so many shoes that we never hear about until they actually come out. Like, how the hell were we not briefed on this?! This shoe's great! It goes on all the time. That's a byproduct of how much product there is in the market. There are so many SKUs, so many points of distribution. I can see how folks in the PR and marketing departments at these brands are like, 'gosh, we only have so much bandwidth, we've got to pick the ones we get behind.' Some just don't get that push. I think that's what you see a lot in the blog space."

In a space where there are so many players, many of which tend to follow the lead of or aggregate the work of thought leaders, there are certainly moments where diversity of thought is lacking, and that has an impact on consumer decision making. If you're unconcerned with hype, perception, and resale value, this trend can be beneficial, as you're able to identify less covered models of an appealing aesthetic. These tend to fall by the wayside; lacking the demand from resellers, they are often destined for clearance. If you have designs of acquiring an already limited product, the hype machine certainly doesn't make it any easier. The abundance of media coverage draws resellers like bees to honey, particularly the less sophisticated resellers lacking direct connection lines to brands or retailers for valuable information on the quantity of supply.

In order to escape the hype machine, Halfhill encourages and challenges staff to identify sneakers they've seen recently that are of interest and under-covered and post on them. He still makes visits to the mall to discover little known product. There is one effort in particular that Halfhill made to differentiate in the early days of Nice Kicks that has had an extremely widespread impact on our broader social media experience.

If you've ever posted a #TBT Instagram photo on Throwback Thursday (and I know you have, come on, admit it), you've participated in an internet trend that derives its origins from sneaker media.

Don't believe me?

Google "Throwback Thursday origins."

Unless that pesky search engine changed its algorithms again, at the top of the page, you should see an excerpt from Quora: "*Sports Illustrated* attributes the origin of the trend to a sneaker-specific blog named Nice Kicks." That's right, just shortly after he launched sneaker blog, Nice Kicks, in April of 2006, founder Matt Halfhill inadvertently sparked a trend that evolved well beyond his intended use, landing in all areas of popular culture and, frankly, of modern life.

Typically, particularly in 2006, the role of sneaker blogs was to inform consumers about upcoming releases – the backstory, where to buy, at what price, and when. For a natural storyteller like Halfhill, however, this basic blocking-and-tackling didn't always provide enough of an outlet, both creatively and as a means of ensuring a robust stream of content on the site.

"I had a slow news day at the time. There wasn't a whole lot to write about. I was like, 'What am I gonna do here?' I loved telling stories. Even when I was talking about Air Force Ones or Bo Jacksons or Jordans, I loved telling the detailed backstory that was way beyond what you saw with the shoe. I thought to myself, why the hell do I need to tell stories based on what's coming out, or some sample that surfaced, or some PE [player edition] that a player had? Why can't I take a look at my collection of shoes and write stories about what I have? These shoes all have stories to them, which is why I have them! So why don't I tell a story people might not have heard before? So, I did that."

It shouldn't come as a surprise that one of the most widespread by-products of sneaker media is the result of a desire to tell robust stories. As we've discussed, storytelling is of critical importance in the sneaker world. Stories are the reason that we buy certain sneakers. They're the reason that similar looking sneakers might be valued hundreds of dollars apart. Without stories, sneakers are pieces of rubber and leather, and some of those pieces of rubber and leather are better looking than others are.

The naming of the Throwback Thursday trend itself, however, was inspired by another product that capitalizes on stories, those written by great athletes over the course of a career.

"I loved throwback jerseys. Throwback jerseys I thought were the greatest thing. When they really hit mainstream in '02, they were really the catalyst for me to learn about some of my favorite basketball players of all time. So, I started going down the Google wormhole when I was 17 years old, reading up on these guys, and I just loved throwbacks even though I never had one. So, I was like 'okay it's Thursday, what do I call this thing? Oh, I'm throwing it back. Throwback Thursday!' That's how it all started."

Almost every single week for years, Halfhill told a robust story around a pair of sneakers, iconic or not, that introduced or revitalized the rich background detail, which made the sneaker special in the first place. The weekly piece persists today, though not always written by Halfhill. Of course, today, the sneaker-focused use of Throwback Thursday is not the most common utilization, a realization that wasn't always met with glee by the person that started the trend.

"Then Instagram happened, and other social media happened, and it morphed and evolved. It was originally about telling stories of old shoes and the people that wore them. My parents would say, 'Yeah, you used to get really angry every Thursday because you were complaining about which celebrity was using the name Throwback Thursday, and it wasn't about shoes!'"

What Halfhill may not have realized at the time, in the midst of the day-to-day grind of writing and operating Nice Kicks, is that he had set in motion a chain of events that would empower and inspire millions of people to tell their own stories on a weekly basis. Over the years, that trace of resentment abated, and he was left with a valuable life lesson: "A lot of times, you create things or do things, and sometimes the greatest thing that happens is not what the original intent or targeted outcome was. When I started Nice Kicks as a teenager, my goal was to make $40 every two weeks when I went to college. Things didn't work out like that. Things change. They went a different direction. First, it was starting to sell things online and I found I preferred storytelling and media over the transactional stuff. Same for Throwback Thursday, which started as one thing and evolved and became something that in a lot of ways is arguably better – it involves way more people telling stories about themselves."

So, the next time a Kardashian posts a Throwback Thursday photo on Instagram, please, I beg of you, remember that they're doing so because Matt Halfhill had a slow news day writing about sneakers. Kidding aside, maybe if Halfhill didn't possess a unique passion for both alliteration and throwback jerseys, our Thursdays may not be as enriched with stories as they are today. The butterfly effect is a crazy thing, and so is sneaker media.

It's a light-hearted anecdote, but it's emblematic. From humble beginnings, sneaker blogs have grown to become trusted and reliable purveyors of news and information that play a critical role in the day-to-day shaping of an enormous industry.

LIGHTS! CAMERA! ACTION!

Sneaker media is anything but limited to the written word, and its purpose extends beyond information and into the realm of pure entertainment.

The capital city of that sneaker-based entertainment? YouTube.

We've touched on the importance of the tactile sneaker experience. You may not get to touch them or try them on through your phone, tablet, or laptop screen, but sneaker YouTube is bringing us as close as possible to this physical sneaker experience. Perhaps the best example of this phenomenon is pop-culture media platform Complex's *Sneaker Shopping* show.

The first episode of *Sneaker Shopping* was published on YouTube in April of 2011, featuring rapper, Jim Jones. *Sneaker Shopping* host, Joe La Puma, currently SVP of Content Strategy for Complex, can be spotted from time to time unsuccessfully attempting to wrangle the attention of the vivacious Jones in the bustling setting of New York City's Flight Club location. With little direction, Jones scans the shelves, comments on a few pairs of sneakers, and lends some crudely worded tips on styling. Two minutes and forty-six chaotic seconds later, a phenomenon of sneaker media was born, though it didn't begin in earnest until 2015.

Fast forward eight years from that Jim Jones episode, and *Sneaker Shopping* boasts several episodes that have eclipsed ten million views. Ten. Million.

Over the years since that first rampageous episode, the show has grown into a well-oiled machine that captures the attention of millions on a near-weekly basis. The premise is relatively simple: Joe La Puma, now somewhat of a celebrity in the sneaker realm due to the show's success, escorts a celebrity guest around the shelves of a popular sneaker shop, often Flight Club or Stadium Goods, asking thoughtful questions about the guest's own experiences with sneakers through the years. La Puma has become highly adept at eliciting the guest's very best sneaker stories, and each episode essentially becomes a walk down the guest's sneaker memory lane, as a stroll along the shelves draws his or her eye to an old favorite or to the pair that got away.

The show is a reminder that sneakers are vehicles for storytelling and that the tactile experience of scouring the shelves remains a highly effective way to develop the connection between consumer and product.

Take for example an episode featuring soccer star, Cristiano Ronaldo, which aired in the summer of 2018 and quickly amassed over five million views in the first three days (in part because it was shortly after the star joined Juventus from his longtime club, Real Madrid). The show opens with La Puma and Ronaldo encountering Cristiano's own Nike Air Max 97 in the store. The sneaker in hand, Ronaldo explains with La Puma's prodding, bears a patchwork design inspired by his childhood, during which he had two pairs of shoes, one for school and one for play. His play sneakers would so often become worn through that his mother would have to patch them up on a regular basis. Nike can tell that story through its own marketing and through the sneaker blogs, but the visual of the person that inspired the sneaker holding it in his hands and telling the associated story is a powerful one.

Notably, in another moment that has become a recurring hallmark of *Sneaker Shopping's* success, La Puma shows his guest a sneaker that he didn't remember or hadn't seen before, and viewers are treated to the sight of Ronaldo's eyes lighting up with excitement: it's a Juventus black-and-white striped colorway of the Air Max 95.

In what is certainly not an uncommon occurrence, Ronaldo goes on to spend well in excess of $3,000 on sneakers to conclude the episode.

Sneaker Shopping episodes shot at consignment shops are the perfect encapsulation of why sneaker resale remains a rocket ship of growth in the present moment. Consumers are presented with incredible breadth of selection. They're armed with robust information provided to them by parties like Complex. They have access to the knowledge of what's hot among various cultural icons and what exactly it is about a shoe that's capturing hearts and imaginations. Because of platforms like Instagram and YouTube, brands and retailers no longer have to rely on the printed and written word to quite literally spell out stories. They can tell them and, better yet, have them told authentically through voices that command attention. The stories are brought to life.

Significant beneficiaries of the *Sneaker Shopping* phenomenon are consignment shops like Stadium Goods and Flight Club which often play host to episodes. In doing so, those shops appear in Complex content, which is aggregated and spread across a vast social media landscape. To a global audience, those locations become tourist destinations, drawing European and Asian demographics into New York City outposts. Not only is this highly impactful, highly unique media inspiring viewers to add the featured store to their must-visit list, it's reinforcing the entire tactile experience of physically sourcing a new pair of sneakers. It's reminding consumers what they love about that journey, of what it's like to have their interest piqued, to feel the grip of nostalgia, and to forge a connection with a product.

Matt Cohen, VP of Business Development and Strategy at the recently merged GOAT and Flight Club, explains how Flight Club focuses on providing a memorable consumer experience, one that essentially allows any regular consumer to walk in and live out their own episode:

"I think the sneaker enthusiast still really appreciates that journey. You walk into Flight Club, and you see shoes that you never thought you would see, some that you didn't even know existed. There are very few people in this world that can come in and tell you about every single shoe in Flight Club. I think that experience is truly unique. If you walk into a traditional brick and mortar store, you may see dozens of selections that could fit your criteria. You walk into Flight Club and you see 4,000 shoes. Flight Club's inventory doesn't even compare to the traditional brick and mortar's. I think that's still a huge "wow" factor, and partially why this industry exists. Additionally, the people on our Flight Club team are super passionate. They love engaging with customers, telling them about different shoes, ultimately making them feel inspired. Our team realizes that there are two stories behind every sneaker purchased. One story rich in the shoe's history and significance, and one more personal story about how that particular shoe makes the customer feel. Visiting Flight Club can make you feel both excitement and emotion, and that is really what the Flight Club experience is all about."

It's that experience that allows brick-and-mortar sneaker resale to not only survive but to thrive. The stores themselves are essentially museums, except the museum exhibits are available for purchase, your favorite celebrities have pointed out really cool parts of the museum that you might've otherwise missed, and they aren't popular field trip destinations *yet* (that I know of). It's an experience that's difficult to replicate via traditional brick and mortar retail, as Cohen alluded to, due mainly to the constraint of offering only primary market product, which points in many ways to the potential future convergence between primary retail and resale.

Sneaker Shopping is marketing perfection for the sneaker brands, whose retros and new releases alike are extolled by various persons of influence, for the consignment shops and retailers, whose in-store experiences are held up for millions to see, and for the sneaker economy as a whole, as the community is reminded of what drives us to this crazy hobby in the first place. Keep in mind, though, that, independent of all of that positive impact, it's also hugely popular media for a website and pop culture media brand, *Complex,* which covers a whole lot more than footwear or even fashion.

It's the efficacy of that media that inspires other content creators to try their own hands at the YouTube medium, and the proliferation of all of this content contributes to the broadening popularity of the sneaker collecting hobby. Undoubtedly though, *Sneaker Shopping* is the flagship property of sneaker media, if for no other reason than how awe-inspiring it is to watch basketball player, PJ Tucker, splash SIXTEEN THOUSAND DOLLARS on sneakers in one episode.

There's a lesson to be learned for brand, retailer, and marketplace alike from *Sneaker Shopping* and other similar content: authenticity is not difficult to spot, and when consumers see it, that's when deeper relationships with product and product stories are formed. *Sneaker Shopping* puts that authentic product connection front and center.

LONG TIME LISTENER, FIRST TIME CALLER

We can't always use our eyes to scan the pages of Sneaker News or Nice Kicks or to take in the latest episode of *Sneaker Shopping*. Driving, commuting, and exercising were once moments reserved for music, radio, or a leave of absence from media of all kinds. In recent years, however, the podcast has risen to new heights of popularity, filling those moments for people all over the world.

According to Edison Research's 2018 Infinite Dial study, 26% of Americans, or 73 million people, listen to a podcast monthly. 48 million Americans listen on a weekly basis, up six million people from the prior year. Podcast fans are now listening to an average of seven different podcasts weekly, up from five in 2017.[92] According to *Wired*, advertising revenue from podcasts was predicted to exceed $220 million by the end of 2017, which would represent an 85% increase over the prior year.[93] In summary, podcasts have absolutely exploded in popularity in recent years, reaching almost 100 million ears weekly.[94]

---

92 Baer, Jay. 2018. "The 13 Critical Podcast Statistics Of 2018 | Baer Facts". *Convince And Convert: Social Media Consulting And Content Marketing Consulting*. https://www.convinceandconvert.com/podcast-research/the-13-critical-podcast-statistics-of-2018/.

93 Quah, Nicholas. 2017. "The Three Fundamental Moments Of Podcasts' Crazy Rise". *WIRED*. https://www.wired.com/story/podcast-three-watershed-moments/.

94 Baer, Jay. 2018. "The 13 Critical Podcast Statistics Of 2018 | Baer Facts". *Convince And Convert: Social Media Consulting And Content Marketing Consulting*.

It comes as little surprise, then, that sneaker media has begun to seep into the podcast world. By no means is this foray on the same level in terms of scale and scope as the blog and YouTube presence – nor should it be, given the importance of visually examining sneakers. Indeed, it's a somewhat unnatural arena for the discussion of such a visual hobby. Still, search "sneakers" in your podcast application of choice, and you'll be greeted by a diverse assortment of listening options to satiate sneaker content cravings arising in moments where your eyes are required for other tasks.

Despite the lack of visual cues, sneaker podcasts have an important role to play: they underscore the sneaker world's intersection with sports, with music, with pop culture, and with broader fashion trends.

It's a nice reminder that the sneaker world, and thus the sneaker economy, certainly doesn't exist in isolation. It has roots in and continues to derive influence from athletics, music, pop culture, and fashion. Given enough time, any discussion of the LeBron 16 is bound to eventually arrive at a spirited debate of MJ vs. LeBron; that's just a scientific fact. Questioning the merits of the decision to release Yeezy's in greater scale lends itself with ease to conversation around Kanye West's latest music, his methods of releasing music, and *of course*, his politics. Detailing Puma's decision to become a WNBA sponsor serves as a natural segue to the discussion around merits of greater pay for that league's athletes and more eyeballs for its games.

The podcast format reminds us of the sneaker-collecting hobby's power as a social force; it sits centrally among many topics that we find interesting. It's why the podcast format can actually work despite the dearth of visuals: it takes that experience of talking shop with friends at the bar or at the sneaker store and makes it downloadable to listen to at your leisure.

Can it provide the self-sustaining, full-time careers that sneaker blogs and video channels have afforded their purveyors? Not likely. However, as a supplemental channel to reach either a bigger audience or your existing audience on a more frequent basis, particularly at times when it would not otherwise be possible? That's where the strategy has real merit, and that's why you see sneaker blogs like Sneaker Bar Detroit producing accompanying podcasts and YouTubers like Jacques Slade and former Nike engineer, Tiffany Beers, joining forces with creative sneaker storyteller, Nick Engvall, on the *Outside the Box* podcast.

It's hyper-targeted content that's reaching the right ears with the right tone, and it won't come as a big surprise when advertisers, whether within the sneaker world or a more tangential party, take greater notice.

***

The sneaker-collecting hobby has captured the passion of its participants with such intensity that a significant amount of people has been able to erect careers, paying jobs, from the dedicated effort to better inform and entertain other enthusiasts. This is truly a remarkable reality, and it speaks to the veracity with which those participants dedicate themselves to the sneaker world.

With the maturation of not only these sneaker media outlets, but also the development of proprietary blogs and content delivered by the secondary marketplaces, the dedicated consumer stands to benefit immensely. Better information, married with keen and astute observation, renders the consumer well-equipped to transact (or abstain) with confidence. No longer should a consumer pay $300 on the secondary market for a sneaker that is known to be restocking at retail in a few weeks' time. They need not rush to buy a sneaker at retail that has scarcely appeared on the blogs and popular Instagram profiles, and can instead sit comfortably and monitor the situation for possible discounts to follow.

Similarly, brands and retailers, in liaising with these outlets, are better able to target and reach consumers, and in some cases, shape perception in ways that were previously not possible. If they want a product launch to be a success, they can rest assured that there are vehicles that will reach those most active of sneaker consumers.

All of this serves to contribute to increased efficiency in a market that was once anything but efficient. The sneaker world is no longer the Wild West, and we have sneaker media to thank for that.

TAKEAWAYS FROM THE SNEAKONOMIST

- Trusted purveyors of news and information contribute to a market that functions more efficiently, as market participants are better armed to transact sensibly.

- In the era of sneaker media, market participants need not pay premiums for a sneaker soon to be available or still available at retail. Nor do they need to rush to buy a product that won't sell out and may be discounted.

- Product is far more efficiently connected with those who want it as a result of reliable sneaker media, whereas easily forging such a connection was previously a tall order.

- Sneaker media is no longer a cottage industry but rather a large and powerful force through which stories can be authentically relayed to interested audiences, the likes of which serve as ideal targets for advertisers.

- The sneaker economy is influenced by and influences vast other areas of popular culture, sitting at the center of a conversation around sports, music, and fashion that renders the hobby such a strong social glue.

CHAPTER 11

ANCILLARY SERVICES –
SAAS (SNEAKERS
AS A SERVICE!)

"Making money is a hobby that will complement any other hobbies you have, beautifully."

—Scott Alexander

When people think of Apple, they think of iPads, Macs, and of course, iPhones. But did you know that the company's services business has the power to generate in excess of $40 billion in revenue annually? While Apple's hardware sales growth is flattening out, the services provided to you on that hardware are a meaningful driver of the company's ability to drive the top line higher.

The App Store, Apple Pay, Apple Care, iTunes, and cloud services all quietly earn revenue from Apple product users on a daily basis, and in some cases, that revenue recurs annually. We opt in without a second thought, eager to preserve or further empower our beloved and expensive devices. We may agonize over the decision between the iPhone XS and XR for days or weeks, but with a few mindless swipes and taps, we pay to store photos, add to our music libraries, and purchase applications.

Sneakers don't have nearly the same utility as Smartphones, especially when the consumer already has enough pairs to fill a closet, but the point is this: wherever there is a market for valuable goods, ancillary services are sure to follow.

Certainly, central to the sneaker economy is the core activity of buying and selling sneakers, but the growth of the sneaker economy is not limited to the retailers and marketplaces, or even the media covering that core activity. Perhaps some of the most fascinating offshoots of the collecting hobby's growth are the ancillary products and services that have been hatched to make the collector's life easier.

The consumer's time is limited, and it's clear digesting all of the information spouted from the various fountains of sneaker-related news is akin to drinking water from a fire hose. Alas, services are spawned to digest and crystallize all of that information into the most critical details: where and when you can buy.

Not to mention, the internet is boundless. Even if we know where to buy, we can't thoroughly explore every e-commerce shop on a daily basis in search of the best deals. Boom, social media accounts and websites aggregating the very best deals are born.

Sneaker collectors like to keep their sneakers in mint condition, and that requires better product than household cleaners. Voila, a small sneaker cleaning and restoration industry is birthed.

It's entrepreneurship in its purest form: those with a passion for a hobby identify unmet needs and creatively work to solve the problem. That's how a community of sneaker collectors grows into a full-blown sneakonomy. It's really quite remarkable when you think about it. Businesses, hatched as true derivatives of the massive market for sneaker trade, are providing careers which, whether highly lucrative or not, pull people away from their perhaps unloved 9-to-5 and into a field where they can focus on their passion.

Do what you love, and you'll never work a day in your life.

NAVIGATING COMPLEXITY

Release day lines have largely come in off the street as queues form online. Sneaker riots are grinding to a halt. These are positive signs of industry maturation. As we now know, that maturation has also introduced a lot of complexity to the limited release system. Complexity can often be eradicated, or at least alleviated, even when it isn't always a top priority for brands or for retailers, who are confronted daily with an abundance of other matters requiring attention. When the complexity relates to products that fly off shelves, physical and virtual, the incentive to alleviate expediently is minimized. Thus, opportunity is born for third parties to devise clever solutions, for entrepreneurship to eradicate friction.

Most sneakerheads associate raffle draws with the inevitability of a loss, and when that's the sentiment of the consumer, it becomes more difficult for retailers to ensure they're cultivating meaningful relationships. Surely, retailers do great business, sell out their stock, and get some Instagram followers and a larger e-mail distribution list in the process, but are they forging lasting bonds and creating competitive advantage, or are they getting complacent?

Andrew Raisman's vision for his application, Copdate, is to help retailers avoid that complacency without sacrificing significant valuable time, effort, and resources. Meaningful customer lifetime value can be created from the release day opportunity, and Copdate aims to aid retailers in that pursuit. At its core, the application offers retailers the ability to make the release experience a more human one, displacing common industry methods, which do little to forge bonds with the consumer.

Those common industry methods are plentiful and largely ineffectual. Take for example the popular draw procedures employed by many retailers. Raisman highlights the drawbacks to the draw: "Unsophisticated raffle systems that the stores are using are like Swiss cheese – you can enter 100 times."

While well-intentioned and perhaps responsible for better social media engagement, the raffle's shortcomings relate mainly to the dehumanization of the process. It's difficult, given the ability for savvy veterans to game the system, to feel treated fairly by this process, even though there's no proactive effort to disadvantage any particular party. The problem, more so, is that there's no proactive effort to ensure that parties are *not* disadvantaged.

The reality is that there's no reasonable way to prevent sneakers from ending up in the hands of a reseller. Anyone among us could become one, even unintentionally. It's not a great leap: you buy a pair of sneakers, and either you don't love them as much as you thought you would, they don't fit properly, or someone offers you $800 on the spot. Just like that, you're a reseller.

It's extraordinarily difficult to prevent *one pair* of sneakers from ending up in the hands of *individual* buyers who may resell. It is, however, possible to level out the playing field so the reseller who typically finds a way to acquire five or six pairs from one retailer ends up with only one – this is part of the Copdate mission. If you don't believe there's a need for such a service, consider one retailer which received an e-mail from a reseller in the wake of the release of the Nike Acronym Presto looking to cancel the THIRTY orders he had placed across multiple e-mails.

Without giving away Copdate's secret sauce, Raisman explains, "We do have a lot of security measures and verification in place systematically and manually and mechanically to validate and flag all sorts of criteria to make sure it's as level a playing field as possible." When things don't go well and consumers feel wronged, the team aims to be front and center in terms of customer service.

Copdate spares consumers from the treachery of long release day lines and flawed draw systems. Copdate RSVP allows retailers to push notifications to their followers, notifying them that reservations for a release are open. Alternatively, retailers can opt for a more sophisticated, transparent raffle system, Copdate Lists, which allows users to enter with a few taps rather than going on a social media tear to secure more entries. Essentially, the offering is "releases-as-a-service."

Many of these boutiques are essentially mom-and-pop shops, not abundantly resourced global organizations, but don't confuse that with low sales volumes. The relatively small staffs of these stores are faced with choices on how to best allocate time daily. While they may want to innovate with regards to the release process, that may not feel like a strong return-on-time decision in the moment. So, just as stores opt to use accounting software rather than learn the nuts and bolts of accounting, they can turn to a subject matter expert on releases, a choice Raisman and the Copdate team believe can drive enhanced lifetime value through relationships which thrive beyond the release transaction.

Copdate is only one example of an ancillary service which has been spawned as a result of the thriving sneaker economy and its unfortunate pain points, and it's an interesting one given its benefits for both business and consumer. Naturally though, many applications mainly cater to the sneaker consumer. One such application is Sneaker Crush, which boasts over 5 million users and ranks in the top 35 free sports applications on the iTunes App Store.

Essentially, the application digests the daily deluge of sneaker news flow and organizes it into a tidy calendar of sneaker release dates. No longer do you have to religiously surf the pages of every single sneaker blog just to keep up with product drops. You likely will anyway, but your informational disadvantage will not be nearly as large as it once was if you chose not to.

For each sneaker listed on the application, there is a "Buy Now" button. Assuming the sneaker hasn't sold out, a click of that button will direct consumers to the sites of both traditional retailers and the likes of Stadium Goods. No Google search and subsequent weeding through results required. At its core, it's aggregation and cataloging of the flood of information emanating from sneaker media outlets daily. It's simple but highly popular and highly effective, as anything which can save a consumer time and effort often is. It provides a rescue vessel from uncertainty, FOMO, and the fear of informational disadvantage.

The relative inattention paid by larger players in any business to a given issue does not mean that there is no value to be extracted from providing an intricate, consumer-friendly solution to that issue. In fact, these are often the areas where the greatest opportunity exists for entrepreneurs to add value.

THE END OF THE BARGAIN HUNT

For a plethora of reasons, not every sneaker release can be limited. As we now know, those which aren't limited can sit on shelves, and, eventually, will be available at a reduced price. In days gone by, waiting for those discounts to come was a risky proposition.

How could you ensure that, when it happened (if it happened), you could be among the quickest to the site or the store to ensure that you picked up a discounted pair before they sold out? How could you even find out that it was happening? Checking the site or store every day? Hoping for an email distribution notifying you of a sale?

Bargain hunting was just that: a hunt.

Today, that hunt is over. The hunters bring the spoils of their work straight to your doorstep, free of any charge to the consumer. Those hunters are the deal sites and social media accounts, like Kicks Deals and Kicks Under Cost, which aggregate the very best deals on the internet, whether directly from a brand, a retail chain, or a boutique retailer. They disseminate these deals, Twitter serving as the primary vehicle, essentially all day every day, with links and relevant promo codes included.

The most diligent consumer will enable Twitter notifications for these accounts, ensuring they're first to the deal they've been patiently awaiting or to a surprise release. They are similarly useful follows on the mornings of big releases, as the Twitter feeds skillfully guide consumers to retailers where supply still exists but may be depleting fast.

These accounts serve a dual-pronged purpose. Of course, they provide consumers with timely information and access to deals they may have otherwise missed or deals they've been waiting for, enabling the purchase of product at favorable prices. However, they also play a valuable role for the brands and for the retailers. They aid in hastening the sell-through of product these parties are eager to offload in order to make room for new product, which can theoretically be sold at full price. With word of a new sale finding its way to the fingertips of the *right* consumers, stock can be cleared faster at that price, rather than potentially requiring further markdowns to clear at the whims of passersby. In a fashion world where speed is important, such expedience is critical and highlights the need for effective affiliate marketing.

Consumers can make note of which products are frequently appearing on the feeds of these deal-centric accounts. This will better inform future buying decisions and may also enable consumers to better place their fingers on the pulse of a brand's current strategic standing. Are they restricting the flow of supply to the market? Trying to clean inventories? Surveying these accounts over time, one can become quite good at predicting at the launch of the product whether or not it will eventually grace the feeds of Kicks Deals or Kicks Under Cost.

Says Kicks Deals founder, Dejan Pralica: "I feel like I have a pretty good knack of being able to predict it [discounting] just based off inventory that's being released or the excitement behind it. You can generally tell when something's going to go on sale, pretty early on for me."

He highlights one trend as an example of what he's noticed over the years. "Generally, the first colorway of a new model, especially with Nike basketball always tends to sell out right away, no matter what the shoe is," Pralica observes. "And I think part of that is it's an exciting new model. The other part of it is Nike, they manage their numbers really well as far as how much inventory, and that's part of a marketing strategy. Now, you're better off making your first one not limited, but limited enough that it's guaranteed that it's going to sell out when you forecast how many units to produce. Your second and third ones [colorways] have a little bit more legs behind them."

Pralica can see when one brand is getting more promotional than another, when product launches are struggling, and when overall brand heat is diminishing. This is the type of information that can be gleaned over time, and increasingly, consumers should begin paying attention. The casual consumer should graduate into a savvy one, if for no other reason than to save meaningful amounts of money. Unfortunately, to their own peril, most consumers haven't done so *yet*.

"So, the average person goes into the mall, looks at some shoes, and says, 'Hey, is there a discount right now?' If it happens to be 25% off this weekend, they'll buy it because they like it, and they'll move on it. To me, if that average consumer graduates to someone who's more into sneakers and can fall under the category of the sneakerhead, then they probably become a little smarter," notes Pralica. "And obviously I think anyone who follows us is a little bit more savvy because they're looking for the best deal possible to maximize savings. They want to know what's happening. They want to know what's going on. But even for us, if you look at it, we're probably the biggest sneaker deals link website on social in the U.S. and in Canada at this point, but our following, it's still nothing compared to the U.S. population and the percentage in math. It's growing. I didn't think it would be this big when we started it in 2011, and here we are and it's just getting bigger and bigger.

As the sneaker-collecting hobby grows, so too will the market for information, and with it, the popularity of Kicks Deals and others.

THE RISE OF THE SNEAKER
DETAILING INDUSTRY

A pair of sneakers is an exhaustible resource with a finite life. Sad, I know, but sneakers are indeed perishable, given enough time and enough wear.

Whether a sneakerhead intends to sell a used pair in the future or not, it physically pains many to notice the signs of their beloved sneakers' inevitable mortality: creasing, scuffs, dirt buildup, color fading, and glue losing its grip. For some, maintaining sneakers in the most pristine state possible is a critical part of the hobby, no matter how often they're worn. Others like to wear their sneakers and eventually sell them, both to finance and to make room for new members of the collection. In situations such as these, maintaining the sneakers in as pristine a condition as possible is of the utmost import in ensuring the realization of palatable value upon sale.

Not surprisingly, the entrepreneurial minds of the sneaker community have spawned businesses to meet the needs of the meticulous sneakerhead, the used reseller, and the one-in-one-out collector.

Of course, there are a plethora of sneaker-specific product offerings catered towards both removing dirt and protecting from stains and water damage. Companies like Crep Protect, Reshoevn8r, and Jason Markk offer a vast assortment of products attending to these specific needs: basic cleaning kits that include cleaning solution, a brush, and a microfiber cloth, sneaker wipes for messes that require immediate clean-up on the go, and repellent sprays. Beyond those detailing essentials are products for more targeted tasks or needs, including suede erasers, odor fresheners, laces pre-treated with repellent, and shoe trees to maintain shape.

The extent to which the sneaker collector can invest in the restoration of his or her collection is remarkable. In fact, SneakersER, based in Glasgow, offers not only many of the aforementioned cleaning products, but also an array of products intended for more demanding resurrections. The company sells dedicated midsole pens, to reinvigorate a dirty white midsole or enrich a fading black one, suede dyes, to make your old Adidas Gazelles look brand new again, and a number of paint pens, perfect for touching up finer details like logos and text.

With the help of these companies and their products, sneakers many years or countless wears old can look near new again.

There are also some products suited for needs that likely seem quite ridiculous to those outside of the sneaker world and even to some within it. For those that get anxious about kneeling or squatting due to the impending horror of creasing their beloved kicks, Sneaker Shields comes to the rescue with a toe insert that aims to reinforce the pristine shape of the shoe. The company offers a variety of inserts, all of which are priced between $10 and $20 and vary based on shoe type, size, rigidity, and comfort. Perhaps more absurdly, an adhesive product dubbed the Sole Protector can be installed on the sole of a sneaker to protect it from yellowing and dirt, which can be particularly bothersome on translucent or transparent soles. It sounds crazy – protecting the *bottom* of your shoes from dirt – but it's actually an extremely clever product for the fastidious sneaker collector and perhaps more importantly for the used reseller – after all, nowhere is significant wear more apparent than on the sole. Uppers and midsoles are fairly easy to clean, but soles? Not so much.

Sneaker detailing products are very much the beneficiaries of social media and of the buzz created by sneaker media outlets. For Jason Markk, the company owes much of its rise in popularity to both factors. Founder, Jason Angsuvarn credits early coverage from Hypebeast and Freshness Mag for the company's quick notoriety. As he conveyed to the *LA Times*, a happy accident documented on Instagram also changed the trajectory of the business: "Angsuvarn had just come out of a Jay-Z and Kanye West concert when he dropped bacon, mustard and onions from a street hot dog on his Air Jordan 3s, staining his beloved shoes. The next day, he documented the cleaning process on Instagram, inspiring a wave of before-and-after shots that has helped Jason Markk earn 215,000 followers on the app. Company sales tripled after the hot dog episode."[95]

---

95   Pierson, David. 2017. "As Sneakers Got More Expensive, Jason Mark Angsuvarn Built An Upscale Shoe-Shining Business". *Los Angeles Times*, 2017.

Correlation is not causation, but if you're going to believe in anything, believe in something dubbed "the hot dog episode" tripling a company's sales.

Today, cleaning videos and before-and-after shots litter the Instagram feeds of sneaker enthusiasts. Often, companies raise the stakes, dousing the most celebrated sneakers of the moment with cringe-inducing substances like ketchup, chocolate sauce, or mud. As it turns out, there's something immensely satisfying about watching a wrecked sneaker become new again before your eyes. It's not magic, but the marketing is.

As we previously discussed with regard to GOAT Clean, the ability to restore and rejuvenate tired sneakers changes the landscape for the resale markets, increasing the supply of palatable sneakers and the value they can fetch, but it can also influence the collector's buying patterns. Replacing grails no longer needs to happen with the same frequency as sneakers avoid the garbage can for a bit longer.

Passionate sneaker enthusiasts with an entrepreneurial mindset saw a sneaker-specific need and rose to satisfy that need with products that are easily tacked on at purchase on various retailer websites or in your local store. It's a simple, but highly effective business.

The sneaker transformation business doesn't begin and end with cleaning and detailing, though. In a sneaker economy filled with consumers hoping to flex and stand out, creative talents have risen to satiate that appetite with custom product, typically sold at highly premium prices. For example, sneaker artist Dan "Mache" Gamache has grown his own custom sneaker service into an enterprise generating six figures annually, often catering to highly visible athletes and celebrities with one-of-a-kind cleats and sneakers.[96] In many ways, he's erased the already blurred line between sneakers and art. Designer Chase Shiel, on the other hand, has launched limited runs of "Mars Yard" Air Max 1s, "Mars Yard" Air Jordan 1s, and "SW Corduroy" Air Jordan 1s in collaboration with Fiamma Studios, taking design inspiration from two of the hottest sneakers in recent memory and applying it in fresh ways to different silhouettes at four figure price tags. These are just two examples in an already bustling and feverishly growing aftermarket sneaker design and customization business.

Whether eager to render old favorites new again or to express themselves with unique pieces, sneaker collectors are well served by their peers, who have channeled their passions into value-additive businesses.

***

---

96   Guzman, Zack. 2018. "This 38-Year-Old Went From His Mom's Basement To Making Six Figures As NFL'S Go-To Sneaker Artist". *CNBC*. https://www.cnbc.com/2018/02/01/dan-mache-gamache-makes-six-figures-as-nfls-go-to-sneaker-artist.html.

Any time a hobby grows with the ferocity of sneaker collecting and consists of intensely passionate followers, diverse opportunities are created to plug the gaps left by the industry's key players. Those same intensely passionate followers are the ones who can rise to embrace the opportunity. In the process, they can create their dream jobs while simultaneously becoming a larger part of the fabric of the community. It's an opportunity not exclusive to the sneaker community, but to any hobby and its authentic participants.

Not every entrepreneur needs to create the next Amazon or even the next StockX or GOAT. Identify a passion. Identify a problem with that passion. Identify a way to solve that problem creatively and chase that solution. Like-minded consumers who share your passion will follow. That's how we got Sneaker News, Kicks Deals, Jason Markk, and countless other valuable contributors to the community – sneakonomic growth at its very finest.

TAKEAWAYS FROM THE SNEAKONOMIST

- With the growth of a market for any object of value comes a market for services related to the preservation or enhancement of that product – complementary services.
- While arenas for sneaker trade will continue to grow explosively, so too will the market for the ancillary services which accompany that activity.

- These complementary services can improve market efficiency by providing better information, better connecting consumer with product, and expediting sales processes.
- Entrepreneurs can plug gaps left by larger players in the sneaker economy, reducing friction in the process of creating their own dream jobs.

CHAPTER 12

HIGH PROFILE HIGH TOPS – THE EVOLVING ROLE OF INFLUENCERS

———

"That's where we really tipped over: when it used to be an emotional attachment to a brand or shoe and became much more about how much will you pay me to wear your product."

—Matt Powell, NPD Group

The rise of the sneaker economy has been invariably intertwined with the popularity of elite athletes and transcendent musicians and their links to sneaker culture on every rung of the ladder. With today's athletes not capturing imaginations in the same way as their predecessors and musicians jumping ship from brand to brand for the promise of greater monetary gain, it's fair to question whether the profile of effective influence is shifting.

Many of the most popular and coveted releases of the past few years have been devised through collaboration with celebrated designers and artists. Undoubtedly, aesthetics have always mattered deeply, but the need for accompanying athlete and musician influence has waned.

In this era, many questions of celebrity influence come to mind:

- Are marketing dollars better spent elsewhere?
- Is Yeezy's success the product of limited quantity, the Kanye West name, Kanye West's design influence, or all of the above?
- Would the needle have moved at all if Drake did follow through on his rumored switch from Nike to Adidas?
- Would the Cactus Jack Air Jordan 4 sell as well without Travis Scott's name attached?
- Can the cottage industry of YouTubers fill the influence void left by the famous?

As we examine the evolving role and face of influence in today's sneaker economy, these are the questions that we'll consider in great detail, arriving at the answers along the way.

THE FADING INFLUENCE OF
ATHLETES & MUSICIANS AND THE
ELUSIVE IMPACT OF YEEZY

Michael Jordan last won an NBA Championship twenty years ago, in 1998. He retired from the sport of basketball (for the last time, at least as far as we know) fifteen years ago, in 2003.

Still, his namesake sneakers, particularly those originating from the decade spanning 1986-1996, remain far and away the most celebrated signature sneakers in existence. We can debate MJ and LeBron's merits on the court until the cows come home, but there's *no* debate around sneaker supremacy. Zero.

LeBron James is a *huge* business for Nike – the Swoosh is currently on the sixteenth edition of the King's signature sneaker – but Jordan Brand is just that: a *brand*. And it's not just any brand; it accounts for approximately 10% of Nike's overall sales.

Now, Michael Jordan is an anomaly, a once in a century confluence of perfect timing, inhuman athletic ability, and commercial appeal. As such, it's difficult to see any athlete of today's era creating a sneaker legacy that even resembles that of His Airness. We have the closest thing possible to Jordan in on-court greatness, and yet we know that LeBron's sneaker legacy won't stack up.

Kyrie Irving and Paul George's signature basketball shoes have been immensely successful for Nike, but we can't say with confidence they'll be worth releasing in retro form a decade or two down the line. Perhaps this is revisionist history, but with Penny Hardaway, Allen Iverson, or even Deion Sanders and Ken Griffey, Jr., the marketing, the personalities, and the designs ensured the longevity of their signature sneakers years after the athlete called it quits.

Today, it's telling that football and baseball players rarely have signature sneakers anymore.

So, what happened? How did athletes lose their broad ability to ignite a fire in the sneaker community?

For one, as performance-focused sneakers have become more technologically advanced, they've simultaneously become less suited for lifestyle wear. At the same time, consumers are generally buying fewer performance-focused sneakers in general.

"If you go back the 40 years or so that this industry really has existed, we've always had at least one performance category that was in fashion that people wore as streetwear," says NPD Group's Matt Powell. "So, you could go back in the seventies and it was tennis. Tennis was this sexy sport. Everybody wanted to be like Jimmy and Chrissy. And then the jogging thing started, and people at cocktail parties were saying to each other, 'do you jog?'"

"Over the 40 years, we've seen the ebb and flow of different sports being in fashion, and I think we've just moved away from that. I think that this is about a fashion change, but I also think that today's consumer is not as serious about sport.

They're definitely serious about health and wellness but are not serious about sport. And so, they don't define themselves as a runner or as a bicycler, but they're doing those activities. I think that because they're much more lighthearted and much less serious in their approach, they don't need an extensive technical product to do those sports. So, I think you layer that on top of it. We're now [in 2018] in the fourth year of not having a single performance category trending positively and that is really uncharted territory for the industry."

With performance product demand waning and brands not eager to develop signature, lifestyle shoes (LeBron's Icon John Elliott collaboration and Nike attempts with Russell Westbrook the exceptions), it's difficult to see a path for the namesakes of today's athletes to take hold in the sneaker community. The broad lack of athlete-centric lifestyle footwear initiative, though, suggests that resources are not best spent trying to convert athlete influence into sales.

Musicians have exerted similarly potent influence in the sneaker community dating back to the roots of modern hip-hop in the 1970s. Perhaps the most visually memorable example of the inextricable link between pop culture and sneakers was Run-D.M.C.'s 1986 hit, "My Adidas," which catapulted Adidas Superstars to a new stratosphere.

Incredibly, that song was written and produced in the absence of an actual endorsement deal. As written by Gary Warnett on fashion retail site, *Mr. Porter*: "A co-manager of the group, future Def Jam honcho Mr. Lyor Cohen, saw the potential to get an endorsement and brought Adidas executive Mr. Angelo Anastasio to witness a moment when the rappers urged the audience to hold up their sneakers as "My Adidas" was performed. At the Madison Square Garden leg of the tour on 19 July 1986, more Adidas executives watched those aloft shoes. Along with Mr. Cohen's brokering and a video in which the group made a brief a capella performance to Adidas and then shouted "GIVE US A MILLION DOLLARS!," this resulted in a then-unprecedented for any musician – let alone a hip-hop act – $1m dollar endorsement deal."[97]

It's extremely noteworthy that the song came first – not the deal. With no deal inked, the group's exaltation of the popular style exuded authenticity, and fans and consumers responded in heaps.

Matt Powell frequently comments on the waning influence of major athletes and musicians in today's retail environment, and it's worth revisiting his quote that began the chapter. "That's where we really tipped over: when it used to be an emotional attachment to a brand or shoe and became much more about how much will you pay me to wear your product," says Powell, on the shift that triggered a downturn in clout. "If you go back on the original beginnings of seeing celebrity influencers, that was about, 'My mom bought me

97   Warnett, Gary. 2016. "How Run-DMC Earned Their Adidas Stripes".
     The Daily | MR PORTER. https://www.mrporter.com/daily/how-run-dmc-earned-their-adidas-stripes/939.

those shoes,' 'That was the first basketball shoe I ever had,' or 'I've worn this brand since I was a kid, and I love this brand!'. So, there was an authenticity, if you will, to the endorsement. I think we've moved away from that to the point where it's just whoever pays me the most, I'm going to wear their shoes."

"I think where we are right now is we've reached the point where the consumer understands how false, how phony this message is and they've started to lose interest."

It calls to mind the recent rumors surrounding Drake's shift from his longstanding relationship with Nike to a new deal with Adidas. While it seems that the transition ultimately fell through, the rumored move was met with confusion. Drake had been an unrelenting, outspoken Nike and Jordan fan for years. If and when he started to wear three stripes, would consumers really be inclined to do the same?

Did they even care he wore Jordan? There's actually concrete evidence to suggest the answer is no. Before the decision to switch became heavily rumored, Jordan brand had a Drake and Toronto themed Jordan IV in the works for release. Images had leaked of the black, purple, and red sneaker with Drake's signature on the tongue. A few months later, the sneaker did indeed release, the signature removed, and they sold out with relative ease anyway.

Perhaps the exception to the trend of waning influence has been Kanye West's Yeezy partnership with Adidas, which was reportedly agreed to in 2013 for a sum of $10 million and later expanded in 2016. Undoubtedly, the partnership has created meaningful buzz for the brand, with Yeezys among the most coveted releases of the last several years. Due to the limited quantities that made them so coveted, though, it's difficult to see the partnership as the financial needle mover for Adidas many would perceive it to be.

At least, that *was* the case until recently, when the strategy shifted toward more democratization, i.e. more supply. Powell has long argued the positive financial ramifications of Yeezy have been less than meaningful to Adidas, and he foresees an impending dilution of the Yeezy brand: "I would argue in the case of Yeezy that we're already starting to see the resale market collapse on that as well because supply is becoming too great. Adidas is trying to get their $10 million investment back and they're going to kill it at some point."

West, of course, would beg to differ. In fact, he went so far as to argue in the spring of 2018 that he makes more money off shoes than Michael Jordan, a claim that was met with great skepticism from, well, pretty much everybody.

There is evidence in the market that suggests the supply increase may saturate the market and weaken brand standing. "I wouldn't be surprised if those Yeezys are not sold out for a couple of days. I personally think they're doing it from a revenue standpoint," says KicksDeals founder Dejan Pralica on the fall 2018 re-release of the white Yeezy 350V2. "Their sales are decelerating. They're discounting heavily. I would have to imagine they're not getting the revenue that they want to right now based on how much they're discounting.

And I think this one's been delayed two or three times now, which to me just probably means they decided to ramp up production."

Indeed, he was correct. Those pairs did not fully sell out for a number of days. Still, it bears wondering whether West's influence has had a positive impact beyond the Yeezy brand itself, and whether that influence is based on his name or his design and stylistic influence. Matt Halfhill, of Nice Kicks, offers a counterpoint to those considering only the sales volume of Yeezy.

"You need a really good lens when you're looking at these things," explains Halfhill. "You have to be able to have your eyes open to the full market when you analyze each small part. And I think that's why there's been strife about whether Kanye is influential: tracking the efficacy of Kanye associated only with Kanye's shoes. That Tubular clearly looked just like a 350, but Kanye doesn't get any credit via statistical analysis. But let's be honest, why was that shoe selling?"

Halfhill refers to the Adidas Tubular Shadow. The Tubular line was relaunched by Adidas in 2014, and in 2016, the brand released a Tubular model, the Shadow, which aesthetically resembled the Adidas Yeezy Boost 350. According to Halfhill, it saw the greatest sell-through of any model from the Adidas Tubular series to date. The aesthetic influence didn't end there, however.

"The Continental clearly received benefit from the success of the Calabasas! People rocking track pants with white tennis sneakers – sure, some people were wearing this style, but it wasn't nearly as popular until after you saw Adidas release the Calabasas tennis sneaker and Calabasas pants. You have to give credit where credit is due! And that doesn't always show up in the Excel spreadsheet."

He raises an important point. The popular Yeezy aesthetic has permeated from the Yeezy brand and into Adidas general releases over the past few years, with some degree of success. The Adidas Tubular Shadow does indeed very closely resemble the Yeezy 350, and the launch of the Adidas Continental did follow very closely in the wake of the Yeezy Powerphase Calabasas. By no means is this aesthetic bleed a new trend, either. Consider, for example, the popularization by Jordan of black and red colorways starting with the "Banned" Jordan 1. Influence isn't confined to aesthetics alone, though. Similarly difficult to quantify but undeniably impactful was Yeezy's influence on the broader popularity of Adidas Boost technology, just as Jordan catalyzed the success of Nike Air.

While follow-on offerings like the Shadow don't carry the Yeezy name and they don't carry the Yeezy resale market, they do still sell in greater volumes, which begs the question: do Yeezy sneakers become just another shoe as supply increases, or can West's influence keep demand (and thus prices) elevated as quantities grow more abundant?

We know that limited quantity alone isn't enough to sell shoes – West's name meant everything to the generation of initial hype surrounding the Yeezy brand. But don't confuse hype and lucrative financial outcomes as synonymous. What seems increasingly likely is that West's influence is not enough to *sustain* the hype as supply floods the market to create such a financial outcome.

As the democratization unfolds, we're seeing early returns suggest that, in the absence of scarcity, Yeezys won't continue to command frenzied crowds. When the "Zebra" Yeezy 350 V2 re-released in November of 2018, the tact seemed similar to that of iconic Jordan re-releases like the Space Jam or the Black Cement 3: enough supply so most who want them can get them, but not enough to completely erode resale premiums. Sizes could be found at retailers in the days following the release, but overall, they were quickly digested by the market. Nonetheless, resale prices that once lingered well above $500 and $600 dropped to the mid $200s.

This release won't tell the whole story – it was the first chance for the vast majority who originally missed out to have an earnest crack at acquisition. The real story comes next, when consumers *know* that they can get a pair.

For the moment though, it seems that the increasingly accessible 350 V2 releases have not hampered the desirability of more scarce newcomers. The Yeezy 700 V2 "Static" and Yeezy 350 V2 "Static Reflective" may both have been in the conversation for sneaker of the year in 2018 if not released in late December, with their resale prices quickly rising to those familiar, elevated levels.

Adidas always faced a tough choice with regard to selecting the right time to better monetize the partnership. It's akin to Mark Zuckerberg and Eduardo Saverin arguing over whether or not to sell advertising space on Facebook in its early days; it would be like ending the party at 11, just when it's getting cool. Taking steps to truly monetize the Yeezy partnership would always make the democratized sneakers less cool as perceived by the broader community.

It's precisely that trade-off that makes it difficult to recognize huge returns on any influencer investment of great scale, not just West's alone.

DESIGNER AS INFLUENCER: WHO KNEW INSPIRED AESTHETICS MATTERED?

No man on earth was more important to the sneaker community in 2017 and 2018 than Virgil Abloh.

In fact, if you ask *TIME*, he was one of the 100 most influential people *on Earth* in 2018 – not the sneaker world, I'm talking about the freaking planet *Earth*.

The honor of being one of *TIME's* most 100 influential people is bestowed for good reason. Abloh did not simply partner with Nike on a collection of sneakers which would become some of the most popular and sought-after in recent years. He demonstrated what it truly means to infuse design with culture, to tell a story through design, and to appreciate the past while viewing it through a lens that is uniquely modern.

Before we delve into Abloh and Nike's smash success that was "The Ten" collection, a reconstruction of ten iconic Nike sneakers, it's important to understand what made Virgil Abloh the no-brainer choice for such a collaboration. Since 2002, Abloh has served as creative director for Kanye West, but his own personal endeavors as a designer began in earnest in 2012 with the launch of his first label, "Pyrex Vision". That label was launched when Abloh screen-printed "Pyrex 23" on Rugby Ralph Lauren flannels that he had acquired at a discount and sold them at a significant premium.[98]

Pyrex's vision differed from that of traditional high-fashion in a significant way, one that's fueled much of Abloh's success: a willingness to allow fashion to be influenced by youth rather than insisting upon the opposite. "We saw kids from Harlem presenting Rick Owens and Raf Simons in a different way that connected directly to culture and Pyrex Vision became the aesthetic of that," Abloh told the *Business of Fashion*. "[Until then] high-fashion was dictating what was happening in culture and for the first time that had been reversed by this generation of influential kids. That, in turn, affected the market."[99]

---

98 Solway, Diane. 2017. "Virgil Abloh And His Army Of Disruptors: How He Became The King Of Social Media Superinfluencers". *W Magazine*. https://www.wmagazine.com/story/virgil-abloh-off-white-kanye-west-raf-simons.

99 Morency, Christopher. 2016. "The Unlikely Success Of Virgil Abloh". *The Business Of Fashion*. https://www.businessoffashion.com/articles/intelligence/the-unlikely-success-of-virgil-abloh-off-white.

One year later, Abloh launched Milan-based "Off-White," named for its place between what had traditionally been a black-and-white, binary choice between high fashion and street culture. The brand has sustained massive success and explosive growth, with celebrities of various import and influence frequently spotted cloaked in Off-White product. The label is geared at elevating street-wear, which at one point had no place in high-fashion, while simultaneously breaking down the traditional barrier between designer and consumer. Off-White is meant to be worn, exuding a look that is simultaneously subtle high-fashion and casual.

As has always been the case, Abloh feeds off youth culture and allows youth culture to drive the label's popularity, maintaining an inner circle of young social media influencers who he encourages to pursue their own design creativity. As Abloh told *GQ*, the old model of industry "gatekeepers" is primed for disruption by youth: "Right now, the whole gatekeeper system is so screwed up. They lost their footing. It's raining. Kids can push them over. I know kids who are half my age who can kill a brand on a whim, make it uncool if they want to."[100]

Abloh's integration with and understanding of culture is not limited to fashion. The renaissance man frequently DJs across the globe. It's not uncommon for Abloh to take the stage at major festivals, including Lollapalooza, Coachella,

---

100 Baron, Zach. 2016. "The Life Of Virgil Abloh, Street-Style Godhead". *GQ*. https://www.gq.com/story/virgil-abloh-profile.

Electric Zoo, and Ultra. The man is somewhat of a nuclear reactor for culture, ingesting it globally through various mediums of art, music, and design, harvesting it, and spreading it through his own art, music, and design.

"You have three minutes to read the room, play a song, and impress the crowd," Abloh told W *Magazine* regarding his DJ experience. "Then you have to figure out how to style this group of songs together so it's one point of view. I'm literally just litmus-testing the culture."[101]

This is exactly the type of figure who can be trusted to reinvigorate brand heat for an array of iconic Nike sneakers, and that's precisely what Nike set out to do in enlisting Abloh for "The Ten" collection. The concept was simple at face value but intricate in execution: reconstruct ten Nike icons to better reflect the culture of today, while still highlighting how the innovation of each sneaker fit into broader Nike history.

In a textbook on the creation of the collection released by Nike, Nike VP of Footwear Design, Andy Caine, describes what the collection accomplished: "Our obsession with serving the athlete and building cutting-edge, pioneering performance products coupled with Virgil's intense curiosity, allowed us to, together, recontextualize these iconic shoes for a new generation of Nike enthusiasts. Many of our icons are classics, and our ability to iterate allows them to remain

---

101 Solway, Diane. 2017. "Virgil Abloh And His Army Of Disruptors: How He Became The King Of Social Media Superinfluencers". W *Magazine*.

as distinctly relevant and as culturally in stride now, as they were when they were first introduced."[102]

In the same book, Abloh details his own vision for the cultural significance of the collection:

"I believe that culture moves on this sort of wavelength. That a young generation possesses ideas that an older generation can now learn from in any genre, whether it's art, fashion, architecture, music. I see it as a renaissance instead of an Armageddon. I wanted to give people the actual information, allow them to see what year these shoes are from, and how they place in the overall history of the brand. So, I looked at this whole project as like passing the baton and doing right by all that innovation, but adding a lifestyle layer to it, to say that these shoes are icons, they transcended into another space, highlighting what emotional attachment these objects [have]... or how we can now look at them in 2017 and understand how important they were in the past. This project to me was especially important, not just for the sneaker itself, but to make a platform that a generation can see themselves in, that we obsess about, but also see a larger story."[103]

The ten sneakers selected for the collection were the Air Jordan 1, the Nike Blazer, the Nike Air Max 90, the Nike Presto, the Nike Air VaporMax, the Converse Chuck Taylor,

---

102 *"TEXTBOOK"*. 2018. Ebook. Nike. https://content.nike.com/content/dam/one-nike/en_us/season-2018-su/NikeLab/TEN/TEXTBOOK.pdf.
103 Ibid.

the Nike Air Max 97, the Nike Air Force 1, the Nike React Hyperdunk, and the Nike Zoom Fly. The former five were developed using a "revealing" design approach, in which Abloh made hefty use of an X-ACTO blade to strip away layers of each sneaker to "reveal" its core design elements and innovations. The latter five were developed using a "ghosting" approach, in which transparent outer layers were used to provide a window into the core of the sneaker. Both approaches led to the creation of sneakers that, while recognizable as the iconic silhouette, were imbued with an unfamiliar but appealing aesthetic.

How do you take an iconic sneaker, something that's already beloved and perceived as design excellence, and change it to contextualize it for a new generation while preserving what prior generations loved about it? Abloh did not downplay the magnitude of such a challenge. "It's potentially career suicide," he explained in the Nike textbook, "taking ten things that are iconic and adding a new lens."[104]

Except, Abloh wasn't about to commit career suicide, because he had a terrific answer to that question.

His solution was to reduce and remove – strip away certain panels and design elements – to highlight the core of the sneaker and to clarify the view of the innovation that made it an icon in the first place. The collection became celebration through simplification. The sneakers are black,

---

104 Ibid.

and the sneakers are white, yes, but they're not simply black and white colorways, a perception Abloh knew he needed to avoid. "When you expose the shoe, it's a design approach that... it was the only thing left," said Abloh in the Nike text. "If you tell some kid off the street that Off-White's doing an Air Force 1, they've seen enough Air Force 1s to say, "Oh it's probably gonna have black and white lines." I was like, I need to over-deliver, find a credible design language and have a reason for it."[105]

It's important to understand many of these icons were an innovation *for the athlete* in one way or another. Often, it has been athletic innovation which has allowed Nike sneakers to become icons, and that's a trend for which Nike would welcome a return to prevalence. In the case of sneakers like the VaporMax or the Zoom Fly, both of which were included in "The Ten," Virgil was empowered to design before either really achieved commercial success in their original form. With these models, he was simultaneously highlighting the properties which make them innovative while also creating an aesthetic which made them feel like decades-long stalwarts of sneaker culture. Just by including them in this group of beloved sneakers, Nike had created a reality in which these models could be icons by association.

The proliferation of "The Ten" into sneaker culture began with Virgil's Air Jordan 1, crafted in the iconic red, black, and

---

105 Ibid.

white "Chicago" colorway, but of course, bearing a vastly distinct aesthetic to the original. Slowly but surely, it seemed that the sneaker found its way onto the foot of every single popular NBA Nike athlete and every hip-hop musician. Every single one of those individuals had been photographed in the sneaker, and every single one of those photographs found its way onto Instagram, and every one of those Instagrams was reproduced and shared in droves.

Simply put: the Off-White Jordan was *everywhere* you looked.

In many cases, Virgil himself had taken a marker to the sneaker, writing the recipient's name or nickname after the "AIR" text on the midsole. For example, the greatest tennis player of all time, famed sneaker collector, and former Nike athlete Roger Federer created significant buzz by practicing in the Off-White Jordans at the 2017 US Open. He proudly traversed the court with his trademark grace in his very own "Air Federers," as transcribed by Virgil Abloh. Drake was spotted in "Air Canadas." A$AP Rocky received "Pretty Flackos," a nod to one of his popular songs.

While other models found their way onto celebrity feet (John Mayer, for example, received "Air Mayer" Air Max 90s – a known favorite of the musician's), it was the distribution of Off-White Jordans to a vast assortment of celebrities which created an unstoppable freight train of hype. The old adage that the richer you become, the more free stuff you receive held particularly true in this case.

By the time the collection was set for release via the Nike SNKRS application in November of 2017, the first real chance for the general public to capture a pair at retail, the hype had reached a fever pitch. The release of each pair was staggered throughout the day. Take it from someone who opened the app and desperately tried to reach "Pending" status for each of the sneakers: November 20th was a tough day for collectors.

Such was the number of desperate competitors (and most certainly, bots) that the application suffered from various, severe performance issues. In fact, due to the overwhelming demand and the technical issues that come with it, Nike had already been forced to cancel a digital raffle via the SNKRS app, originally scheduled for November 9th.

Needless to say, this writer took an L on all nine pairs (the Converse Chuck Taylors did not release until 2018), and I was hardly alone in my failure.

The unprecedented demand, countered by carefully man-aged supply from Nike, created extreme secondary market fervor. That extreme fervor, not necessarily uncommon for one style, was unheard of for an entire *collection*. Sneaker and streetwear blog, *Highsnobiety*, chronicled and analyzed the resale value of the collection on the StockX marketplace. The Air Jordan 1 peaked at over $2300. The Presto cleared $1500. The VaporMax and Air Force 1 both eclipsed $1000, while the Blazer came up just short of four figures, and the Air Max 90, Air Max 97, and Zoom Fly all nestled in between $700 and

$900. The Hyperdunk brings up the rear in the mid $600s.[106] The Converse Chuck Taylor, which released later, peaked at a somewhat fluky $2500 on StockX, but we can safely assume that the top of its 12-month trading range, $1,026, is a more apt measure of its resale ceiling.

"The Ten" collection was not just a boon for resellers, however. In some ways, Nike was leaning on this collaboration with Virgil Abloh to reignite a cooling Jordan Brand and its storytelling. "When we connect the right product with the strength of the Jordan's storytelling, the results are incredible," explained Trevor Edwards on the company's Q2 2018 earnings call. "For instance, the Air Jordan 1 was the most coveted product in The Ten collection, cementing its position as 2017's Shoe of the Year."[107]

Mark Parker elaborated further: "We saw incredible demand for the Virgil Abloh collaboration with respect to 10 of NIKE's most iconic styles, ranging from the Jordan 1 to the Air Force 1, to the Presto to the Blazer and beyond. All of these launches of new innovative products in Q2 were met with extraordinary demand, expanding and creating new energy within NIKE's unrivaled portfolio of power franchises."[108]

---

106 Gorsler, Fabian. 2018. "OFF-WHITE X Nike Sneakers: An Analysis Of Resell Prices". *Highsnobiety*. https://www.highsnobiety.com/p/off-white-nike-resell-price-analysis/.

107 "FY 2018 Q2 Earnings Release Conference Call Transcript". 2017. *Nike, Inc. – Investor Relations.*

108 Ibid.

Abloh and Off-White had provided the brand and its consumers with a fresh lens through which icons could be viewed, context which could re-energize old franchises and provide a launch pad for newer ones expected to take up the mantle of iconic Nike innovation. It comes as little surprise, then, that the original "The Ten" collection would not be the last and only iterations of the Nike and Off-White collaboration. Instead, a steady stream of Off-White releases has persisted.

The newer releases do not stack up to their predecessors in terms of resale market flourish, perhaps due to gravity bringing the hype back to earth from unsustainable heights, but more likely due to increased supply (as was almost certainly the case for the University Blue Jordans in comparison to the "Chicago" Off-White original). Nonetheless, they remain incredibly sought-after commodities.

For context, more recently released models such as the aforementioned University Blue Jordan 1, and the all-white and all-black Prestos, sell for half or a little bit less than half of their predecessor's going rate on the secondary market. Keep in mind, however, we're talking about half of $2500 or $1500; the point being that these remain among the most highly coveted sneaker releases of the year and that saturation remains a laughably distant fear.

For the moment, the collaboration shows few signs of slowing. Abloh was tabbed to dress one of the most dominant athletes of all time, male or female, Serena Williams, for the

2018 US Open. The collection features new colorways of The Ten's Nike Blazer and Nike Air Max 97. As he so often does, Virgil understood very well the desired look of the intended subject, aiming to create an aesthetic which would be about "expressing Serena's spirit with each swing of the racket", as he conveyed to *Vogue*.[109] The satisfied tennis star relayed the success of his efforts, noting "It really embodies what I always say: that you can be strong and beautiful at the same time."[110]

The collaboration's success can be attributed to both Abloh's cultural fluency and his reverence for what makes each icon such a critical piece of the Nike story. It's this cultural fluency and the ability to modernize icons which makes the designer such a comet of popularity in today's fashion world.

Abloh let the *Business of Fashion* in on one of his goals back in September of 2016: "The end goal is to modernise fashion and steer a [fashion] house, because I believe in the modernisation of these storied brands. I want to prove this new iteration of fashion and use Off-White as a case study for these new ideas that relate to current consumers, because at the end of the day it's an industry I believe in."[111]

109 Newbold, Alice. 2018. "What Are Serena Williams And Virgil Abloh Up To?". *Vogue.Co.Uk*. https://www.vogue.co.uk/article/serena-williams-off-white-virgil-abloh-trainer-collaboration.

110 Yotka, Steff. 2018. "Serena Williams Will Return To The U.S. Open In Virgil Abloh X Nike". *Vogue*. https://www.vogue.com/article/serena-williams-us-open-virgil-abloh-x-nike.

111 Morency, Christopher. 2016. "The Unlikely Success Of Virgil Abloh". *The Business Of Fashion*.

Mission accomplished. Goal attained.

In March of 2018, Louis Vuitton named Virgil Abloh its new artistic director of menswear. In the process, he became the first black man in the label's 164-year history to assume the role and certainly the first from Rockford, Illinois. With Louis Vuitton, he will be tasked again with melding luxury and high fashion with his impeccable understanding of streetwear and relatability. Sneakers will play a role in the new gig, and his first design for Louis Vuitton, a leather high top, bears clear classic inspiration.

Once again, the designer, becoming more iconic in his own right every day, will apply his cultural fluency and his respect for the classics to the process of recontextualization for a new audience under a new banner. While he's doing that, his Nike collaborations will continue to capture the undivided interest of the sneaker community at large.

A modern-day renaissance man indeed.

***

Certainly, Virgil is the most successful example of this growing trend – the increasing prevalence of designer as influencer. But there are countless other examples where it's clear the designer's vision and story conveyed through the sneaker's design have captured the attention and hearts of the consumer. John Elliott's collaboration with Nike on the LeBron Icon quickly sold out despite a high retail price of

$250. Just Don Jordan 2s, devised by streetwear designer Don C, command huge prices on the secondary market, and his 2018 collaboration with Nike on the Jordan Legacy 312 flew off shelves at retail, despite waning resale values.

Streetwear designer Jerry Lorenzo's Nike Air Fear of God 1 was one of the most coveted releases of 2018, and bears an extremely distinct and fresh aesthetic. In fact, it's somewhat of a rarity for a collaborator to design an entirely new silhouette from the ground up. Typically, they are enlisted to put their own spin on an existing model.

Artists too can have a huge influence on product sales and on value. The NikeCraft Mars Yard sneaker is among the most expensive on the secondary market, garnering in excess of $2,000. The sneaker was designed by contemporary artist, Tom Sachs, as a high-performance, high-durability sneaker, with inspiration from his interactions with NASA. Material choice was absolutely critical to the design and the overall aesthetic, with many materials included in their natural, undyed state. "I have always embraced flaws," Sachs told Nike. "The natural polyurethane midsole shows wear. The shoe shows evidence of experiences, even the little bits of tongue that may flake off are like forensic bread crumbs. People wear their scars with pride, so that's another reason why we don't polish the materials away — it's storytelling.

Rock your shoes dirty to say, 'I wear my shoes. I do things with my life. Behold the evidence of my actions.'"[112]

American artist and designer, KAWS, collaborated with Jordan on two colorways of the Jordan 4, one grey suede and one black suede. The grey version commands eye-popping four figure prices on the secondary market. To the untrained eye, it looks like an unspectacular, monochromatic grey Jordan 4, and yet it's a $1000+ sneaker. Such adoration speaks to the influence that artists and designers can now affect on the sneaker community at large.

That Virgil, KAWS, and Tom Sachs can generate such hype suggests we've entered a new era, in which design ethos and storytelling matter more than the simple attachment of a famous name to a product. It may be for just the same reason in part, for the contributions in *design* Kanye West has made with Yeezy rather than the simple association of his name with Adidas, that the line has known such success and adoration.

AUTHENTIC VOICES GROW LOUDER

Today, influence need not come only from a famous name or from a truly inspired product design. Rather, it can also originate from the voices of a new class of trusted voices, those who have authentically built devoted and sincere followings, seemingly from nothing, which are transportable

---

112 "Nike And Tom Sachs Introduce The Nikecraft Mars Yard 2.0". 2017. *Nike News.* https://news.nike.com/news/tom-sachs-mars-yard-2-0.

across YouTube and Instagram. Individuals like Jacques Slade (1mm YouTube subscribers and counting) and Foamer Simpson (375k subscribers) provide their respective (enormous) communities with content on a nearly daily basis.

We're not talking about individuals rambling into their iPhone cameras about what they like or dislike about a shoe, setting new marks every day for how many times they can say "these are super dope." Don't get me wrong, there's A LOT of that out there. But those who have risen above the crop have found ways to produce differentiated content of an extremely high-quality. They eschew the traditional 'confessional' model, avoid the mundane narration of a few sneaker pictures, and produce videos replete with cut scenes, music, thought-provoking commentary, and diversity of visuals.

The core tenets of the content don't vary tremendously; it all generally centers around sneaker unboxings, reviews, and product comparisons. The differentiation comes via the time and effort put into shooting and editing, but more importantly, through the authenticity of voice. They share their passion for sneakers and articulate it in unique and entertaining ways to build and maintain audiences of scale.

Given these captive audiences, it's not surprising to see sneaker brands and especially retailers (the chains like Champs Sports, Hibbett Sports, and Foot Locker are frequent donors) sending product to these voices on a regular basis. In doing so, they gain instant visibility with hundreds of thousands of their most likely customers for just the cost of a handful of pairs of free sneakers. It's highly targeted, largely inexpensive marketing. Consequently, influencer marketing is an area many of these parties are focusing on with increased vigor – often dedicating staff members specifically to the efforts. That low cost comes at the expense of complete control of the story. While it's not likely these personalities will absolutely pan a free product that's been sent to their doorstep, it's absolutely critical they be honest about what they like, and more importantly, dislike about the product.

Without that honesty and a fair but critical eye, they would be nothing but mouthpieces for the brands.

Matt Powell describes the drivers of the efficacy of this new class of influencer: "It's the sincerity of the smaller influencers, the people who really care about the product, who aren't compensated, or are and get some free stuff, but there's no real compensation here."

Consumers today have a more accurate BS meter – they know when they're being sold to. They know when somebody is being paid to sling product. That's not a program that they're going to tune into on a daily basis. This of course speaks to the authenticity of those that have amassed followings. These followings grant them access to enviable assortments of product, and yet, the followings persist when those products appear in content because they are treated with an honest and fair voice.

It's additionally noteworthy that many of these voices are *reachable* to their audiences. These are not musicians and athletes, sequestered from the rest of society and seemingly untouchable. These are individuals who are interacting with their followings in the comment sections and on Instagram. They participate in *dialogues*, not just monologues. It's a two-way conversation, they contribute to and learn from their communities. That connectivity is critical to building a reputation for authenticity, and it's not brain surgery. It's simply being a human being.

The messaging from these voices is not phony, and in a world where athletes and musicians trade allegiance for dollars, there are many ears eager to listen to the voice of an authentic, real, and entertaining peer.

***

The use of marketing dollars on influencers of various kinds bears watching in the years to come. The evidence is beginning to suggest the juice isn't worth the squeeze.

Dollars shadily spent on recruiting high school basketball athletes to schools affiliated with certain brands no longer seem worthwhile, even when you *exclude* the FBI involvement, NCAA violations, and reputational damage that came with the discovery of those practices. Musicians aren't capable of bringing an increasingly smart consumer with them as they switch from brand to brand; that consumer doesn't want to follow the fattening of the musician's wallet with the thinning of their own. Puma made a PR splash in winning the race to ink the newest NBA rookies on the block to contracts, but what does that say about the other brands? Surely, Nike and Adidas could outspend if they so chose, but they conceded those spoils to Puma. Puma needs backing to re-launch its basketball efforts from scratch, but those endorsement dollars can only take them so far. They must be followed by inspired, aesthetically appealing product.

As we know, storytelling matters in sneakers, and with these high-profile individuals comes the potential for powerful storytelling. Where that storytelling is beginning to fall short, however, is authenticity.

The consumer is aware of the monetary value of sneaker contracts. It's not enough for a player or a musician to get paid, wear the sneakers, and look cool doing it. There has to be an authentic voice attached and an aesthetic that matches that voice for an effective story to be told. Otherwise, the sizable investment is wasted.

TAKEAWAYS FROM THE SNEAKONOMIST

- Athlete endorsement no longer carries the same influence it used to, due to both waning authenticity around deals and a consumer who is not receptive to today's performance product.
- Musicians, who have demonstrated a willingness to skip from brand to brand based on compensation, can't drive meaningful financial outcomes on their names alone.

Their name must be accompanied by inspired aesthetics and powerful storytelling.

- Designers and artists have filled the influence void left by athletes and musicians, captivating consumers with rich design ethos and fresh aesthetics.
- Hype and lucrative financial outcomes are not inter-changeable concepts. Hype can ensure limited releases sell-out swiftly, but influence and the corresponding hype may not drive meaningful financial gain to the brand unless it can be successfully maintained in step with mass-market supply.
- On the flip side of that coin, the efficacy of influence can't be measured in the financial outcomes for signature shoes alone – it often manifests itself in products which don't bear the influencer's name. Consequently, holistic ROI is difficult to measure.
- A new class of influencer has emerged – the internet influ-encer – captivating large audiences by offering authen-tic and honest product opinions through high quality content, all while maintaining a dialogue with followers. This influencer channel can be leveraged efficiently by brands and retailers alike, at the expense of sacrificing storytelling control.

CONCLUSION

THE TOUR CONCLUDES, BUT THE FUTURE AWAITS

———

With that, our tour concludes, but the sneaker economy's journey is just beginning.

It's come an undeniably long way, bursting out of the underground and into the mainstream, hooking new consumers and spawning new businesses with all the momentum of a snowball rampaging downhill. Make no mistake though; this snowball is amassing dollars. With startling velocity, sneakerheads both new and old are eagerly exchanging dollars for kicks, building and tweaking their portfolios with an eye toward the next worthy addition.

Brands and retailers continue to scratch that itch with skill, and yet, those traditional relationships are just the tip of the sneaker economy iceberg. From street corners, to online forums, to eBay and beyond, sneaker resale has blossomed into a full-fledged industry capable of commanding well in excess of $100 million in investment funding in 2018 alone. Consumers are faced with a seemingly boundless variety of sneakers to choose from at any given moment, from the latest Yeezy to hit stores to Jordans that were chaotically released years earlier – and they're all available at a few clicks of a button. Not all of the resale players will win, but those that do will handsomely validate the conviction of their investors in the form of lucrative returns.

Such secondary market growth also means that the sneakerhead's latest purchase need not be only a physical object to be worn, consumed, exhausted, and discarded. No, that was the case back when sneakers were just shoes. Rather, that sneaker box has become a store of cash – an asset – its value communicated via market activity in real time at all hours of the day. It may not be an investment, yet at the same time, no longer has a consumer "spent" money the second they hit the purchase button. They've merely reallocated resources.

Of course, any time cash is exchanged for an asset, risk increases, and such is the case with sneakers. Vastly more often than not, that cash-for-sneaker exchange will result in a loss of capital. Yet, more than ever before, that initial cash outlay does not represent a complete loss of principal. Due to a robust, increasingly friction-free secondary market function, the savvy market participant can convert sneakers to cash and back in a reasonable amount of time with less erosion of value, utilizing the firm bids on offer across the resale market.

Savvy, however, is required. Slowly but surely, as the difference between primary and secondary sneaker markets melts away, the supply of sneakers available for purchase relentlessly builds. When supply builds without a commensurate increase in demand, prices come under pressure. Though new demand has been skillfully generated, sneaker releases find their way not onto feet but onto the secondary market with increasing frequency, and thus the high level of supply is digested at a slower pace. With the forces of supply and demand placing downward – albeit mild but downward nonetheless – pressure on broad prices, the uninformed reseller is slowly being squeezed out of the market, crippled by stores of the wrong inventory. The result, though, is not the pop of a bubble, because a bubble this is not.

Thanks to the present moment in which scores of information and data are available at just a few taps of a finger, the sneaker market differs meaningfully from other collectibles, which popped with great fanfare. Beanie Babies crashed back to Earth when collectors sought the realization of their mouth-watering gains, only to realize nobody actually wanted to buy. The sneaker economy is replete with *real, complete* sales data, and also real indications of demand – the buyers here are not theoretical. Baseball cards collapsed in the nineties when the card companies pigged out, but also because consumers were blissfully unaware of the fact so many others had also acquired their presumed treasures. The sneaker manufacturers, however, are wary of diluting their brands, and act accordingly and thoughtfully to protect the future of the market, counterbalancing short-term obligations to shareholders. Moreover, sneaker media – the blogs, Instagrams, YouTubes, and podcasts – render us far more wary of market dynamics. If a sneaker has been mass-produced, consumers are increasingly aware and avoid buying high.

Many in sneaker media have carved full-time careers out of not only aiding consumers in better discovering their next pair and strategizing on acquisition, but also entertaining us and regaling us with the stories which make sneakers so special. They ensure the right product finds mindshare with the right consumers, both through the daily blocking-and-tackling of detailing releases and the rich, creative content designed to amuse. Sneaker media is a highly valuable – and likely underrated – piece of the sneaker ecosystem, providing benefits to all other constituents: brand, consumer, retailer, and marketplace alike.

Such is also the case for the ancillary services that have risen to better serve the sneaker consumers burdened by the wealth of information and data available to them and by the challenge of getting their hands on the next target in their sights. Unsung heroes these parties may be, but they play a large part in ensuring that the sneaker market advances in efficiency and avoids the perils of the collectibles that have previously failed.

The sneaker economy has *matured* but it is not *mature*, and it will continue to grow as the bright minds of the industry drive it into the future. The reach of what has been, is being, and will be accomplished here extends well beyond the world of sneakers. The achievements of the sneaker economy will play a role in shaping the future of retail, eschewing traditional models, relationships, and structures in the pursuit of the one all-important goal at the core of retail success: better connecting product with consumer.

Take for example the convergence of primary and secondary sneaker markets. Secondary sneaker markets won't simply expedite the discounting process of brands and retailers – they'll lead a slow but inevitable charge towards the death of MSRP and the proliferation of truly variable, market-based pricing. That doesn't necessarily mean only cheaper prices for consumers – it means faster discovery and satisfaction of market demand.

Sneaker manufacturers are revolutionizing their processes to bring product to consumers faster because that's what today's consumer demands. Beneath the surface, though, they're enabling highly responsive, nimble supply, and eliminating the longstanding balancing act between avoiding steep discounts and leaving revenue on the table. Product is provided to the consumer who wants it, when they want it, where they want it.

Those two forces alone – more variable pricing leading to quicker demand discovery and advanced manufacturing providing near perfect supply – remove previously unfathomable amounts of friction. Eliminating the highly scientific but still imperfect guesswork that shaped retail for years has immensely positive financial implications to the brands.

And what of the retailers? We know that in the sneaker economy they're not shuttering their doors and going home. No, they're ensuring they are not purveyors of product alone, but of memorable consumer *experiences*. In an internet-centric world, the sneaker economy's retailers, particularly boutiques, demonstrate the value of embracing culture to become an authentic part of the fabric of a community. Many associate, often fairly, the forces of capitalism with the erosion of culture but the sneaker economy proves that need not be the case. Those businesses that can identify with their consumers and forge authentic connections *based on culture* are poised for greater success. There's a reason the large sneaker brands continue to collaborate with boutique retailers. Boutiques add value in ways that large corporations find difficult, namely by developing truly symbiotic consumer relationships, especially at the local level.

All of these interactions – between brand and consumer, retailer and consumer, consumer and marketplace – are gently guided at their core by the strength of storytelling. It's those who can tell rich, colorful stories, breathing life into product, that are better able to successfully connect product with consumer. Profound differences in value, hundreds or even thousands of dollars between sneakers of a highly similar aesthetic, can often be attributed directly to those stories and to accompanying scarcity or lack thereof.

Without rich stories, sneakers are...well...just shoes – pieces of rubber and leather sold at a handsome markup to protect our feet in style.

But we know better now.

We know that tactful scarcity and colorful storytelling have made all the difference in the world, transforming those pieces of leather and rubber into the full-blown phenomenon now known as sneakonomic growth.

ACKNOWLEDGEMENTS

———

In the preparation of this book, I received immeasurable levels of support and guidance, both from those very close to me and from complete strangers eager to help.

I made the critical discovery during this process that the individuals comprising the sneaker community are not only very bright and very thoughtful, but they're also extremely generous, both with their time and their insights. To all of the great sneaker minds who were willing to spend time talking shop with a curious author, I am sincerely grateful for your generosity and feedback. You truly went above and beyond. There were also a number of people who were enormously helpful in facilitating those terrific discussions, and for that I am equally appreciative.

To the entire team at New Degree Press, you helped me turn an imprecise concept into a finished, tangible product.

I am immensely grateful for the guidance, the revision work, the constructive feedback, and all of the efforts that made this book a reality. Most critically, I thank you for providing me with the constant motivation to continue charging towards the finish line.

To my friends and family, who acted as sounding boards throughout the process, advanced readers in the latter stages, and key supporters from day one, I offer my deepest gratitude. Perhaps more importantly, I thank you for resisting the urge to ridicule my fascination with sneakers to no end.

WORKS REFERENCED

_____

INTRODUCTION

Panzarino, Matthew. 2018. "Sneaker Market GOAT Hires COO Lizzie Francis And Makes A Play For Women Sneaker Shoppers". *Techcrunch*. https://techcrunch.com/2018/06/19/sneaker-market-goat-hires-coo-lizzie-francis-and-makes-a-play-for-women-sneaker-shoppers/.

Shapiro, Bee. 2018. "How Much Is That Sneaker In The Window?". *New York Times*. https://www.nytimes.com/2018/05/12/business/how-much-is-that-sneaker-in-the-window.html.

Thompson, Ryan. 2015. "The Footsy Index: How Sneakers Became Very Big Business | Financial Times". *Ft.Com*. https://www.ft.com/content/

b3ea93b2-d48d-11e4-9bfe-00144feab7de#axzz3WBgYk-
YUg.

Wolf, Cam. 2018. "Ebay Wants To Be The Place You Sell
Your Sneakers—Again". *GQ*. https://www.gq.com/story/
ebay-sneaker-resale-competition.

CHAPTER 1

Lazarus, George. 1985. "Michael Jordan Shoe Also Having Big
Rookie Season". *The Chicago Tribune*, 1985. https://www.
chicagotribune.com/news/ct-xpm-1985-05-14-8501300378-
story.html.

Lev, Michael. 1996. "'Air Max Hunting' Shocks Japan – Holdups, Beatings Blamed On Mania For Used Sneakers". *The
Chicago Tribune*, 1996. http://community.seattletimes.
nwsource.com/archive/?date=19961117&slug=2360191.

Vandermey, Anne. 2015. "Lessons From The Great Beanie
Babies Crash". *Fortune*. http://fortune.com/2015/03/11/
beanie-babies-failure-lessons/.

CHAPTER 2

Block, Justin. 2018. "Jeff Staple's Oral History Of The 2005
Nike SB "Pigeon" Riot In NYC". *Medium*. https://medium.

com/@jblock49_6777/jeff-staples-oral-history-of-the-
2005-nike-sb-pigeons-riot-in-nyc-446f518a7fe3.

"Nike Shoe Launch Sparks Melee At Florida Mall". 2012. *Twin
Cities*. https://www.twincities.com/2012/02/23/nike-shoe-
launch-sparks-melee-at-florida-mall/.

Rosario, Frank, and Aaron Feis. 2014. "Sneaker Release
Nearly Causes Riot At Soho Store". *The New York Post*,
2014. https://nypost.com/2014/04/03/sneaker-release-
nearly-causes-riot-at-soho-store/.

CHAPTER 3

"Art: An Asset Class To Be Reckoned With – The Sovereign
Group". 2018. *The Sovereign Group*. https://www.sover-
eigngroup.com/press-room/art-asset-class-reckoned/.

Cuban, Mark. 2008. "Talking Stocks | Blog Maverick". *Blog-
maverick.Com.* http://blogmaverick.com/2008/09/08/
talking-stocks-and-money/.

Gibson, Richard. 1998. "Ready For A Bear Market? Some
Worry That The Beanie Baby Craze Is Going Soft".
Wall Street Journal. https://www.wsj.com/articles/
SB906611121666496500?mod=article_inline.

Kaur, Tarandip. 2017. "Ones To Watch: How To Trade Time-pieces For Impressive Returns". *Forbes.Com*. https://www.forbes.com/sites/tarandipkaur/2017/09/24/ones-to-watch-how-to-trade-timepieces-for-impressive-returns/#518e3d-81b1a8.

Mahtani, Shibani. 2018. "Sorry, Collectors, Nobody Wants Your Beanie Babies Anymore". *Wall Street Journal*. https://www.wsj.com/articles/sorry-collectors-no-body-wants-your-beanie-babies-anymore-1519234039.

"New Alternative Asset Class". 2018. *Pwccmarketplace.Com*. https://www.pwccmarketplace.com/alternative-invest-ment.

"PWCC Market Indices". 2018. *Pwccmarketplace.Com*. https://www.pwccmarketplace.com/market-indices.

Sullivan, Paul. 2018. "Trading Cards: A Hobby That Became A Multimillion-Dollar Investment". *New York Times*. https://www.nytimes.com/2018/03/23/your-money/trad-ing-cards-investment.html.

Wolff-Mann, Ethan. 2018. "Watches Are Bad Investments—With One Notable Exception". *Money*. http://time.com/money/4058109/watches-value-rolex-investment/.

Woodham, Doug. 2018. "What You Need To Know About Investing In Fine Art". *Artsy*. https://www.artsy.net/article/artsy-editorial-investing-fine-art-investing-traditional-asset-classes.

CHAPTER 4

"Adidas Ag's (ADDYY) CEO Herbert Hainer On Q4 2015 Results – Earnings Call Transcript". 2016. *Seeking Alpha*. https://seekingalpha.com/article/3953386-adidas-ags-addyy-ceo-herbert-hainer-q4-2015-results-earnings-call-transcript.

"Adidas's (ADDYY) CEO Kasper Rorsted On Q1 2017 Results – Earnings Call Transcript". 2017. *Seeking Alpha*. https://seekingalpha.com/article/4069286-adidass-addyy-ceo-kasper-rorsted-q1-2017-results-earnings-call-transcript?part=single.

"Adidas's (ADDYY) CEO Kasper Rorsted On Q2 2017 Results – Earnings Call Transcript". 2017. *Seeking Alpha*. https://seekingalpha.com/article/4095577-adidass-addyy-ceo-kasper-rorsted-q2-2017-results-earnings-call-transcript?part=single.

"Adidas AG ADR (ADDYY) CEO Kasper Rorsted On Q2 2018 Results – Earnings Call Transcript". 2018. *Seeking Alpha*.

https://seekingalpha.com/article/4197285-adidas-ag-adr-
addyy-ceo-kasper-rorsted-q2-2018-results-earnings-call-
transcript?part=single.

Allaire, Christian. 2014. "Shoe Of The Year: Adidas Stan
Smith". *Footwear News.* https://footwearnews.com/2014/
influencers/power-players/fnaa-2014-shoe-of-the-year-
adidas-stan-smith-388/.

"Foot Locker's (FL) CEO Dick Johnson On Q2 2017 Results –
Earnings Call Transcript". 2017. *Seeking Alpha.* https://
seekingalpha.com/article/4100368-foot-lockers-fl-
ceo-dick-johnson-q2-2017-results-earnings-call-tran-
script?part=single.

"Foot Locker's (FL) CEO Ric Johnson On Q1 2017 Results –
Earnings Call Transcript". 2017. *Seeking Alpha.* https://
seekingalpha.com/article/4074866-foot-lockers-fl-
ceo-ric-johnson-q1-2017-results-earnings-call-tran-
script?part=single.

Fox, Imogen. 2015. "How 2015 Was The Year The Stan Smith
Went Mass". *The Guardian.* https://www.theguardian.
com/fashion/2015/dec/22/2015-stan-smith-went-mass-
adidas-sneakers-trainer.

"FY 2017 Q1 Earnings Release Conference Call Transcript". 2016. *Nike, Inc. – Investor Relations.* https://s1.q4cdn. com/806093406/files/doc_financials/2017/Q1/NIKE-Inc. Q117-OFFICIAL-Transcript-with-QA_FINAL.pdf.

"FY 2017 Q2 Earnings Release Conference Call Transcript". 2016. *Nike, Inc. – Investor Relations.* https://s1.q4cdn. com/806093406/files/doc_financials/2017/Q2/NIKE-Inc. Q217-OFFICIAL-Transcript-with-QA-FINAL.pdf.

"FY 2017 Q3 Earnings Release Conference Call Transcript". 2017. *Nike, Inc. – Investor Relations.* https://s1.q4cdn. com/806093406/files/doc_financials/2017/Q3/NIKE-Inc. Q317-OFFICIAL-Transcript-with-QA-FINAL.pdf.

"FY 2018 Q1 Earnings Release Conference Call Transcript". 2017. *Nike, Inc. – Investor Relations.* https://s1.q4cdn. com/806093406/files/doc_financials/2018/Q1/NIKE-Inc.- Q118-OFFICIAL-Transcript-with-QA.pdf.

"FY 2018 Q2 Earnings Release Conference Call Transcript". 2017. *Nike, Inc. – Investor Relations.* https://s1.q4cdn. com/806093406/files/doc_financials/2018/q2/NIKE-Inc.- Q218-OFFICIAL-Transcript-with-QA-FINAL.pdf.

"FY 2018 Q3 Earnings Release Conference Call Transcript". 2018. *Nike, Inc. – Investor Relations.* https://s1.q4cdn.

com/806093406/files/doc_events/2018/NIKE-Inc.-Q318-
OFFICIAL-Transcript-with-QA-FINAL.pdf.

"FY 2018 Q4 Earnings Release Conference Call Transcript".
2018. *Nike, Inc. – Investor Relations.* https://s1.q4cdn.
com/806093406/files/doc_financials/2018/Q4/NIKE-
Inc.-Q418-OFFICIAL-Transcript-with-QA-FINAL.pdf.

Schwartzberg, Lauren. 2017. "Stan Smith Knows You Think
He's Just A Sneaker". *The Cut.* https://www.thecut.
com/2017/02/stan-smith-knows-you-think-hes-just-a-
sneaker.html.

CHAPTER 5

Burns, Matt. 2016. "Dan Gilbert And Campless Founder
Launch A Marketplace For Sneakers". *Techcrunch.* https://
techcrunch.com/2016/02/08/dan-gilbert-and-campless-
founder-launch-a-marketplace-for-sneakers/.

Schwartzberg, Lauren. 2016. "This 16-Year-Old Has Made
Millions Selling Rare Sneakers". *The Cut.* https://www.
thecut.com/2016/08/benjamin-kickz-sneaker-don.html.

Shapiro, Bee. 2018. "How Much Is That Sneaker In The
Window?". *New York Times.* https://www.nytimes.

com/2018/05/12/business/how-much-is-that-sneaker-in-the-window.html.

CHAPTER 6

The Newsroom. "The Greater Fool." 1.10. Directed by Greg Mottola. Written by Aaron Sorkin. HBO, August 26 2012.

"Sixers & Stubhub Launch Revolutionary New Ticketing Platform | Philadelphia 76ers". 2016. *Philadelphia 76ers*. https://www.nba.com/sixers/news/sixers-stubhub-launch-revolutionary-new-ticketing-platform.

CHAPTER 7

Danforth, Chris. 2018. "Nike's SNKRS App Is Making Sneaker Releases Fun Again". *Highsnobiety*. https://www.highsnobiety.com/p/nike-snkrs-ron-farris-interview/.

"Foot Locker's (FL) CEO Richard Johnson On Q4 2017 Results – Earnings Call Transcript". 2018. *Seeking Alpha*. https://seekingalpha.com/article/4152868-foot-lockers-fl-ceo-richard-johnson-q4-2017-results-earnings-call-transcript.

"Foot Locker, Inc. (FL) CEO Dick Johnson On Q1 2018 Results – Earnings Call Transcript". 2018. *Seeking Alpha*.

https://seekingalpha.com/article/4177373-foot-locker-inc-fl-ceo-dick-johnson-q1-2018-results-earnings-call-transcript.

Green, Dennis. 2018. "Adidas Just Opened A Futuristic New Factory — And It Will Dramatically Change How Shoes Are Sold". *Business Insider*. https://www.businessinsider.com/adidas-high-tech-speedfactory-begins-production-2018-4.

"Nike Investor Day 2017". 2017. *Nike*. https://s1.q4cdn.com/806093406/files/doc_events/2017/10/updtd/NIKE-Inc.-2017-Investor-Day-Transcript-With-Q-A-FINAL.pdf.

"The Finish Line's (FINL) CEO Sam Sato On Q2 2018 Results – Earnings Call Transcript". 2017. *Seeking Alpha*. https://seekingalpha.com/article/4108914-finish-lines-finl-ceo-sam-sato-q2-2018-results-earnings-call-transcript?part=single.

CHAPTER 8

"Foot Locker (FL) Q3 2017 Results – Earnings Call Transcript". 2017. *Seeking Alpha*. https://seekingalpha.com/article/4126064-foot-locker-fl-q3-2017-results-earnings-call-transcript.

"Foot Locker's (FL) CEO Richard Johnson On Q4 2017
Results – Earnings Call Transcript". 2018. *Seeking Alpha.*
https://seekingalpha.com/article/4152868-foot-lockers-fl-
ceo-richard-johnson-q4-2017-results-earnings-call-tran-
script.

"Foot Locker, Inc. (FL) CEO Dick Johnson On Q1 2018
Results – Earnings Call Transcript". 2018. *Seeking Alpha.*
https://seekingalpha.com/article/4177373-foot-locker-inc-
fl-ceo-dick-johnson-q1-2018-results-earnings-call-tran-
script.

"FY 2018 Q3 Earnings Release Conference Call Transcript".
2018. *Nike, Inc. – Investor Relations.* https://s1.q4cdn.
com/806093406/files/doc_events/2018/NIKE-Inc.-Q318-
OFFICIAL-Transcript-with-QA-FINAL.pdf.

"FY 2018 Q4 Earnings Release Conference Call Transcript".
2018. *Nike, Inc. – Investor Relations.* https://s1.q4cdn.
com/806093406/files/doc_financials/2018/Q4/NIKE-
Inc.-Q418-OFFICIAL-Transcript-with-QA-FINAL.pdf.

"FY 2019 Q1 Earnings Release Conference Call Transcript".
2018. *Nike, Inc. – Investor Relations.* https://s1.q4cdn.
com/806093406/files/doc_financials/2019/Q1/NIKE-Inc.-
Q119-OFFICIAL-Transcript-with-QA-FINAL.pdf.

Ofiaza, Renz. 2017. "Adidas & Concepts Open Exclusive Boutique In Boston". *Highsnobiety*. https://www.highsnobiety.com/2017/08/25/adidas-concepts-store/.

Stebbings, Harry. 2018. "GOAT's Eddy Lu On Pivoting From Failing Social Dining App To The World's Largest Sneaker Marketplace, How The Best Founders Pick Their Investors & Why It Is Better To Be Hated Than Unknown". Podcast. *The Twenty Minute VC*.

"The Finish Line's (FINL) CEO Sam Sato On Q3 2018 Results – Earnings Call Transcript". 2017. *Seeking Alpha*. https://seekingalpha.com/article/4133328-finish-lines-finl-ceo-sam-sato-q3-2018-results-earnings-call-transcript.

Verry, Peter. 2017. "What Sneaker Fans Can Expect From Adidas' Co-Branded Store With Concepts". *Footwear News*. https://footwearnews.com/2017/focus/athletic-outdoor/adidas-concepts-store-boston-410840/.

CHAPTER 9

Abel, Katie. 2018. "Why The Women's Sneaker Market Is Finally On The Cusp Of A Revolution". *Footwear News*. https://footwearnews.com/2018/fashion/athletic-outdoor/womens-sneakers-nike-unlaced-paris-fashion-week-selfridges-510156/.

Burns, Matt. 2018. "Detroit's Stockx Raises $44M From GV And Battery To Expand Marketplace Internationally". *Techcrunch.* https://techcrunch.com/2018/09/12/detroits-stockx-raises-44m-from-gv-and-battery-to-expand-marketplace-internationally/.

Hughes, Aria. 2018. "Stadium Goods To Open Concept Space Inside Nordstrom". *WWD.* https://wwd.com/menswear-news/mens-retail-business/stadium-goods-to-open-store-inside-nordstrom-1202633799/.

Kawamura, Yuniya. 2016. *Sneakers: Fashion, Gender, And Subculture.* 1st ed. Bloomsbury Academic.

Milnes, Hilary. 2018. "How Stadium Goods Is Seizing China's Streetwear Opportunity – Digiday". *Digiday.* https://digiday.com/marketing/stadium-goods-seizing-chinas-streetwear-opportunity/.

Northman, Tora. 2018. "How Come Brands Still Aren't Making Sneakers In Women's Sizes?". *HYPEBAE.* https://hypebae.com/2018/8/lack-of-womens-sneaker-sizes-nike-adidas.

Panzarino, Matthew. 2018. "Sneaker Market GOAT Hires COO Lizzie Francis And Makes A Play For Women Sneaker Shoppers". *Techcrunch.* https://techcrunch.

com/2018/06/19/sneaker-market-goat-hires-coo-lizzie-francis-and-makes-a-play-for-women-sneaker-shoppers/.

Street, Mikelle. 2018. "Nordstrom's First Standalone Men's Store Is Banking On 'High Heat' Product And Prime Customer Service For Success". *Fashionista*. https://fashionista.com/2018/04/nordstrom-mens-store-nyc.

Wolf, Cam. 2018. "The $60 Million Sneaker Merger". *GQ*. https://www.gq.com/story/goat-flight-club-sneaker-merger-60-million.

Zakkour, Michael. 2018. "When Alibaba Met Stadium Goods: The Case For Foreign Smes To Try And Crack Chinese E-Commerce". *Forbes.Com*. https://www.forbes.com/sites/michaelzakkour/2018/01/22/when-alibaba-met-stadium-goods-the-case-for-foreign-smes-to-try-and-crack-chinese-e-commerce/#414b5342631c.

CHAPTER 10

Baer, Jay. 2018. "The 13 Critical Podcast Statistics Of 2018 | Baer Facts". *Convince And Convert: Social Media Consulting And Content Marketing Consulting*. https://www.convinceandconvert.com/podcast-research/the-13-critical-podcast-statistics-of-2018/.

Quah, Nicholas. 2017. "The Three Fundamental Moments Of Podcasts' Crazy Rise". *WIRED*. https://www.wired.com/story/podcast-three-watershed-moments/.

CHAPTER 11

Guzman, Zack. 2018. "This 38-Year-Old Went From His Mom's Basement To Making Six Figures As NFL'S Go-To Sneaker Artist". *CNBC*. https://www.cnbc.com/2018/02/01/dan-mache-gamache-makes-six-figures-as-nfls-go-to-sneaker-artist.html.

Pierson, David. 2017. "As Sneakers Got More Expensive, Jason Mark Angsuvarn Built An Upscale Shoe-Shining Business". *Los Angeles Times*, 2017. https://www.latimes.com/business/la-fi-himi-jason-markk-20171105-htmlstory.html.

CHAPTER 12

Baron, Zach. 2016. "The Life Of Virgil Abloh, Street-Style Godhead". *GQ*. https://www.gq.com/story/virgil-abloh-profile.

"FY 2018 Q2 Earnings Release Conference Call Transcript". 2017. *Nike, Inc. – Investor Relations*. https://s1.q4cdn.

com/806093406/files/doc_financials/2018/q2/NIKE-Inc.-
Q218-OFFICIAL-Transcript-with-QA-FINAL.pdf.

Gorsler, Fabian. 2018. "OFF-WHITE X Nike Sneakers: An
Analysis Of Resell Prices". *Highsnobiety*. https://www.
highsnobiety.com/p/off-white-nike-resell-price-analysis/.

Morency, Christopher. 2016. "The Unlikely Success Of Virgil
Abloh". *The Business Of Fashion*. https://www.businessof-
fashion.com/articles/intelligence/the-unlikely-success-of-
virgil-abloh-off-white.

Newbold, Alice. 2018. "What Are Serena Williams And Virgil
Abloh Up To?". *Vogue.Co.Uk*. https://www.vogue.co.uk/
article/serena-williams-off-white-virgil-abloh-train-
er-collaboration.

"Nike And Tom Sachs Introduce The Nikecraft Mars Yard
2.0". 2017. *Nike News*. https://news.nike.com/news/tom-
sachs-mars-yard-2-0.

Solway, Diane. 2017. "Virgil Abloh And His Army Of Disruptors: How He Became The King Of Social Media Superinfluencers". *W Magazine*. https://www.wmagazine.com/
story/virgil-abloh-off-white-kanye-west-raf-simons.

"TEXTBOOK". 2018. Ebook. Nike. https://content.nike.com/
content/dam/one-nike/en_us/season-2018-su/NikeLab/
TEN/TEXTBOOK.pdf.

Warnett, Gary. 2016. "How Run-DMC Earned Their Adidas
Stripes". *The Daily | MR PORTER*. https://www.mrporter.
com/daily/how-run-dmc-earned-their-adidas-stripes/939.

Yotka, Steff. 2018. "Serena Williams Will Return To The U.S.
Open In Virgil Abloh X Nike". *Vogue*. https://www.vogue.
com/article/serena-williams-us-open-virgil-abloh-x-nike.